The DLM Early Childhood EXPRESS

Teacher's Edition

Unit 8
Healthy Food/Healthy Body

Nell Duke • Douglas Clements • Julie Sarama • William Teale

McGraw Hill **Wright Group**

The McGraw·Hill Companies

Authors

Nell K. Duke
Professor of Teacher Education and Educational Psychology and Co-Director of the Literacy Achievement Research Center Michigan State University, East Lansing, MI

Douglas H. Clements
Professor of Early Childhood and Mathematics Education University at Buffalo, State University of New York, New York

Julie Sarama
Associate Professor of Mathematics Education University at Buffalo, State University of New York, New York

William Teale
Professor of Education University of Illinois at Chicago, Chicago, IL

Contributing Authors

Kim Brenneman, PhD
Assistant Research Professor of Psychology at Rutgers University, National Institute for Early Education Research Rutgers University, New Brunswick, NJ

Peggy Cerna
Early Childhood Consultant Austin, TX

Dan Cieloha
Educator and President of the Partnership for Interactive Learning Oakland, CA

Paula Jones
Early Childhood Consultant Lubbock, TX

Bobbie Sparks
Educator and K-12 Science Consultant Houston, TX

Rita Abrams
Composer, Lyricist, Educator, Author, and two-time Emmy Award winner Mill Valley, CA

Image Credits: Cover (toothbrush)Raimund Koch/Getty Images, (traincar)Ryan McVay/Getty Images, (wheels)felinda/istockphoto, (all other)The McGraw-Hill Companies; **5** blue jean images/Getty Images; **9** Seth Joel/Photographer's Choice RF/Getty Images; **18-19** Martin Barraud/Getty Images; **19** Image Source/CORBIS; **24** JGI/Jamie Grill/Getty Images; **25** Olya Telnova/iStockphoto; **30** Royalty-Free/CORBIS; **36** TSI Graphics; **42** (t)Jack Hollingsworth/Getty Images, (b)gulfimages/Alamy; **46** Masterfile Royalty-Free/Getty Images; **48** Steve Mack; **48 54** TSI Graphics; **56-57** Jamie Grill/Getty Images; **57** Mike Kemp/Getty Images; **62** The McGraw-Hill Companies/Ken Karp, photographer; **63** Image Source/Getty Images; **64** Getty Images; **68** Steve Mack; **70** Absodels/Getty Images; **74** Daniel Griffo; **76** Eileen Hine; **80** Andersen Ross/Getty Images; **90** Ariel Skelley/Getty Images; **94-95** Bounce/Getty Images; **95** Jeremy Woodhouse/Getty Images; **100** Royalty-Free/Masterfile; **101** Lawrence Manning/CORBIS; **102** Holli Conger; **106** Blend Images/Alamy; **108** Hector Borlasca; **110** image100/PunchStock; **114** Comstock Images; **118** Valeria Cis; **120** Melissa Iwai; **126** Tim Beaumont; **130** Brand X Pictures/PunchStock; **132-133** John Lund/Drew Kelly/Getty Images; **133** JGI/Jamie Grill/Getty Images; **138** The McGraw-Hill Companies/Ken Karp, photographer; **139** Thinkstock/Getty Images; **140** Ingram Publishing / Fotosearch; **146** Miki Sakamoto; **151** Steve Mack; **152** Rubberball/Getty Images; **154** Daniel Griffo; **156 157** Jan Bryan-Hunt; **162** Melissa Iwai; **164** Stockbyte/Getty Images; **168** Jan Bryan-Hunt; **171** (br)The McGraw-Hill Companies, Inc./Ken Cavanagh photographer; **172** Jim Esposito Photography L.L.C./Getty Images; **174** Michael Donnelly/Getty Images; **178** D. Berry/PhotoLink/Getty Images; **181** (t)Steve Mack, (c)Ingram Publishing/Alamy, (b)Daniel Griffo; **183** (t)Susan LeVan/Getty Images, (b)Laura Gonzalez; **185** Mike Wesley; **186** (t)The McGraw-Hill Companies, Inc., (b)Eileen Hine; **192** Photodisc Collection/Getty Images; **BackCover** (all wheels)felinda/istockphoto, (pencil)Andy Crawford/Getty Images, (rust wicker)Comstock/CORBIS, (bell)Stockbyte/Getty Images, (webcam)Medioimages/Photodisc/Getty Images, (pencilmirror)Yasuhide Fumoto/Getty Images, (U3roof)Ryan McVay/Getty Images, (elephant)PhotoLink/Getty Images, (looking glass) CMCD/Getty Images, (alligator)Siede Preis/Getty Images, (alligatorbelly)Ryan McVay/Getty Images, (U5traincar)83owl/Getty Images, (toothbrush)Raimund Koch/Getty Images, (U8traincar)Ryan McVay/Getty Images, (brush)Brand X Pictures/PunchStock, (all other)The McGraw-Hill Companies.

The McGraw·Hill Companies

www.WrightGroup.com

Wright Group

Printed in the United States of America.

Send all inquiries to:
Wright Group/McGraw-Hill
P.O. Box 812960
Chicago, IL 60681

ISBN 978-0-07-658086-6
MHID 0-07-658086-5

3 4 5 6 7 8 9 WEB 16 15 14 13 12 11

Acknowledgment

Building Blocks was supported in part by the National Science Foundation under Grant No. ESI-9730804, "Building Blocks— Foundations for Mathematical Thinking, Pre-Kindergarten to Grade 2: Research-based Materials Development" to Douglas H. Clements and Julie Sarama. The curriculum was also based partly upon work supported in part by the Institute of Educational Sciences (U.S. Dept. of Education, under the Interagency Education Research Initiative, or IERI, a collaboration of the IES, NSF, and NICHHD) under Grant No. R305K05157, "Scaling Trajectories and Technologies" and by the IERI through a National Science Foundation NSF Grant No. REC-0228440, "Scaling Up the Implementation of a Pre-Kindergarten Mathematics Curricula: Teaching for Understanding with Trajectories and Technologies." Any opinions, findings, and conclusions or recommendations expressed in this material are those of the authors and do not necessarily reflect the views of the funding agencies.

Reviewers

Tonda Brown, *Pre-K Specialist*, Austin ISD; Deanne Colley, *Family Involvement Facilitator*, Northwest ISD; Anita Uphaus, *Retired Early Childhood Director*, Austin ISD; Cathy Ambridge, *Reading Specialist*, Klein ISD; Margaret Jordan, *PreK Special Education Teacher*, McMullen Booth Elementary; Niki Rogers, *Adjunct Professor of Psychology/Child Development*, Concordia University Wisconsin

Table of Contents

Getting Started

Getting Started with *The DLM Early Childhood Express*

The DLM Early Childhood Express is a holistic, child-centered program that nurtures each child by offering carefully selected and carefully sequenced learning experiences. It provides a wealth of materials and ideas to foster the social-emotional, intellectual, and physical development of children. At the same time, it nurtures the natural curiosity and sense of self that can serve as the foundation for a lifetime of learning.

The lesson format is designed to present information in a way that makes it easy for children to learn. Intelligence is, in large part, our ability to see patterns and build relationships out of those patterns, which is why *DLM* is focused on helping children see the patterns in what they are learning. It builds an understanding of how newly taught material resembles what children already know. Then it takes the differences in the new material and helps the children convert them into new understanding.

Each of the eight Teacher Edition units in *DLM* is centered on an Essential Question relating to the unit's theme. Each week has its own more specific focus question. By focusing on essential questions, children are better able to connect their existing knowledge of the world with the new concepts and ideas they are learning at school. Routines at the beginning and end of each day help children focus on the learning process, reflect on new concepts, and make important connections. The lessons are designed to allow children to apply what they have learned.

Social and Emotional Development
Social-emotional development is addressed everyday through positive reinforcement, interactive activities, and engaging songs.

Language and Communication
All lessons are focused on language acquisition, which includes oral language development and vocabulary activities.

Emergent Literacy: Reading
Children develop literacy skills for reading through exposure to multiple read-aloud selections each day and through daily phonological awareness and letter recognition activities.

Emergent Literacy: Writing
Children develop writing skills through daily writing activities and during Center Time.

Mathematics
The math strand is based on *Building Blocks,* the result of NSF-funded research, and is designed to develop children's early mathematical knowledge through various individual and group activities.

Science
Children explore scientific concepts and methods during weekly science-focused, large-group activities, and Center Time activities.

Social Studies
Children explore Social Studies concepts during weekly social studies-focused, large-group activities, and Center Time activities.

Fine Arts
Children are exposed to art, dance, and music through a variety of weekly activities and the Creativity Center.

Physical Development
DLM is designed to allow children active time for outdoor play during the day, in addition to daily and weekly movement activities.

Technology Applications
Technology is integrated throughout each week with the use of online math activities, computer time, and other digital resources.

English Language Learners
Today's classrooms are very diverse. *The DLM Early Childhood Express* addresses this diversity by providing lessons in both English and Spanish. The program also offers strategies to assist English Language Learners at multiple levels of proficiency.

Flexible Scheduling

With *The DLM Early Childhood Express*, it's easy to fit lessons into your day.

Typical Full-Day Schedule

10 min	Opening Routines
15 min	Language Time
60-90 min	Center Time
15 min	Snack Time
15 min	Literacy Time
20 min	Active Play (outdoors if possible)
30 min	Lunch
15 min	Math Time
	Rest
15 min	Circle Time: Social and Emotional Development
20 min	Circle Time: Content Connection
30 min	Center Time
25 min	Active Play (outdoors if possible)
15 min	Let's Say Good-Bye

Typical Half-Day Schedule

10 min	Opening Routines
15 min	Language Time
60 min	Center Time
15 min	Snack Time
15 min	Circle Time (Literacy, Math, or Social and Emotional Development)
30 min	Active Play (outdoors if possible)
20 min	Circle Time (Content Connection, Literacy, Math, or Social and Emotional Development)
15 min	Let's Say Good-Bye

Welcome to *The DLM Early Childhood Express.*

Add your own ideas. Mix and match activities. Our program is designed to offer you a variety of activities on which to build a full year of exciting and creative lessons.

Happy learning to you and the children in your care!

Themes and Literature

With *The DLM Early Childhood Express,* children develop concrete skills through experiences with music, art, storytelling, hands-on activities and teacher-directed lessons that, in addition to skills development, emphasize practice and reflection. Every four weeks, children are introduced to a new theme organized around an essential question.

Literature selections and cross-curricular content are linked to the theme to help children reinforce lesson concepts. Children hear and discuss an additional read-aloud selection from the *Teacher Treasure Book* at the beginning and end of each day. At the end of each unit, children take home a *My Theme Library Book* reader of their own.

Unit 1: All About Pre-K
Why is school important?

	Focus Question	Literature
Week 1	What happens at school?	*Welcome to School* *Bienvenidos a la escuela*
Week 2	What happens in our classroom?	*Yellowbelly and Plum Go to School* *Barrigota y Pipón van a la escuela*
Week 3	What makes a good friend?	*Max and Mo's First Day at School* *Max y Mo van a la escuela*
Week 4	How can we play and learn together?	*Amelia's Show and Tell Fiesta/Amelia y la fiesta de "muestra y cuenta"*
Unit Wrap-Up	**My Library Book**	*How Can I Learn at School?* *¿Cómo puedo aprender en la escuela?*

Unit 2: All About Me
What makes me special?

	Focus Question	Literature
Week 1	Who am I?	*All About Me* *Todo sobre mí*
Week 2	What are my feelings?	*Lots of Feelings* *Montones de sentimientos*
Week 3	What do the parts of my body do?	*Eyes, Nose, Fingers, and Toes* *Ojos, nariz, dedos y pies*
Week 4	What is a family?	*Jonathan and His Mommy* *Juan y su mamá*
Unit Wrap-Up	**My Library Book**	*What Makes Us Special?* *¿Qué nos hace especiales?*

Unit 3: My Community
What is a community?

	Focus Question	Literature
Week 1	What are the parts of a community?	*In the Community* *En la comunidad*
Week 2	How does a community help me?	*Rush Hour,* *Hora pico*
Week 3	Who helps the community?	*Quinito's Neighborhood* *El vecindario de Quinito*
Week 4	How can I help my community?	*Flower Garden* *Un jardín de flores*
Unit Wrap-Up	**My Library Book**	*In My Community* *Mi comunidad*

Unit 4: Let's Investigate
How can I learn more about things?

	Focus Question	Literature
Week 1	How can I learn by observing?	*Let's Investigate* *Soy detective*
Week 2	How can I use tools to investiagte?	*I Like Making Tamales* *Me gusta hacer tamales*
Week 3	How can I compare things?	*Nature Spy* *Espía de la naturaleza*
Week 4	How do objects move?	*What Do Wheels Do All Day?* *¿Qué hacen las ruedas todo el día?*
Unit Wrap-Up	**My Library Book**	*How Can We Investigate?* *¿Cómo podemos investigar?*

Unit 5: Amazing Animals
What is amazing about animals?

	Focus Question	Literature
Week 1	What are animals like?	*Amazing Animals* *Animales asombrosos*
Week 2	Where do animals live and what do they eat?	*Castles, Caves, and Honeycombs* *Castillos, cuevas y panales*
Week 3	How are animals the same and different?	*Who Is the Beast?* *Quien es la bestia?*
Week 4	How do animals move?	*Move!* *¡A moverse!*
Unit Wrap-Up	**My Library Book**	*Hello, Animals!* *¡Hola, animales!*

Unit 6: Growing and Changing
How do living things grow and change?

	Focus Question	Literature
Week 1	How do animals grow and change?	*Growing and Changing* *Creciendo y cambiando*
Week 2	How do plants grow and change?	*I Am a Peach* *Yo soy el durazno*
Week 3	How do people grow and change?	*I'm Growing!* *Estoy creciendo!*
Week 4	How do living things grow and change?	*My Garden* *Mi jardin*
Unit Wrap-Up	**My Library Book**	*Growing Up* *Creciendo*

Unit 7: The Earth and Sky
What can I learn about the earth and the sky?

	Focus Question	Literature
Week 1	What can I learn about the earth and the sky?	*The Earth and Sky* *La Tierra y el cielo*
Week 2	What weather can I observe each day?	*Who Likes Rain?* *¿A quién le gusta la lluvia?*
Week 3	What can I learn about day and night?	*Matthew and the Color of the Sky* *Matias y el color del cielo*
Week 4	Why is caring for the earth and sky important?	*Ada, Once Again!* *¡Otra vez Ada!*
Unit Wrap-Up	**My Library Book**	*Good Morning, Earth!* *¡Buenos días, Tierra!*

Unit 8: Healthy Food/Healthy Body
Why is healthy food and exercise good for me?

	Focus Question	Literature
Week 1	What are good healthy habits?	*Staying Healthy* *Mantente sano*
Week 2	What kinds of foods are healthy?	*Growing Vegetable Soup* *A sembrar sopa de verduras*
Week 3	Why is exercise important?	*Rise and Exercise!* *A ejercitarse, ¡uno, dos, tres!*
Week 4	How can I stay healthy?	*Jamal's Busy Day* *El intenso día de Jamal*
Unit Wrap-Up	**My Library Book**	*Healthy Kids* *Niños sanos*

Tools for Teaching

The *DLM Early Childhood Express* is packed full of the components you'll need to teach each theme and enrich your classroom. The *Teacher Treasure Package* is the heart of the program, because it contains all the necessary materials. Plus, the *Teacher's Treasure Book* contains all the fun components that you'll love to teach. The *Literature Package* contains all the stories and books you need to support children's developing literacy. You'll find letter tiles, counters, and puppets in the *Manipulative Package* to connect hands-on learning skills with meaningful play.

Teacher Treasure Package

This package contains all the essential tools for the teacher such as the *Teacher's Treasure Book*, *Teacher's Editions*, technology, and other resources no teacher would want to be without!

Alphabet Wall Cards (English and Spanish)

ABC Picture Cards (English and Spanish)

Sequence Cards (English and Spanish)

Oral Language Development Cards (English and Spanish)

Photo Library CD-ROM

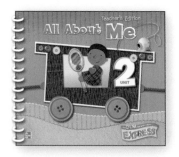

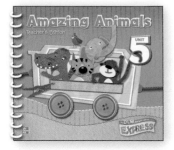

▲ Each lesson's instruction uses a variety of cards to help children learn. *Alphabet Wall Cards* and *ABC Picture Cards* help build letter recognition and phonemic awareness. *Oral Language Development Cards* teach new vocabulary, and are especially helpful when working with English Language Learners. *Sequencing Cards* help children learn how to order events and the vocabulary associated with time and sequence.

▲ There is one bilingual *Teacher's Edition* for each four-week theme. It provides the focus questions for each lesson as well as plans for centers and suggestions for classroom management.

▶ The bilingual *Teacher's Treasure Book* features 500+ pages of the things you love most about teaching Early Childhood, such as songs, traditional read alouds, folk tales, finger plays, and flannelboard stories with patterns.

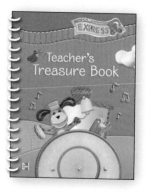

▶ An *ABC Take-Home Book* with blackline masters is provided for each letter of the English and Spanish alphabets.

ABC Take-Home Book (English and Spanish)

▶ Flip charts and their Audio CDs support the activities in each lesson. Children practice literacy and music skills using the **Rhymes and Chants Flip Chart,** which supports oral language development and phonological awareness in both English and Spanish. An Audio CD is included and provides a recording of every rhyme or chant. The **Making Good Choices Flip Chart** provides illustrations to allow students to explore social and emotional development concepts while facilitating classroom activities and discussion. 15 lively songs recorded in both English and Spanish address key social emotional development themes such as: joining in, helping others, being fair, teasing, bullying, and much more. The **Math and Science Flip Chart** is a demonstration tool that addresses weekly math and science concepts through photos and illustrations.

▶ Other key resources include a **Research & Professional Development Guide,** and a bilingual **Home Connections Resource Guide** which provides weekly letters home and take-home story books.

Building Blocks

Building Blocks, the result of NSF-funded research, develops young children's mathematical thinking using their bodies, manipulatives, paper, and computers.

Building Blocks online management system guides children through research-based learning trajectories. These activities-through-trajectories connect children's informal knowledge to more formal school mathematics. The result is a mathematical curriculum that is not only motivating for children but also comprehensive.

▶ **DLMExpressOnline.com** includes the following:

● e-Books of student and teacher materials

● Audio recordings of the **My Library** and **Literature Books** (Big/Little) in English and Spanish

● Teacher planning tools and assessment support

Tools for Teaching

Literature Package

This package contains the literature referenced in the program. Packages are available in several variations so you can choose the package that best meets the needs of your classroom. The literature used in the program includes expository selections, traditional stories, and emergent readers for students. All literature is available in English or Spanish.

▶ *My Library Books* are take-home readers for children to continue their exploration of unit themes. (English and Spanish)

Baby animals need help to grow big and strong. Baby animals need a safe place to live.

▶ *Concept Big Books* are nonfiction selections that introduce the essential questions for each unit and help children make connections between their background knowledge and unit themes. (English and Spanish)

▶ The *ABC Big Book* helps children develop phonemic awareness and letter recognition. (English and Spanish)

▶ The **Big Books** and **Little Books** reinforce each week's theme and the unit theme. Selections include stories originally written in Spanish, as well as those written in English.

▶ The stories in the **Big Books and Little Books** are recorded on the **Listening Library Audio CDs**. They are available in English and Spanish.

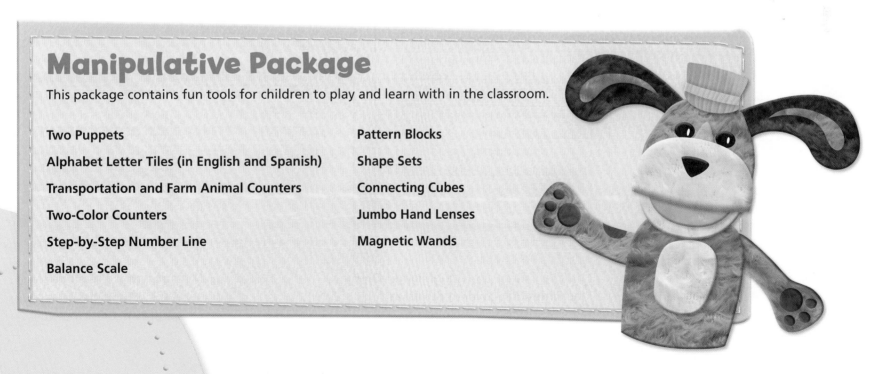

Manipulative Package

This package contains fun tools for children to play and learn with in the classroom.

Two Puppets

Alphabet Letter Tiles (in English and Spanish)

Transportation and Farm Animal Counters

Two-Color Counters

Step-by-Step Number Line

Balance Scale

Pattern Blocks

Shape Sets

Connecting Cubes

Jumbo Hand Lenses

Magnetic Wands

A Typical Weekly Lesson Plan

Each week of *The DLM Early Childhood Express* is organized the same way to provide children with the structure and routines they crave. Each week begins with a weekly opener that introduces the focus question for the week and includes a review of the week's Learning Goals, the Materials and Resources needed for the week, a Daily Planner, and a plan for the Learning Centers children will use throughout the week.

Each day's lesson includes large-group Circle Time and small-group Center Time. Each day includes Literacy, Math, and Social and Emotional Development activities during Circle Time. On Day 1, children explore Science. On Days 2 and 4, they work on more in-depth math lessons. On Day 3, Social Studies is the focus. Fine Art or Music/Movement activities take place during Circle Time on Day 5.

You will find the **Program Materials** and **Other Materials** needed for each day on the Materials and Resources page.

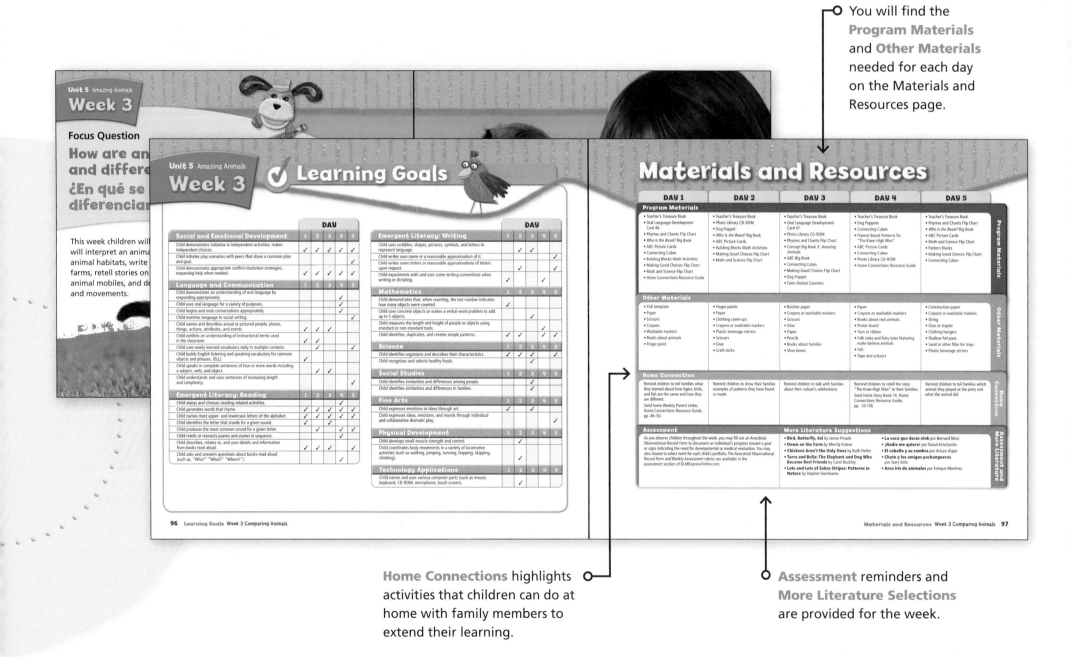

Home Connections highlights activities that children can do at home with family members to extend their learning.

Assessment reminders and **More Literature Selections** are provided for the week.

The **Daily Planner** provides a Week-at-a-Glance view of the daily structure and lesson topics for each week.

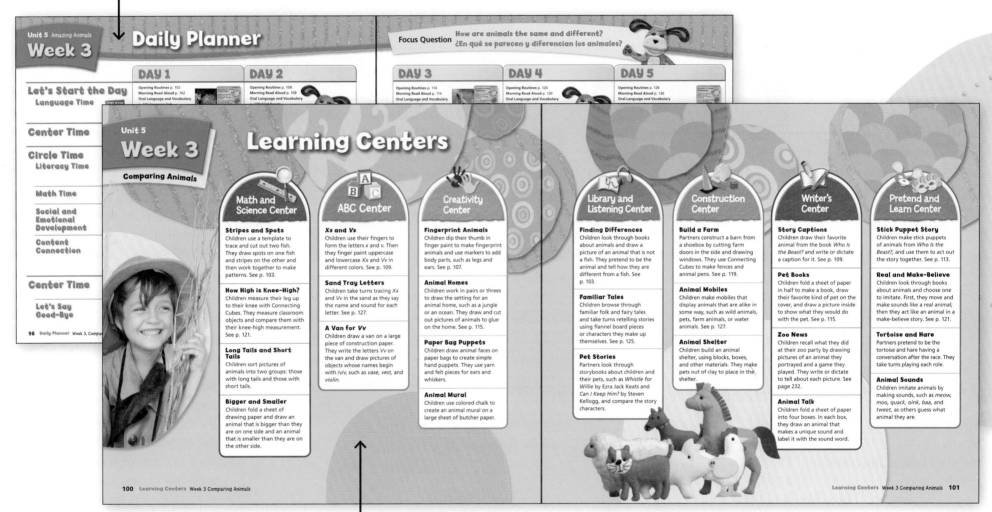

Learning Centers should be used throughout the week during Center Time. This page provides an overview of center activities to set up for children. Additional information about some center activities is provided in the daily lessons. The Learning Centers are intended to remain open for the entire week. These centers provide the opportunity for children to explore a wide range of curricular areas.

Lesson Overview

Our **Teacher's Editions** are organized by theme, week, and day. Each day's lesson is covered in six page spreads. The lessons integrate learning from the skill domain areas of: Social Emotional Development, Language and Communication, Emergent Literacy Reading and Writing, Mathematics, Science, Social Studies, Fine Arts, Physical Development, and Technology.

Each day begins with **Opening Routines** and a **Read Aloud** selection. This structured time helps children settle into their day.

The **Learning Goals** met by the lesson are listed on each page.

Observational Checks at point of use help to focus learning. These informal assessment questions help to ensure children are meeting lesson objectives.

Language Time is the first large-group activity of the day. It includes Oral Language and Vocabulary Development as well as Phonological Awareness activities.

Instructional questions are provided in both **English and Spanish.**

Tips for working with **English Language Learners** are shown at point of use throughout the lessons. Teaching strategies are provided to help children of of all language backgrounds and abilities meet the lesson objectives.

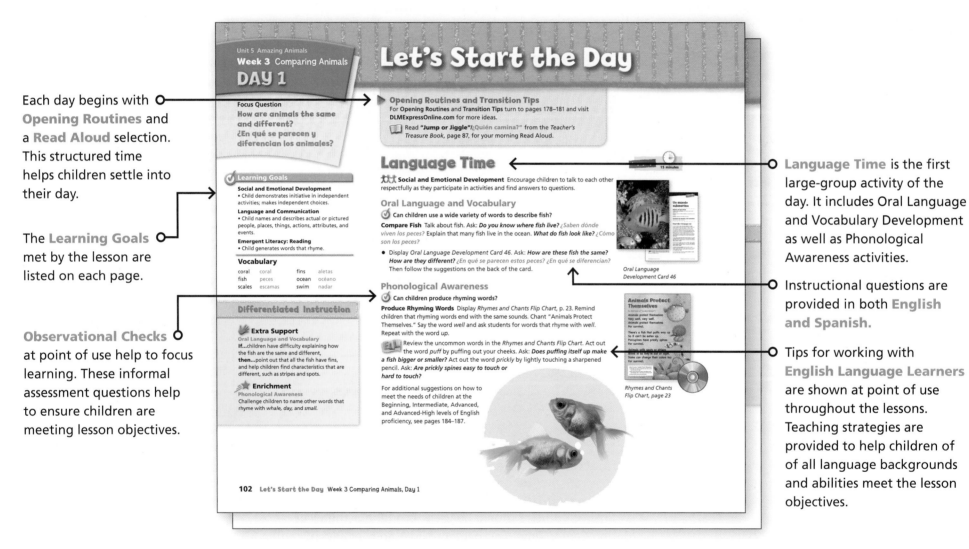

Unit 5 Amazing Animals
Week 3 Comparing Animals
DAY 1

Focus Question
How are animals the same and different?
¿En qué se parecen y diferencian los animales?

Learning Goals

Social and Emotional Development
• Child demonstrates initiative in independent activities; makes independent choices.

Language and Communication
• Child names and describes actual or pictured people, places, things, actions, attributes, and events.

Emergent Literacy: Reading
• Child generates words that rhyme.

Vocabulary

coral	coral	fins	aletas
fish	peces	ocean	océano
scales	escamas	swim	nadar

Differentiated Instruction

Extra Support
Oral Language and Vocabulary
If...children have difficulty explaining how the fish are the same and different,
then...point out that all the fish have fins, and help children find characteristics that are different, such as stripes and spots.

Enrichment
Phonological Awareness
Challenge children to name other words that rhyme with *whale*, *day*, and *small*.

Let's Start the Day

Opening Routines and Transition Tips
For **Opening Routines** and **Transition Tips** turn to pages 178–181 and visit DLMExpressOnline.com for more ideas.
Read **"Jump or Jiggle"/¿Quién camina?"** from the *Teacher's Treasure Book*, page 87, for your morning Read Aloud.

Language Time

15 minutes

Social and Emotional Development Encourage children to talk to each other respectfully as they participate in activities and find answers to questions.

Oral Language and Vocabulary

Can children use a wide variety of words to describe fish?

Compare Fish Talk about fish. Ask: *Do you know where fish live?* ¿Saben dónde viven los peces? Explain that many fish live in the ocean. *What do fish look like?* ¿Cómo son los peces?

• Display *Oral Language Development Card 46*. Ask: *How are these fish the same? How are they different?* ¿En qué se parecen estos peces? ¿En qué se diferencian? Then follow the suggestions on the back of the card.

Oral Language Development Card 46

Phonological Awareness

Can children produce rhyming words?

Produce Rhyming Words Display *Rhymes and Chants Flip Chart*, p. 23. Remind children that rhyming words end with the same sounds. Chant "Animals Protect Themselves." Say the word *well* and ask students for words that rhyme with *well*. Repeat with the word *up*.

Review the uncommon words in the *Rhymes and Chants Flip Chart*. Act out the word *puff* by puffing out your cheeks. Ask: *Does puffing itself up make a fish bigger or smaller?* Act out the word *prickly* by lightly touching a sharpened pencil. Ask: *Are prickly spines easy to touch or hard to touch?*

For additional suggestions on how to meet the needs of children at the Beginning, Intermediate, Advanced, and Advanced-High levels of English proficiency, see pages 184–187.

Rhymes and Chants Flip Chart, page 23

Center Time provides additional information for teacher-guided small-group activities and suggestions for independent activities children will complete during weekly Center Rotation.

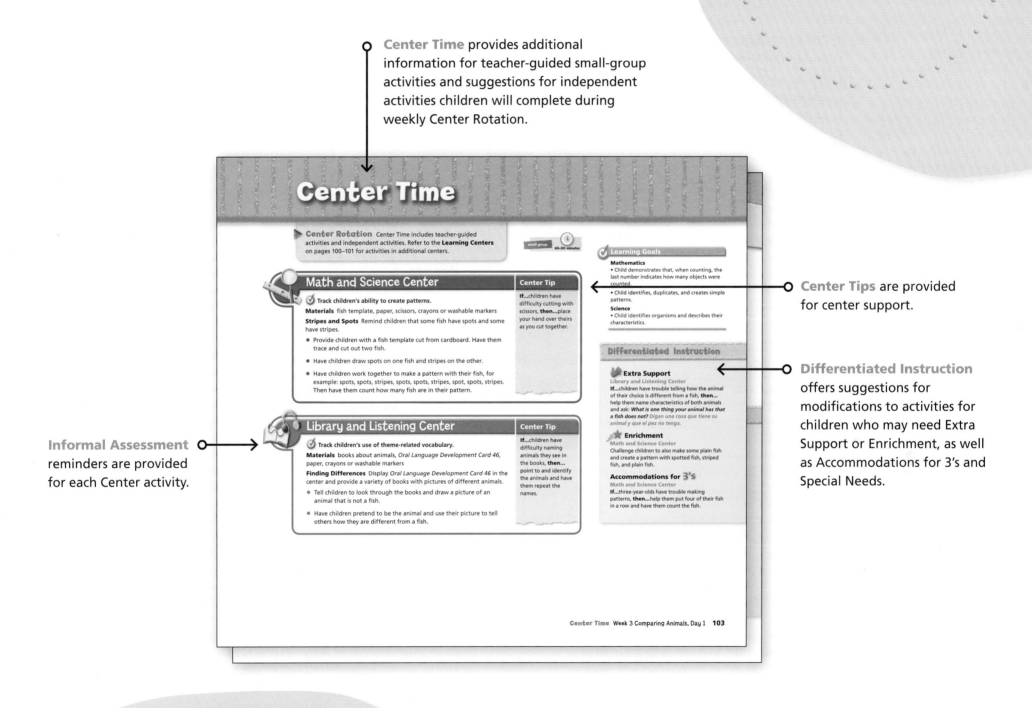

Center Time

▶ **Center Rotation** Center Time includes teacher-guided activities and independent activities. Refer to the **Learning Centers** on pages 100–101 for activities in additional centers.

small group | 60–90 minutes

Math and Science Center

☑ Track children's ability to create patterns.

Materials fish template, paper, scissors, crayons or washable markers

Stripes and Spots Remind children that some fish have spots and some have stripes.

- Provide children with a fish template cut from cardboard. Have them trace and cut out two fish.
- Have children draw spots on one fish and stripes on the other.
- Have children work together to make a pattern with their fish, for example: spots, spots, stripes, spots, spots, stripes, spot, spots, stripes. Then have them count how many fish are in their pattern.

Center Tip
If...children have difficulty cutting with scissors, **then**...place your hand over theirs as you cut together.

Library and Listening Center

☑ Track children's use of theme-related vocabulary.

Materials books about animals, *Oral Language Development Card 46*, paper, crayons or washable markers

Finding Differences Display *Oral Language Development Card 46* in the center and provide a variety of books with pictures of different animals.

- Tell children to look through the books and draw a picture of an animal that is not a fish.
- Have children pretend to be the animal and use their picture to tell others how they are different from a fish.

Center Tip
If...children have difficulty naming animals they see in the books, **then**... point to and identify the animals and have them repeat the names.

✓ Learning Goals

Mathematics
- Child demonstrates that, when counting, the last number indicates how many objects were counted.
- Child identifies, duplicates, and creates simple patterns.

Science
- Child identifies organisms and describes their characteristics.

Differentiated Instruction

Extra Support
Library and Listening Center
If...children have trouble telling how the animal of their choice is different from a fish, **then**... help them name characteristics of both animals and ask: **What is one thing your animal has that a fish does not?** *Digan una cosa que tiene su animal y que el pez no tenga.*

Enrichment
Math and Science Center
Challenge children to also make some plain fish and create a pattern with spotted fish, striped fish, and plain fish.

Accommodations for 3's
Math and Science Center
If...three-year-olds have trouble making patterns, **then**...help them put four of their fish in a row and have them count the fish.

Center Time Week 3 Comparing Animals, Day 1   **103**

Center Tips are provided for center support.

Differentiated Instruction offers suggestions for modifications to activities for children who may need Extra Support or Enrichment, as well as Accommodations for 3's and Special Needs.

Informal Assessment reminders are provided for each Center activity.

Lesson Overview

Children have **Literacy Time** every day. During this time, children listen to and discuss a second Read Aloud from a nonfiction **Concept Big Book** or a **Big Book/Little Book** literature selection.

Building Blocks online activities are provided each week during Math Time.

Children work in large groups on 15 minute math activities during daily **Math Time.**

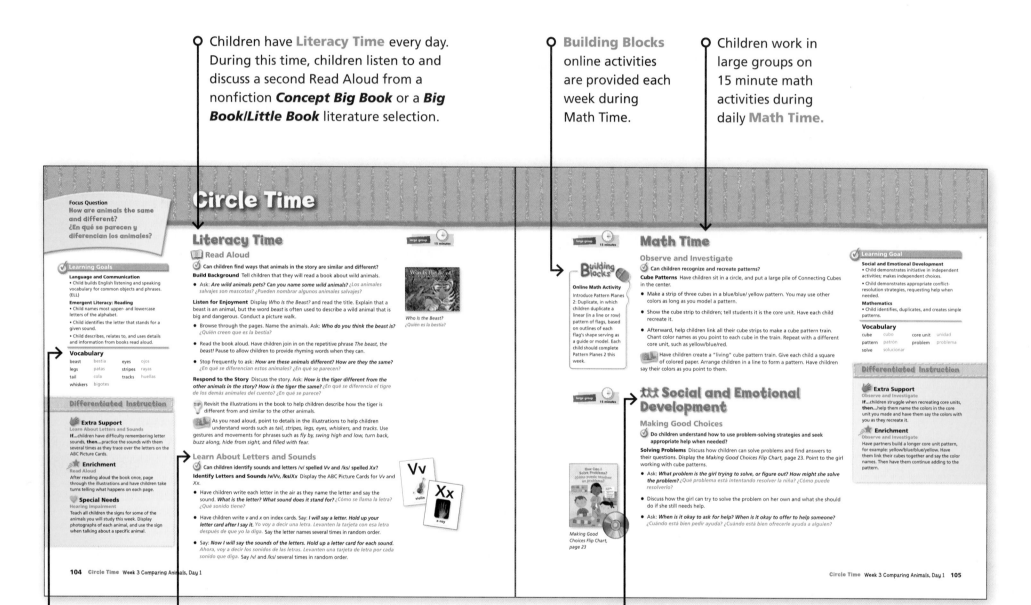

Focus Question
How are animals the same and different?
¿En qué se parecen y diferencian los animales?

Circle Time

Literacy Time

📖 Read Aloud

✓ Can children find ways that animals in the story are similar and different?
Build Background Tell children that they will read a book about wild animals.

- Ask: **Are wild animals pets? Can you name some wild animals?** ¿Los animales salvajes son mascotas? ¿Pueden nombrar algunos animales salvajes?

Listen for Enjoyment Display *Who Is the Beast?* and read the title. Explain that a beast is an animal, but the word *beast* is often used to describe a wild animal that is big and dangerous. Conduct a picture walk.

- Browse through the pages. Name the animals. Ask: **Who do you think the beast is?** ¿Quién creen que es la bestia?

- Read the book aloud. Have children join in on the repetitive phrase *The beast, the beast!* Pause to allow children to provide rhyming words when they can.

- Stop frequently to ask: **How are these animals different? How are they the same?** ¿En qué se diferencian estos animales? ¿En qué se parecen?

Respond to the Story Discuss the story. Ask: **How is the tiger different from the other animals in the story? How is the tiger the same?** ¿En qué se diferencia el tigre de los demás animales del cuento? ¿En qué se parece?

TIP Revisit the illustrations in the book to help children describe how the tiger is different from and similar to the other animals.

🔵🔵 As you read aloud, point to details in the illustrations to help children understand words such as *tail, stripes, legs, eyes, whiskers,* and *tracks.* Use gestures and movements for phrases such as *fly by, swing high and low, turn back, buzz along, hide from sight,* and *filled with fear.*

Learn About Letters and Sounds

✓ Can children identify sounds and letters /v/ spelled *Vv* and /ks/ spelled *Xx*?
Identify Letters and Sounds /v/*Vv,* /ks/*Xx* Display the ABC Picture Cards for *Vv* and *Xx.*

- Have children write each letter in the air as they name the letter and say the sound. **What is the letter? What sound does it stand for?** ¿Cómo se llama la letra? ¿Qué sonido tiene?

- Have children write *v* and *x* on index cards. Say: *I will say a letter. Hold up your letter card after I say it.* Yo voy a decir una letra. Levanten la tarjeta con esa letra después de que yo la diga. Say the letter names several times in random order.

- Say: *Now I will say the sounds of the letters. Hold up a letter card for each sound.* Ahora, voy a decir los sonidos de las letras. Levanten una tarjeta de letra por cada sonido que diga. Say /v/ and /ks/ several times in random order.

Who Is the Beast?
¿Quién es la bestia?

Vv
violin

Xx
x-ray

✓ Learning Goals

Language and Communication
- Child builds English listening and speaking vocabulary for common objects and phrases. (ELL)

Emergent Literacy: Reading
- Child names most upper- and lowercase letters of the alphabet.
- Child identifies the letter that stands for a given sound.
- Child describes, relates to, and uses details and information from books read aloud.

Vocabulary

beast	bestia	eyes	ojos
legs	patas	stripes	rayas
tail	cola	tracks	huellas
whiskers	bigotes		

Differentiated Instruction

📖 Extra Support
Learn About Letters and Sounds
If...children have difficulty remembering letter sounds, **then**...practice the sounds with them several times as they trace over the letters on the ABC Picture Cards.

⭐ Enrichment
Read Aloud
After reading aloud the book once, page through the illustrations and have children take turns telling what happens on each page.

🔵 Special Needs
Hearing Impairment
Teach all children the signs for some of the animals you will study this week. Display photographs of each animal, and use the sign when talking about a specific animal.

Math Time

large group / 15 minutes

Observe and Investigate

✓ Can children recognize and recreate patterns?
Cube Patterns Have children sit in a circle, and put a large pile of Connecting Cubes in the center.

- Make a strip of three cubes in a blue/blue/ yellow pattern. You may use other colors as long as you model a pattern.

- Show the cube strip to children; tell students it is the core unit. Have each child recreate it.

- Afterward, help children link all their cube strips to make a cube pattern train. Chant color names as you point to each cube in the train. Repeat with a different core unit, such as yellow/blue/red.

🔵🔵 Have children create a "living" cube pattern train. Give each child a square of colored paper. Arrange children in a line to form a pattern. Have children say their colors as you point to them.

Building Blocks

Online Math Activity
Introduce Pattern Planes 2: Duplicate, in which children duplicate a linear (in a line or row) pattern of flags, based on outlines of each flag's shape serving as a guide or model. Each child should complete Pattern Planes 2 this week.

large group / 15 minutes

🧑🧑 Social and Emotional Development

Making Good Choices

✓ Do children understand how to use problem-solving strategies and seek appropriate help when needed?
Solving Problems Discuss how children can solve problems and find answers to their questions. Display the *Making Good Choices Flip Chart,* page 23. Point to the girl working with cube patterns.

- Ask: **What problem is the girl trying to solve, or figure out? How might she solve the problem?** ¿Qué problema está intentando resolver la niña? ¿Cómo puede resolverlo?

- Discuss how the girl can try to solve the problem on her own and what she should do if she still needs help.

- Ask: **When is it okay to ask for help? When is it okay to offer to help someone?** ¿Cuándo está bien pedir ayuda? ¿Cuándo está bien ofrecerle ayuda a alguien?

Making Good Choices Flip Chart, page 23

✓ Learning Goal

Social and Emotional Development
- Child demonstrates initiative in independent activities; makes independent choices.
- Child demonstrates appropriate conflict-resolution strategies, requesting help when needed.

Mathematics
- Child identifies, duplicates, and creates simple patterns.

Vocabulary

cube	cubo	core unit	unidad
pattern	patrón	problem	problema
solve	solucionar		

Differentiated Instruction

📖 Extra Support
Observe and Investigate
If...children struggle when recreating core units, **then**...help them name the colors in the core unit you made and have them say the colors with you as they recreate it.

⭐ Enrichment
Observe and Investigate
Have partners build a longer core unit pattern, for example: yellow/blue/blue/yellow. Have them link their cubes together and say the color names. Then have them continue adding to the pattern.

Vocabulary is provided in English and Spanish to help expand children's ability to use both languages.

Children learn about **Letters and Sounds** every day. The sound is introduced with the letter. Children also practice letter formation.

Social and Emotional Development concepts are addressed every day to help children better express their emotions and needs, and establish positive relationships.

Circle Time is devoted to longer activities focusing on different cross-curricular concepts each day. Day 1 is Science Time. Days 2 and 4 are Math Time. On Day 3, children have Social Studies Time. Fine arts are covered in Art Time or Music and Movement Time on Day 5.

An end-of-the-day **Writing** activity is provided each day.

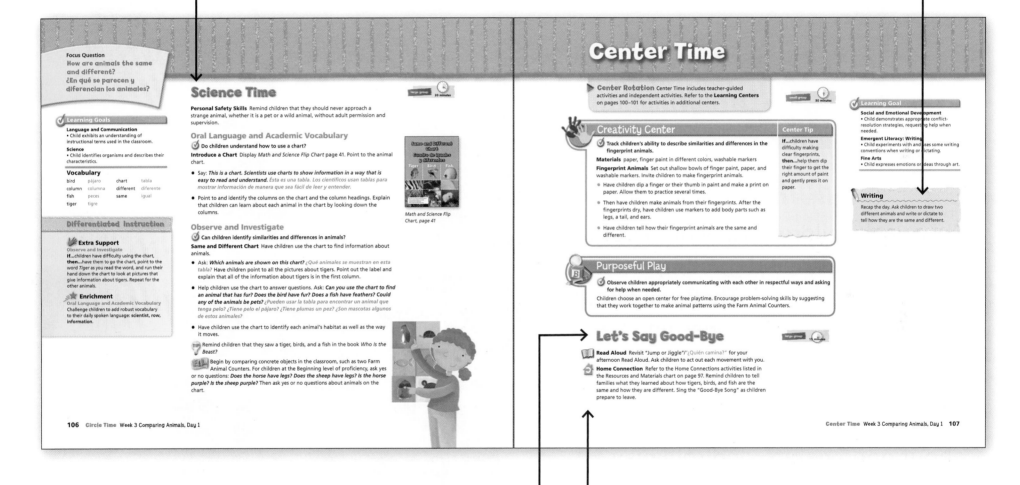

Focus Question
How are animals the same and different?
¿En qué se parecen y diferencian los animales?

Learning Goals

Language and Communication
• Child exhibits an understanding of instructional terms used in the classroom.
Science
• Child identifies organisms and describes their characteristics.

Vocabulary
bird — pájaro   chart — tabla
column — columna   different — diferente
fish — peces   same — igual
tiger — tigre

Differentiated Instruction

Extra Support
Observe and Investigate
If...children have difficulty using the chart, then...have them to go the chart, point to the word *Tiger* as you read the word, and run their hand down the chart to look at pictures that give information about tigers. Repeat for the other animals.

Enrichment
Oral Language and Academic Vocabulary
Challenge children to add robust vocabulary to their daily spoken language: scientist, row, information.

Science Time
large group — 20 minutes

Personal Safety Skills Remind children that they should never approach a strange animal, whether it is a pet or a wild animal, without adult permission and supervision.

Oral Language and Academic Vocabulary
☑ Do children understand how to use a chart?
Introduce a Chart Display *Math and Science Flip Chart* page 41. Point to the animal chart.

• Say: *This is a chart. Scientists use charts to show information in a way that is easy to read and understand. Ésta es una tabla. Los científicos usan tablas para mostrar información de manera que sea fácil de leer y entender.*

• Point to and identify the columns on the chart and the column headings. Explain that children can learn about each animal in the chart by looking down the columns.

Observe and Investigate
☑ Can children identify similarities and differences in animals?
Same and Different Chart Have children use the chart to find information about animals.

• Ask: *Which animals are shown on this chart? ¿Qué animales se muestran en esta tabla?* Have children point to all the pictures about tigers. Point out the label and explain that all of the information about tigers is in the first column.

• Help children use the chart to answer questions. Ask: *Can you use the chart to find an animal that has fur? Does the bird have fur? Does a fish have feathers? Could any of the animals be pets? ¿Pueden usar la tabla para encontrar un animal que tenga pelo? ¿Tiene pelo el pájaro? ¿Tiene plumas un pez? ¿Son mascotas algunos de estos animales?*

• Have children use the chart to identify each animal's habitat as well as the way it moves.

TIP Remind children that they saw a tiger, birds, and a fish in the book *Who Is the Beast?*

ELL Begin by comparing concrete objects in the classroom, such as two Farm Animal Counters. For children at the Beginning level of proficiency, ask yes or no questions: *Does the horse have legs? Does the sheep have legs? Is the horse purple? Is the sheep purple?* Then ask yes or no questions about animals on the chart.

Math and Science Flip Chart, page 41

106 Circle Time Week 3 Comparing Animals, Day 1

Center Time

▶ **Center Rotation** Center Time includes teacher-guided activities and independent activities. Refer to the **Learning Centers** on pages 100–101 for activities in additional centers.
small group — 30 minutes

Creativity Center
☑ Track children's ability to describe similarities and differences in the fingerprint animals.
Materials paper, finger paint in different colors, washable markers
Fingerprint Animals Set out shallow bowls of finger paint, paper, and washable markers. Invite children to make fingerprint animals.

• Have children dip a finger or their thumb in paint and make a print on paper. Allow them to practice several times.

• Then have children make animals from their fingerprints. After the fingerprints dry, have children use markers to add body parts such as legs, a tail, and ears.

• Have children tell how their fingerprint animals are the same and different.

Center Tip
If...children have difficulty making clear fingerprints, then...help them dip their finger to get the right amount of paint and gently press it on paper.

Purposeful Play
☑ Observe children appropriately communicating with each other in respectful ways and asking for help when needed.

Children choose an open center for free playtime. Encourage problem-solving skills by suggesting that they work together to make animal patterns using the Farm Animal Counters.

Let's Say Good-Bye
large group

Read Aloud Revisit "Jump or Jiggle"/"¿Quién camina?" for your afternoon Read Aloud. Ask children to act out each movement with you.
Home Connection Refer to the Home Connections activities listed in the Resources and Materials chart on page 97. Remind children to tell families what they learned about how tigers, birds, and fish are the same and how they are different. Sing the "Good-Bye Song" as children prepare to leave.

Learning Goal

Social and Emotional Development
• Child demonstrates appropriate conflict-resolution strategies, requesting help when needed.
Emergent Literacy: Writing
• Child experiments with and uses some writing conventions when writing or dictating.
Fine Arts
• Child expresses emotions or ideas through art.

Writing
Recap the day. Ask children to draw two different animals and write or dictate to tell how they are the same and different.

Center Time Week 3 Comparing Animals, Day 1 107

Let's Say Good-Bye includes the closing routines for each day. The Read Aloud from the beginning of the day is revisited with a focus on skills practiced during the day.

Each day provides a **Home Connection**. At the start of each week, a letter is provided to inform families of the weekly focus and offer additional literature suggestions to extend the weekly theme focus.

Week 1

Focus Question

What are good healthy habits?

¿Cuáles son los hábitos saludables?

This week children will learn about personal health and good hygiene at home and school. They will discuss healthy habits such as washing hands and brushing teeth, listen to stories about healthy routines, learn about medical professionals, create posters about good habits, and role play a check-up with a doctor or dentist.

✓ Learning Goals

Social and Emotional Development	Day 1	2	3	4	5
Child accepts responsibility for and regulates own behavior.	✓	✓	✓	✓	✓
Child maintains concentration/attention skills until a task is complete.	✓		✓	✓	✓

Language and Communication	1	2	3	4	5
Child demonstrates an understanding of oral language by responding appropriately.			✓	✓	
Child follows two- and three-step oral directions.		✓			
Child follows basic rules for conversations (taking turns, staying on topic, listening actively).				✓	
Child names and describes actual or pictured people, places, things, actions, attributes, and events.	✓	✓	✓		✓
Child uses newly learned vocabulary daily in multiple contexts.	✓		✓	✓	✓
Child speaks in complete sentences of four or more words including a subject, verb, and object.				✓	
Child uses regular and irregular plurals, regular past tense, personal and possessive pronouns, and subject-verb agreement.		✓			✓

Emergent Literacy: Reading	1	2	3	4	5
Child enjoys and chooses reading-related activities.				✓	
Child blends two phonemes to form a word.	✓	✓	✓	✓	✓
Child names most upper- and lowercase letters of the alphabet.	✓	✓	✓	✓	✓
Child identifies the letter that stands for a given sound.	✓	✓	✓	✓	✓
Child produces the most common sound for a given letter.			✓		✓
Child retells or reenacts poems and stories in sequence			✓	✓	
Child describes, relates to, and uses details and information from books read aloud.	✓	✓			✓

Emergent Literacy: Writing	Day 1	2	3	4	5
Child uses scribbles, shapes, pictures, symbols, and letters to represent language.			✓		✓
Child writes own name or a reasonable approximation of it.			✓		

Mathematics	1	2	3	4	5
Child uses concrete objects or makes a verbal word problem to add up to 5 objects.	✓	✓	✓	✓	
Child uses concrete objects or makes a verbal word problem to subtract up to 5 objects from a set.	✓	✓		✓	✓

Science	1	2	3	4	5
Child follows basic health and safety rules.					✓
Child practices personal hygiene skills independently (for example, washes hands, blows nose, covers mouth, brushes teeth).	✓	✓			✓
Child recognizes and selects healthy foods.			✓	✓	

Social Studies	1	2	3	4	5
Child identifies similarities and differences in families.			✓		
Child understands basic human needs for food, clothing, shelter.			✓		

Fine Arts	1	2	3	4	5
Child expresses emotions or ideas through art.			✓		✓
Child expresses ideas, emotions, and moods through individual and collaborative dramatic play.		✓			

Physical Development	1	2	3	4	5
Child develops small-muscle strength and control.		✓			

Materials and Resources

DAY 1	DAY 2	DAY 3	DAY 4	DAY 5
Program Materials				
• Teacher's Treasure Book • Oral Language Development Card 71 • Rhymes and Chants Flip Chart • Concept Big Book 4: *Staying Healthy* • ABC Big Book • Building Blocks Math Activities • Making Good Choices Flip Chart • Math and Science Flip Chart • Home Connections Resource Guide	• Teacher's Treasure Book • Dog Puppets • ABC Picture Cards • Concept Big Book 4: *Staying Healthy* • ABC Big Book • Two-Color Counters • Building Blocks Math Activities • Making Good Choices Flip Chart	• Teacher's Treasure Book • Oral Language Development Card 72 • Rhymes and Chants Flip Chart • ABC Picture Cards • ABC Big Book • Two-Color Counters • Making Good Choices Flip Chart • Photo Library CD-ROM	• Teacher's Treasure Book • Dog Puppets • Flannel Board and Patterns for "The Three Little Kittens" • ABC Picture Cards • ABC Big Book • Math and Science Flip Chart • Two-Color Counters	• Teacher's Treasure Book • Oral Language Development Card 73 • Sequence Cards: "Brushing Your Teeth" • Rhymes and Chants Flip Chart • Photo Library CD-ROM • Concept Big Book 4: *Staying Healthy* • ABC Big Book • Making Good Choices Flip Chart
Other Materials				
• health-related books • paper and crayons • doctor/dentist play items • tooth patterns • white construction paper • markers • scissors	• pictures of objects whose names have two phonemes (see p. 32) • paper • paints in various colors • games played with dot cubes	• construction paper and crayons • art materials • tape • paper plate or paper circle • dark cloth • pictures of families from around the world • clothing and job-related toys	• pictures of objects (same as Day 2) • nursery rhyme books • flannel patterns • drawing materials • picture/drawing of apple slice • sock puppets • paper plates and raisins • sticky notes	• magazines • glue, crayons, and scissors • construction paper • ABC puzzles and books • paper plates and fish crackers • paints and posterboard • blocks • medical toys
Home Connection				
Encourage children to tell their families what they learned about visiting a doctor. Send home Weekly Family Letter, Home Connections Resource Guide, pp. 69–70.	Encourage children to tell their families about healthy habits, such as washing their hands.	Encourage children to tell their families about the things that all families need.	Encourage children to tell their families about the three little kittens and their troubles. Send home: ABC Song, ABC Take-Home Book, (English) p. 6 or (Spanish) p. 34. Blank Book Template, ABC Take-Home Book, (English) p. 33, or (Spanish) p. 64	Encourage children to tell their families what they learned this week about healthy habits.

Assessment

As you observe children throughout the week, you may fill out an Anecdotal Observational Record Form to document an individual's progress toward a goal or signs indicating the need for developmental or medical evaluation. You may also choose to select work for each child's portfolio. The Anecdotal Observational Record Form and Weekly Assessment rubrics are available in the assessment section of DLMExpressOnline.com.

More Literature Suggestions

- **Oh the Things You Can Do That Are Good for You!** by Tish Rabe
- **Janey Junkfood's Fresh Adventure** by Barbara Storper
- **The Monster Health Book: A Guide to Eating Healthy, Being Active & Feeling Great for Monsters & Kids!** by Edward Miller
- **Healthy Me: Fun Ways to Develop Good Health and Safety Habits** by Michelle O'Brien
- **Shark Swimathon** by Stuart J. Murphy
- **Sopa de vegetales** por Ann Morris
- **Abecedario nutritivo** por Yanitzia Canetti
- **Somos un equipo** por Sharon Gordon
- **My Way/A mi manera** por Lynn Reiser
- **¿Para qué usas la lengua?** por María del Carmen Sánchez Mora

	DAY 1	**DAY 2**
Let's Start the Day **Language Time**	**Opening Routines** p. 26 **Morning Read Aloud** p. 26 **Oral Language and Vocabulary** p. 26 Healthy Habits **Phonological Awareness** p. 26 Blending Phonemes 	**Opening Routines** p. 32 **Morning Read Aloud** p. 32 **Oral Language and Vocabulary** p. 32 Healthy Habits **Phonological Awareness** p. 32 Blending Phonemes 
Center Time	**Focus On:** **Library and Listening Center** p. 27 **Pretend and Learn Center** p. 27	**Focus On:** **ABC Center** p. 33 **Creativity Center** p. 33
Circle Time **Literacy Time**	**Read Aloud** *Staying Healthy/* *Mantente sano* p. 28 **Learn About Letters and Sounds:** Reviewing the Alphabet p. 28  	**Read Aloud** *Staying Healthy/* *Mantente sano* p. 34 **Learn About Letters and Sounds:** Reviewing the Alphabet p. 34  
Math Time	**Finger Games** p. 29	**Snapshots (Adding)** p. 35
Social and Emotional Development	**Managing One's Behavior** p. 29 	**Managing One's Behavior** p. 35 
Content Connection	**Science:** **Oral Language and Academic Vocabulary** p. 30 Talking About Healthy Habits **Observe and Investigate** p. 30 Visiting a Doctor 	**Math:** **Finger Count** p. 36 **Finger Games** p. 36
Center Time	**Focus On:** **Math and Science Center** p. 31 **Purposeful Play** p. 31	**Focus On:** **Math and Science Center** p. 37 **Purposeful Play** p. 37
Let's Say Good-Bye	**Read Aloud** p. 31 **Writing** p. 31 **Home Connection** p. 31	**Read Aloud** p. 37 **Writing** p. 37 **Home Connection** p. 37

DAY 3

Opening Routines p. 38

Morning Read Aloud p. 38

Oral Language and Vocabulary
p. 38 Healthy Habits

Phonological Awareness
p. 38 Blending Phonemes

Focus On:

Writer's Center p. 39

Creativity Center p. 39

Read Aloud
"A Special Surprise"/"Una sorpresa especial" p. 40

Learn About Letters and Sounds: Reviewing the Alphabet p. 40

Hidden Toppings p. 41

Managing One's Behavior p. 41

Social Studies:

Oral Language and Academic Vocabulary
p. 42 Talking About Families

Understand and Participate
p. 42 Looking at Family Pictures

Focus On:

Pretend and Learn Center p. 43

Purposeful Play p. 43

Read Aloud p. 43

Writing p. 43

Home Connection p. 43

DAY 4

Opening Routines p. 44

Morning Read Aloud p. 44

Oral Language and Vocabulary
p. 44 Animal Families

Phonological Awareness
p. 44 Blending Phonemes

Focus On:

Library and Listening Center p. 45

Pretend and Learn Center p. 45

Read Aloud
"The Three Little Kittens"/ "Los tres gatitos"
p. 46

Learn About Letters and Sounds: Reviewing the Alphabet p. 46

Healthy Kids and Raisins p. 47

Managing One's Behavior p. 47

Math:

p. 48 Making Word Problems

p. 48 Farm Scene

Focus On:

Math and Science Center p. 49

Purposeful Play p. 49

Read Aloud p. 49

Writing p. 49

Home Connection p. 49

DAY 5

Opening Routines p. 50

Morning Read Aloud p. 50

Oral Language and Vocabulary
p. 50 Healthy Habits

Phonological Awareness
p. 50 Blending Phonemes

Focus On:

Writer's Center p. 51

ABC Center p. 51

Read Aloud
Staying Healthy/ Mantente sano p. 52

Learn About Letters and Sounds: Reviewing the Alphabet p. 52

Gone Fishing p. 53

Managing One's Behavior p. 53

Art Time:

Oral Language and Academic Vocabulary
p. 54 Healthy Habits

Explore and Express p. 54 Health Poster

Focus On:

Construction Center p. 55

Purposeful Play p. 55

Read Aloud p. 55

Writing p. 55

Home Connection p. 55

Learning Centers

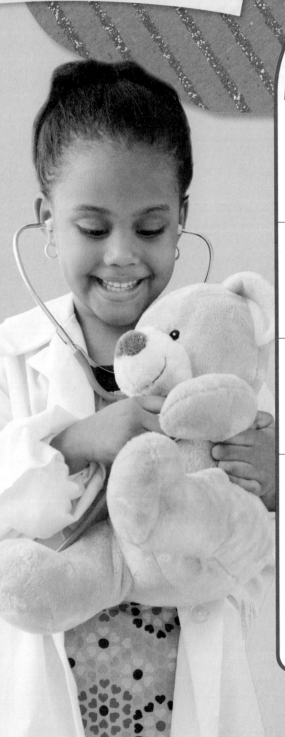

Math and Science Center

Counting Teeth
Children use paper teeth to create and solve addition and subtraction problems. See p. 31.

Dot Cube Game
Children use dot cubes to play games. They add the number of dots to move their game pieces. See p. 37.

Place Scenes
Child pairs create and solve addition and subtraction word problems with counters. See p. 49.

Warm Weather Count
Children draw a picture of themselves dressed for hot, sunny weather. They count the number of protective items and clothing added to go outside in hot weather, such as hats, sunglasses, and sunscreen, and discuss why dressing for the weather keeps them healthy.

ABC Center

Letter Sort
Children sort letter cards into three categories: letters made with lines, with curves, and with lines and curves. They name the letters and their sounds. See p. 33.

ABC Puzzles and ABC Books
Children name letters and make letter sounds as they complete ABC puzzles. They look through alphabet books and name the letters and their sounds. See p. 51.

Matching Initial Letters
Children sort word cards by initial letters.

Letter and Sound Movement Match
Partners make up movements to accompany letter sounds, such as rubbing a tummy for the /m/ sound. As one partner says the sound and makes the movement, the other names the letter that makes the sound.

Creativity Center

Hand Print Designs
Children use their hands as stamps to form a design and then demonstrate thorough hand washing. See p. 33.

Cozy Quilts
Children create a paper patchwork quilt and discuss healthy sleeping habits. See p. 39.

Proper Attire
Children decorate paper dolls to show which clothes should be worn in rainy, cold, or hot weather to keep the dolls healthy.

Keeping Cool
Child pairs make accordion folds in paper to create fans. They discuss with a partner when they might need to use the fan.

Library and Listening Center

Browsing Health-Related Books
Children look at books about health, choose a healthy habit, draw it, and explain why it is important. See p. 27.

Browsing Nursery-Rhyme Books
Children look at nursery-rhyme books and identify realistic and make-believe animal families. See p. 45.

Healthy Cupboard
Child pairs recite the nursery rhyme "Old Mother Hubbard." They list healthy foods Mother Hubbard could stock in her cupboard.

Good Advice
Partners retell nursery rhymes such as "Jack Be Nimble" or "Wee Willie Winkie." They discuss with their partner what the characters did that was not healthy or safe and what the characters could do to be healthy or safe.

Construction Center

Doctor/Dentist Office
Children use blocks and art materials to create a doctor or dentist's office. They describe the office and use it to pretend to be doctors, dentists, and patients. See p. 55.

Make a Bed
Children use blocks and tissues to make a model bed. They tuck in toy animals or people and describe why they need sleep to stay healthy.

Health Center
Child pairs use blocks and art materials to build a Health Center, where they can play doctors, dentists, and nurses, or pretend to sell healthy items in a store, such as a fruit and vegetable stand.

Writer's Center

Hear My Name
Children write their names on paper and decorate their names. They draw pictures of animals or objects that have names beginning with the same letters and letter sounds as their names. See p. 39.

"I Know My ABCs" Book
Children write upper and lower case letters of the alphabet and illustrate with pictures of items that have names with the same initial letter sounds. See p. 51.

Healthy Reminder Card
Children copy the sentence "It is time for your check up." and illustrate it with a picture of a doctor or dentist check up. They discuss when they should get check ups and why they are important.

Pretend and Learn Center

Say Ahh!
Children pretend to be doctors and dentists. They describe how they help patients. See p. 27.

Role-Play Jobs
Children pretend to do the job of a family member. They describe the job. See p. 43.

Retell and Act Out Stories
Children use pictures or drawings of apple slices to retell "A Special Surprise." They use the flannel board patterns or make and use sock puppets to retell "The Three Little Kittens." See p. 45.

Good Guardians
Children pretend to care for young children. As they play, they explain how washing, dressing, and feeding routines help children stay healthy.

DAY 1

Let's Start the Day

Focus Question

What are good healthy habits?

¿Cuáles son los hábitos saludables?

Learning Goals

Social and Emotional Development
• Child accepts responsibility for and regulates own behavior.

Language and Communication
• Child uses newly learned vocabulary daily in multiple contexts.

Emergent Literacy: Reading
• Child blends two phonemes to form a word.

Vocabulary

hands	manos	health	salud
sink	lavamanos	soap	jabón
wash	lavar		

Differentiated Instruction

✋ Extra Support

Phonological Awareness
If...children have difficulty blending two discrete phonemes to make a word, **then...** stretch the sounds, singing them together (e.g., *sssseeee* for *see*). Ask what the word is.

⭐ Enrichment

Phonological Awareness
Challenge children to blend three phonemes to make words, such as /f/ /u/ /n/ for *fun*.

Accommodations for 3's

Phonological Awareness
If...children have difficulty blending sounds, **then...**have them blend larger word parts, such as the two parts of a compound word. For example, have children listen as you say "tooth" and "brush." Ask children to put the parts together and say the word they make.

▶ **Opening Routines and Transition Tips**
For **Opening Routines** and **Transition Tips** turn to pages 178–181 and visit **DLMExpressOnline.com** for more ideas.

 Read **"A Spring Walk"**/**"Una caminata en primavera"** from the *Teacher's Treasure Book*, page 187, for your morning Read Aloud.

Language Time

 large group · 15 minutes

👤👤👤 **Social and Emotional Development** Have children wait until they are called on before responding to questions during the group discussion.

Oral Language and Vocabulary

✓ **Can children explain the importance of washing their hands?**

Healthy Habits Talk about the importance of washing your hands to stay healthy and prevent illnesses. Tell children they should wash their hands with warm, soapy water for as long as it takes to sing the "ABC Song." Ask: ***When do you wash your hands? How do you wash them?*** *¿Cuándo se lavan las manos? ¿Cómo se las lavan?*

● Display *Oral Language Development Card 71*. Name what the girl is doing (washing her hands) and what she is using (water). Then follow the suggestions on the back of the card.

Oral Language Development Card 71

Phonological Awareness

✓ **Can children blend sounds to form words?**

Blending Phonemes Display *Rhymes and Chants Flip Chart* page 33. Sing "A Healthy You!" to the tune of "Head, Shoulders, Knees, and Toes." Tell children that you will say the sounds that make up a word. You want them to put the sounds together to say the whole word. Model with the sounds /s/ /ē/ to make *see*. Say: ***I see children in the picture. What are they doing?*** *Veo unos niños en esta ilustración. ¿Qué están haciendo?* Repeat with /ē/ /t/ (eat). Ask children to blend the sounds, then find a child in the picture doing what the word describes (eating).

ELL Use the *Rhymes and Chants Flip Chart* to revisit the body-part words *hands, teeth,* and *fingernails*. Point to your hands. Say: ***These are my hands.*** Have children repeat as they hold out their hands. Ask: ***What are these?*** Have children chorally respond. Continue with the remaining body-part words. Then, have children name other body parts they can identify in English.

For additional suggestions on how to meet the needs of children at the Beginning, Intermediate, Advanced, and Advanced-High levels of English proficiency, see pages 184–187.

Rhymes and Chants Flip Chart, page 33

Center Time

▶ **Center Rotation** Center Time includes teacher-guided activities and independent activities. Refer to the **Learning Centers** on pages 24–25 for activities in additional centers.

 small group | 60–90 minutes

Library and Listening Center

Center Tip

✓ **Listen for children's descriptions and understandings of healthy habits.**

Materials health-related books, paper, crayons

Browsing Health-Related Books Have children browse through health-related books and choose one healthy habit. Help them name the habit and explain its importance.

● Have children draw their chosen healthy habit and share their drawings.

● Ask: *How will doing this keep you healthy? ¿Cómo te mantendrás sano al hacer esto?*

Center Tip

If...children have difficulty describing a healthy habit, **then...**give them clues by pointing to specifics in the photo, such as a toothbrush or toothpaste.

Pretend and Learn Center

Center Tip

✓ **Verify that children sustain their attention to complete a task.**

Materials doctor or dentist play items (clothing; tools such as stethoscope, bandage, tongue depressor, thermometer, scale, toothbrush)

Say Ahh! Tell children that they will be a doctor or dentist. They will have several patients today who need their help.

● Help children choose the appropriate play items (clothing and tools).

● Prompt them with questions related to these play items to expand on their dialogue and sustain their attention to the task.

Center Tip

If...children have difficulty using specific play items, **then...** explain the purpose of medical tools and materials, such as a stethoscope, bandage, tongue depressor, thermometer, and scale.

 Learning Goals

Social and Emotional Development
• Child maintains concentration/attention skills until a task is complete.

Language and Communication
• Child uses newly learned vocabulary daily in multiple contexts.

Science
• Child practices personal hygiene skills independently (for example, washes hands, blows nose, covers mouth, brushes teeth).

Differentiated Instruction

 Extra Support
Library and Listening Center
If...children have difficulty drawing or coloring healthy habit pictures, **then...**have them review the healthy habit picture in the book, and describe it in specific words, such as tools used.

 Enrichment
Library and Listening Center
Challenge children by saying an item's name sound-by-sound for them to blend and then find in one of the book's pictures (e.g., /s/ /ō/ /p/).

 Special Needs
Cognitive Challenges
Model how each of the doctor play items is used. For example: *I hold a stethoscope to my heart to hear it beat. Thump. Thump. Thump! Pongo el estetoscopio sobre mi corazón para escuchar su latido. ¡Bum, bum, bum!*

Focus Question

What are good healthy habits?

¿Cuáles son los hábitos saludables?

 Learning Goals

Emergent Literacy: Reading
- Child names most upper- and lowercase letters of the alphabet.
- Child identifies the letter that stands for a given sound.
- Child describes, relates to, and uses details and information from books read aloud.

Science
- Child practices personal hygiene skills independently (for example, washes hands, blows nose, covers mouth, brushes teeth).

Vocabulary

brushing	cepillarse	check-up	chequeo
habits	hábitos	healthy	sano
strong	fuerte	washing	lavarse

Differentiated Instruction

 Extra Support

Learn About Letters and Sounds

If...children have difficulty remembering the name or sound of any of the letters, **then...** focus on those letters during Center Time. Provide additional instruction and practice.

⭐ **Enrichment**

Learn About Letters and Sounds

Challenge children to write words using the letter-sounds they know. Focus on 2- and 3-letter words. Model how to segment the word sound-by-sound (e.g., /m/ /o/ /m/) and attach a known letter to each sound.

Accommodations for 3's

Learn About Letters and Sounds

Children may need more time and practice to learn letter-sounds. Focus on naming and writing the letters in the child's first name, as well as the first sound in the name.

Literacy Time

 large group / 15 minutes

📖 Read Aloud

✓ **Can children describe healthy habits, using information from the book and their own experiences?**

Build Background Tell children that you will be reading a book about healthy habits, or ways they can prevent illness and grow big and strong.

- Ask: **What do you do to stay healthy?** *¿Qué hacen para mantenerse sanos?*

Listen for Enjoyment Display *Concept Big Book 4: Staying Healthy,* and read the title. Conduct a picture walk.

- Browse through the pages. Name and describe each healthy habit.

- Ask: **Why is it important to _____?** *¿Por qué es importante _____?*

Respond to the Story Have children name the healthy habits you pointed out. Ask: **What healthy habits do we have at school?** *¿Qué hábitos saludables tenemos en la escuela?*

💡 **TIP** Be sure children can relate information in the book to their daily lives.

ELL As you browse the book, point to specific items or actions in the photos as you explain the healthy habit pictured. Encourage children to point to the photos and name items or actions they know.

Learn About Letters and Sounds

✓ **How many letter-sounds can children identify?**

Reviewing the Alphabet Sing the "ABC Song" with children as you page through the *ABC Big Book*. Tell children that they have now learned all the letters of the alphabet and a sound that each letter stands for.

- Have children find the *ABC Big Book* page containing the first letter in their name.

- Have them write their name on a self-sticking note and place it on the page. Prompt them to say the sound.

- Page through the *ABC Big Book* again. This time say, for example, "A is for Alicia" for each letter that begins a child's name.

Staying Healthy
Mantente sano

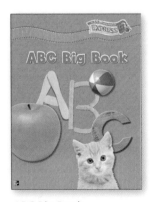

ABC Big Book

Math Time

Observe and Investigate

 Can children quickly recognize the total of two small groups?

Finger Games Children make numbers with their fingers (hands should be placed in their laps between tasks).

- Ask children to show 5 with their fingers, and discuss responses: *How many did you show on one hand? How many did you show on the other? How many fingers are showing altogether?* ¿*Cuánto mostraste en una mano?* ¿*Cuánto mostraste en la otra?* ¿*Cuántos dedos hay en total?* Ask them to show another way to make 5, using both hands if they have not yet, and repeat the questions.

- Repeat, always asking children to describe their actions, and alternate the following: (1) show 4 using both hands, and then show 4 a different way; (2) show 4 with the same number on each hand; and (3) show 4 with a different number on one hand than the other. Repeat with other numbers, adjusting finger combinations as needed.

ELL Focus on the concepts of *same* and *different* to help children during the math activity. Use classroom manipulatives. Show two that are identical. Say: *These are the same.* Have children repeat. Then show two that are different. Say: *These are not the same. These are different.* Continue showing pairs of items. Ask: *Are these the same or different?*

Building Blocks

Online Math Activity

Introduce Piece Puzzler 4: Compose Shapes, in which children solve more complex puzzles containing larger areas to fill, as well as fewer lines to guide their work. Each child should complete Piece Puzzler 4 this week.

✕✕✕ Social and Emotional Development

Making Good Choices

 Do children regulate their own behavior during classroom activities?

Managing One's Behavior Discuss classroom procedures during discussions, transitions, and Center Time. Display the *Making Good Choices Flip Chart*, page 33. Point to the boy playing with the blocks.

- Ask: *No one else is playing in the Block Center. What should the boy do?* *No hay nadie más jugando en el centro de bloques.* ¿*Qué debe hacer el niño?*

- Then discuss waiting for friends to finish other activities. Highlight the child raising a hand during the circle discussion.

Making Good Choices Flip Chart, page 33

✓ Learning Goals

Social and Emotional Development
- Child accepts responsibility for and regulates own behavior.

Mathematics
- Child uses concrete objects or makes a verbal word problem to add up to 5 objects.
- Child uses concrete objects or makes a verbal word problem to subtract up to 5 objects from a set.

Vocabulary

altogether	total	different	diferente
how many	cuánto	number	número
same	igual		

Differentiated Instruction

👋 **Extra Support**
Observe and Investigate
If...children struggle during Finger Games, **then...**use smaller numbers. Focus on showing the same number on each hand.

⭐ **Enrichment**
Observe and Investigate
Challenge children to quickly make and compare sets of larger numbers (up to 10). Use Counting Cards or manipulatives.

Accommodations for 3's
Observe and Investigate
If...children struggle during Finger Games, **then...**have them show the number on one hand only. Then hold up your hand with the same number. Ask: *Are these the same?* ¿*Son iguales?*

Focus Question
What are good healthy habits?
¿Cuáles son los hábitos saludables?

Learning Goals

Language and Communication
• Child names and describes actual or pictured people, places, things, actions, attributes, and events.

Science
• Child practices personal hygiene skills independently (for example, washes hands, blows nose, covers mouth, brushes teeth).

Vocabulary

check-up	chequeo	doctor	doctor
habit	hábito	healthy	sano
ill/sick	sano /enfermo	office	consultorio

Differentiated Instruction

✋ Extra Support

Oral Language and Academic Vocabulary
If...children have difficulty describing why a healthy habit is important, **then...**explain the consequences of not using these habits (e.g., cause/effect relationships), such as getting cavities if they don't regularly brush their teeth. Ask: **What can happen if you don't brush your teeth regularly?** *¿Qué puede suceder si no te cepillas los dientes con regularidad?*

⭐ Enrichment

Oral Language and Academic Vocabulary
Challenge children to add robust vocabulary to their spoken language repertoire: **illness, disease, germs.**

Science Time

large group — 20 minutes

Personal Health Skills Have children wash their hands before snack time and meals. Model proper washing, as needed.

Oral Language and Academic Vocabulary

☑ **Can children describe the importance and use of healthy habits?**

Talking About Healthy Habits Point to the photo of the girl in the doctor's office on the *Math and Science Flip Chart,* page 61. Say: ***This girl goes once a year to the doctor to get a check-up. She also goes to the doctor when she is ill, or sick. The doctor checks our bodies and how we are growing.*** *Esta niña visita al doctor una vez al año para hacerse un chequeo. También visita al doctor cuando está enferma. El doctor nos revisa el cuerpo para ver cómo estamos creciendo.*

- Explain that a yearly check-up at the doctor's office is one way to stay healthy and prevent illness.

- Ask: ***Do you remember having a check-up? What are some of the things a doctor does during a check-up?*** *¿Recuerdan si se hicieron un chequeo? ¿Qué cosas hace el doctor durante un chequeo?*

- Discuss the other healthy habits shown on the chart. Ask children to describe each one and how it protects us and helps us stay healthy. Make sure to discuss how some of the habits get rid of germs or stop them from being passed to others.

Observe and Investigate

☑ **Can children explain what a doctor does?**

Visiting a Doctor Take children to visit the school nurse or invite a doctor or nurse to visit the classroom.

- Ask the doctor or nurse to describe the tools he or she uses. Ask children if they know what the tools are used for. Have the doctor or nurse explain the tools' uses (e.g., stethoscope, bandages, thermometer, scale).

- If the doctor or nurse agrees, let children take turns holding the tools and model their use. Have children describe what they are checking when they use each tool.

- Ask the doctor or nurse for expert advice: ***What can we do to stay healthy?*** *¿Qué podemos hacer para mantenernos sanos?*

💡 **TIP** Tell children that they will have more opportunities to use the doctor's tools in the Pretend and Learn Center.

ELL Begin by asking children yes/no or one-word answer questions about healthy habits. ***Is this a bandage or a thermometer? Do you brush your teeth before or after eating?*** To help children use health-related words, have them role-play visiting a doctor. Narrate their role-play, stopping to ask questions. For example: ***Are you in a doctor's office? Where are you?***

Staying Healthy
Estar sano

Math and Science Flip Chart, page 61

Center Time

▶ **Center Rotation** Center Time includes teacher-guided activities and independent activities. Refer to the **Learning Centers** on pages 24–25 for activities in additional centers.

 small group · 30 minutes

Math and Science Center

	Center Tip

☑ Observe children as they illustrate word problems using their math manipulatives.

Materials tooth pattern, white construction paper, markers, scissors

Counting Teeth Prepare a tooth pattern for children to trace. Have children cut out 5 teeth. Ask them to number the teeth from 1–5.

● Children work with a partner to create word problems. Each child displays a chosen number of teeth. The pair then adds them. Ask: *What problem did you make? How many teeth altogether?* *¿Cuántos dientes hay en total?*

● For subtraction, have children first add the total number of teeth, then have each child remove a chosen number. Ask: *What problem did you make? How many teeth are remaining?* *¿Qué problema crearon? ¿Cuántos dientes quedan?*

Center Tip

If...children need help creating a word problem, **then...** provide a total number for them (the answer). Say, for example: *Show 3 teeth. Each of you must show a different number to add up to 3. Muestren 3 dientes. Cada uno de ustedes debe mostrar un número diferente para llegar a 3.*

Purposeful Play

☑ Observe children attending to tasks until they are completed.

Children choose an open center for free playtime. Encourage cooperation skills by suggesting they work together to role-play a visit to a doctor or dentist.

Let's Say Good-Bye

 large group · 15 minutes

 Read Aloud Revisit "A Spring Walk"/ *"Una caminata en primavera"* for your afternoon Read Aloud. Remind children to listen for reasons why a spring walk is fun and healthy.

 Home Connection Refer to the Home Connections activities listed in the Resources and Materials chart on page 21. Remind children to tell families about visiting a doctor or nurse. Sing the "Good-Bye Song"/"Hora de ir a casa" as children prepare to leave.

Learning Goals

Social and Emotional Development
• Child maintains concentration/attention skills until a task is complete.

Language and Communication
• Child names and describes actual or pictured people, places, things, actions, attributes, and events.

Mathematics
• Child uses concrete objects or makes a verbal word problem to add up to 5 objects.
• Child uses concrete objects or makes a verbal word problem to subtract up to 5 objects from a set.

Writing

Recap the day. Have children name common healthy habits. Ask: *What can you do to stay healthy?* *¿Qué pueden hacer para mantenerse saludables?* Record their answers. Read them back as you track the print, and emphasize that print is read from left to right and from top to bottom.

DAY 2

Focus Question

What are good healthy habits?
¿Cuáles son los hábitos saludables?

Learning Goals

Language and Communication
• Child follows two- and three-step oral directions.
• Child names and describes actual or pictured people, places, things, actions, attributes, and events.

Emergent Literacy: Reading
• Child blends two phonemes to form a word.

Fine Arts
• Child expresses ideas, emotions, and moods through individual and collaborative dramatic play.

Vocabulary

healthy	sano	habit	hábitos
sneezing	estomudar	sick	enfermo
washing	lavar		

Differentiated Instruction

 Extra Support

Oral Language and Vocabulary
If...children have difficulty describing a healthy habit, **then...**offer questions about specific habit details, such as: *What do you use to wash your hands? Do you use warm or cold water? Soap? When do you wash your hands? ¿Qué usan para lavarse las manos? ¿Agua tibia o agua fría? ¿Jabón? ¿Cuándo se lavan las manos?*

 Enrichment

Oral Language and Vocabulary
Expand children's vocabularies during the discussion by adding words such as *germs* or *prevent*. Briefly define each word and reinforce during Center Time play.

Let's Start the Day

Opening Routines and Transition Tips
For **Opening Routines** and **Transition Tips** turn to pages 178–181 and visit DLMExpressOnline.com for more ideas.

Read **"Little Red Riding Hood"/**"Caperucita Roja" from the *Teacher's Treasure Book*, page 162, for your morning Read Aloud.

Language Time

large group   15 minutes

Social and Emotional Provide 3-step directions for children to follow throughout the day's lessons, such as "Put your toys away, come to circle, and sit on the mat."

Oral Language and Vocabulary

✓ **Can children identify and recreate healthy habits?**

Healthy Habits Talk about the many things you can do to stay healthy. Ask: *What do we do to keep us from getting sick? ¿Qué hacemos para evitar que enfermarnos?*

● Have children describe in detail each healthy habit, such as washing their hands or sneezing into their arms. Ask: *Why is this important? When do we wash our hands? How? ¿Por qué es importante? ¿Cuándo nos lavamos las manos? ¿Cómo nos las lavamos?*

● Encourage children to role-play a healthy habit for their classmates to guess. Once it is identified, review why the habit helps prevent illness.

Phonological Awareness

✓ **Can children blend sounds to form words?**

Blending Phonemes Display a Dog Puppet and a photo depicting an object or animal whose name contains two sounds (e.g., *knee, bee, tie, pie, boy, egg, row, shoe, tea, ice, key, toe, zoo*). Tell children that the puppet will say the sounds in the word pictured. They must blend together the sounds to see if the puppet was correct. Occasionally say the incorrect sounds and ask children to provide the correct sounds.

ELL Teach the names of the photos used in the Phonological Awareness activity in small groups with English Language Learners prior to using them in the whole group lesson. This will help these children more fully participate in the lesson.

Center Time

 small group · 60–90 minutes

> **Center Rotation** Center Time includes teacher-guided activities and independent activities. Refer to the **Learning Centers** on pages 24–25 for activities in additional centers.

ABC Center

✓ **Keep track of the letter-sounds children are beginning to master.**

Materials *ABC Picture Cards*

Letter Sort Have children sort the upper case letters on the *ABC Picture Cards* into three piles: (1) letters made with lines, (2) letters made with circles or curves, and (3) letters made with lines and curves.

- Once the letters are sorted, ask: *What is the name of this letter? What is its sound? ¿Cómo se llama esta letra? ¿Qué sonido tiene?*

- Then have children find the letters in words they know, such as their name.

- Repeat the activity with lower case letters.

Center Tip

If... children have difficulty sorting the letters, **then...**provide one example letter for each pile, such as E, C, and P. Help children compare each letter to the example letter.

Creativity Center

✓ **Monitor children's ability to use art tools and effectively wash their hands.**

Materials large sheets of paper, various colors of paints

Hand Print Designs Tell children that they will make hand print designs.

- Have children begin by thoroughly washing their hands. Then model for them how to make a hand print.

- Have children create a hand print design, using many colors. Suggest they overlap some of the hands to mix the colors.

- When completed, ask: *What do we do now? How can we get our hands clean? ¿Qué hacemos ahora? ¿Cómo podemos limpiarnos las manos?*

Center Tip

If...children have difficulty thoroughly washing their hands, **then...**model for them using warm, soapy water. Sing the "ABC Song" as you wash to demonstrate appropriate length of washing.

 Learning Goals

Emergent Literacy: Reading
- Child names most upper- and lowercase letters of the alphabet.
- Child produces the most common sound for a given letter.

Science
- Child practices personal hygiene skills independently (for example, washes hands, blows nose, covers mouth, brushes teeth).

Physical Development
- Child develops small-muscle strength and control.

Differentiated Instruction

 Extra Support

ABC Center

If...children have difficulty identifying curved letters, **then...**have them trace/copy the letter with a piece of yarn or flexible stick. Ask: *Do you have to bend the yarn/flexible stick to make the letter? ¿Tienen que doblar el hilo/palito para formar la letra?*

Enrichment

ABC Center

Point to each *ABC Picture Card* in turn. Challenge children to name words that begin with the letter-sound.

Accommodations for 3's

ABC Center

If...children have difficulty sorting letters, **then...**limit the sort to a smaller set of *ABC Picture Cards* and focus on only letters with just lines versus letters with circles or curves.

Focus Question
What are good healthy habits?
¿Cuáles son los hábitos saludables?

 Learning Goals

Language and Communication
• Child understands and uses regular and irregular plural nouns, regular past tense verbs, personal and possessive pronouns, and subject-verb agreement.

Emergent Literacy: Reading
• Child names most upper- and lowercase letters of the alphabet.

• Child describes, relates to, and uses details and information from books read aloud.

Science
• Child practices personal hygiene skills independently (for example, washes hands, blows nose, covers mouth, brushes teeth).

Vocabulary

brushing	cepillarse	check-up	chequeo
habits	hábitos	healthy	sano
strong	fuerte	washing	lavarse

 Differentiated Instruction

✋ Extra Support

Learn About Letters and Sounds
If...children have difficulty hopping to the letters in their names, **then...**have them hop only to the first letter in their names, or provide directional clues such as "Hop backwards two letters."

⭐ Enrichment

Learn About Letters and Sounds
Have children say the sound of each letter as they hop the ABC path.

Literacy Time

 large group · 15 minutes

📖 Read Aloud

✓ Can children describe healthy habits, using information from the book and their own experiences?

Build Background Tell children that you will be rereading a book about healthy habits, or ways they can prevent illness and grow big and strong.

● Ask: **What do we do at school to stay healthy?** *¿Qué hacemos en la escuela para mantenernos sanos?*

Listen for Understanding Display *Concept Big Book 4: Staying Healthy,* page 17, and read the title.

● Read pages 18–21. Point to the photographs and describe each healthy habit in detail, such as the proper way to sneeze or when to wash your hands.

● Ask: **What did you learn about staying healthy? Why is staying healthy important?** *¿Qué aprendieron sobre mantenerse sanos? ¿Por qué es importante mantenerse sanos?*

Respond to the Story Have children name the healthy habits depicted. Ask: **When do we wash our hands at school? What healthy habits do you have at home? Show me with your finger how we read the words on this page.** *¿Cuándo nos lavamos las manos en la escuela? ¿Qué hábitos saludables tienen en casa? Muéstrenme con el dedo cómo leer las palabras de esta página.*

ELL As you read the book, point to specific items and actions in the photos as you explain each healthy habit. Ask follow-up yes/no or short answer questions, such as: **Is this a toothbrush? Is the boy washing his hands or brushing his teeth?** Make sure children understand that "teeth" is the plural of "tooth" and can use the words appropriately.

For additional suggestions on how to meet the needs of children at the Beginning, Intermediate, Advanced, and Advanced-High levels of English proficiency, see pages 184–187.

Learn About Letters and Sounds

✓ How many letters can children identify?

Reviewing the Alphabet Sing the "ABC Song" with children as you page through the *ABC Big Book.* Praise children for their efforts.

● Using *ABC Picture Cards*, make an ABC path on the floor.

● Have one child walk the path as everyone sings the "ABC Song." Repeat with other children.

● Then ask each child to hop to the letters in his or her name in order.

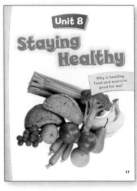

Staying Healthy
Mantente sano

Aa

apple   acorn

ABC Picture Cards

Math Time

large group 15 minutes

Observe and Investigate

✓ **Can children quickly recognize the total number in two small groups?**

Snapshots (Adding) Secretly put three counters in one of your hands and three counters in the other. Show your closed hands, and then open them for two seconds, closing them immediately after.

Building Blocks

Online Math Activity

Introduce Number Snapshots 3, in which children match a group up to 5 to its numeral when shown only briefly. Each chlid should complete the activity this week.

large group 15 minutes

- Ask: *How many counters did you see in each hand? How many counters did you see altogether?* ¿Cuántas fichas vieron en cada mano? ¿Cuántas fichas vieron en total? Open both hands, and count the counters with children to check.

- Repeat with as many counters as children's ability allows.

🏃 Social and Emotional Development

Making Good Choices

✓ **Do children regulate their own behavior during classroom activities?**

Managing One's Behavior Revisit the *Making Good Choices Flip Chart* page 33, "What Happens in Our Classroom?"

Making Good Choices Flip Chart, page 33

- Display one of the Dog Puppets. Say: *Tell the puppet ways the children in the picture are waiting their turn.* Cuéntenle al títere la forma en que los niños de la ilustración están esperando su turno.

- Provide each child a turn to tell the puppet the ways the pictured children wait until it is their turn to answer a question or engage in an activity. Remind children that waiting their turn shows kindness towards their classmates.

- Play the song "Pushy, Pushy, Pushy"/"La cancion del empujon" from the Making Good Choices Audio CD. Ask children how the people in the song could make better choices.

ELL Provide sentence frames to help during the conversation with the dog puppet. Use these and others: *The child is _____ because _____. You raise your hand when _____.* Model the use of each frame. Have children repeat, then apply using their own words. Some children may feel more comfortable just repeating the completed frame you provided.

Learning Goals

Social and Emotional Development
- Child accepts responsibility for and regulates own behavior.

Mathematics
- Child uses concrete objects or makes a verbal word problem to add up to 5 objects.
- Child uses concrete objects or makes a verbal word problem to subtract up to 5 objects from a set.

Vocabulary

add	sumar	altogether	en total
count	contar	how many	cuánto
number	número		

Differentiated Instruction

✋ **Extra Support**

Observe and Investigate
If...children struggle with adding the counters, **then...**show the counters for a longer period of time before closing your hands.

⭐ **Enrichment**

Observe and Investigate
Challenge children by increasing the number of counters in one hand and then the other.

💜 **Special Needs**

Vision Loss
To adapt the Snapshots activity, replace counters with dot cards that use dots made of felt or hook and loop tape. The child can feel the dots and count them.

Learning Goals

Social and Emotional Development
• Child accepts responsibility for and regulates own behavior.

Mathematics
• Child uses concrete objects or makes a verbal word problem to add up to 5 objects.

• Child uses concrete objects or makes a verbal word problem to subtract up to 5 objects from a set.

Vocabulary

add	sumar	altogether	contar
how many	cuántos	number	número
subtract	restar		

Differentiated Instruction

 Extra Support

Observe and Investigate

If...children have difficulty determining how many fingers to show on either hand, **then...**have them always show 5 fingers on their left hand for sums 6 or above. For sums under five have them always show 1 finger on their left hand.

 Enrichment

Observe and Investigate

Challenge children to make word problems with answers larger than 10. Children will show one number with their fingers, and think of the other number in their heads. For example, children can show 5 fingers and ask: **What is 5 plus 10?** *¿Cuánto es 5 más 10?*

Math Time

  large group 20 minutes

Social Emotional Skills Ask children why it would be a good idea to wait until everyone has had time to figure out the math problem before showing or stating their answer.

 Can children count to 10?

Finger Count Have children hold up their fingers as they count from 1–10.

● Ask: *How many fingers are on one hand? How many fingers do you have altogether? ¿Cuántos dedos tienen en una mano? ¿Cuántos dedos tienen en total?*

● Have children hold up one finger on one hand and one finger on the other. Ask: *How many altogether? ¿Cuántos son en total?* Then say: *If I want to show 3 fingers, what do I need to do? Si quiero mostrar 3 dedos, ¿qué tengo que hacer?* Model for children how to show a given number using a chosen number of fingers from both hands.

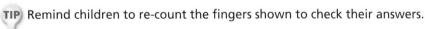 **Can children add and subtract numbers?**

Finger Games Children make numbers with their fingers (hands should be placed in their laps between tasks).

● Ask children to show 5 with their fingers, and discuss responses: *How many did you show on one hand? How many did you show on the other hand? How many fingers are showing altogether? ¿Cuántos mostraron con una mano? ¿Cuántos mostraron con la otra? ¿Cuántos dedos mostraron en total?*

● Repeat, always asking children to describe their actions, and alternate the following: (1) do not allow thumbs in responses; (2) challenge children by asking them to show 3, 5, or 7 using the same number on each hand, discuss why it cannot be done (odd numbers), and then model equal numbers per hand using 4, 6, 8, and 10; and, (3) show 4 on one hand by asking how many fingers up and how many down, and repeat with 0, 1, 2, 3, and 5.

 TIP Remind children to re-count the fingers shown to check their answers.

ELL Point to a Counting Card with the number in the task (e.g., 7) as you say the number.

Center Time

▶ **Center Rotation** Center Time includes teacher-guided activities and independent activities. Refer to the **Learning Centers** on pages 24–25 for activities in additional centers.

   small group 30 minutes

Learning Goals

Social and Emotional Development
• Child accepts responsibility for and regulates own behavior.

Language and Communication
• Child follows two- and three-step oral directions.

Mathematics
• Child uses concrete objects or makes a verbal word problem to add up to 5 objects.

Math and Science Center

✓ **Observe children as they count using dot cubes, and regulate behavior during a game.**

Materials simple games that use dot cubes

Dot Cube Games Provide various dot cube games for children to play.

• Explain or model the rules for each game. Have children play with a partner or in a small group. Say: ***Remember to wait your turn before rolling the cube or moving your game piece.*** *Recuerden esperar su turno para lanzar el dado o mover una ficha.*

• Help children count and add the numbers on the dot cubes. Children may need help with the numbers 11 and 12. Show these two numbers using the dot cubes before children begin playing.

Center Tip

If...children need help following game directions, **then...** play the game with them for a few minutes until they feel comfortable with the rules.

Writing

Recap the day. Have children name healthy habits they keep at school.
Ask: ***How do we stay healthy at school?*** *¿Cómo nos mantenemos saludables en la escuela?* Ask them to draw a picture showing an example of a healthy habit and label it.

Purposeful Play

✓ **Observe children completing center activities.**

Children choose an open center for free playtime. Encourage cooperation skills by suggesting they continue to role-play healthy habits in the Play and Learn Center from Day 1.

Let's Say Good-Bye

  large group 15 minutes

 Read Aloud Revisit the story "Little Red Riding Hood"/"Caperucita Roja" for your afternoon Read Aloud. Remind children to listen for the lesson that Little Red Riding Hood learned.

 Home Connection Refer to the Home Connections activities listed in the Resources and Materials chart on page 21. Remind children to tell families about healthy habits, such as washing hands. Sing the "Good-Bye Song"/"Hora de ir a casa" as children prepare to leave.

DAY 3

Focus Question

What are good healthy habits?
¿Cuáles son los hábitos saludables?

 Learning Goals

Language and Communication
• Child uses newly learned vocabulary daily in multiple contexts.

Emergent Literacy: Reading
• Child blends two phonemes to form a word.

Vocabulary

alarm	alarma	bed	cama
blanket	cobija	clock	reloj
nighttime	noche	pillow	almohada
sleep/rest	dormir/descansar		

Differentiated Instruction

 Extra Support

Phonological Awareness
If...children have difficulty blending two discrete phonemes to make a word, then...stretch the sounds, singing them together (e.g., *ssssoooo* for *so*). Ask: *What's the word? ¿Cuál es la palabra?*

Enrichment

Phonological Awareness
Challenge children to blend three phonemes to make words, such as /r/ /u/ /n/ for *run*.

Accommodations for 3's

Phonological Awareness
If...children have difficulty blending sounds, then...have them blend larger word parts, such as the two parts of a compound word. For example, say: *Listen to these word parts: night...time. Put them together. What's the word? Escuchen estas dos partes: night...time. Ahora únanlas. ¿Cuál es la palabra?*

 # Let's Start the Day

> ## Opening Routines and Transition Tips
> For **Opening Routines** and **Transition Tips** turn to pages 178–181 and visit DLMExpressOnline.com for more ideas.
>
> Read **"The Lion's Haircut"/**"El corte de pelo del león" from the *Teacher's Treasure Book*, page 271, for your morning Read Aloud.

Language Time

large group **15 minutes**

Social and Emotional Development Have children wait for your signals before they transition from one activity to another.

Oral Language and Vocabulary

✓ **Can children explain the importance of getting proper sleep?**

Healthy Habits Talk about the importance of getting proper rest to stay healthy. Tell children they should get at least eight hours of sleep a night to grow big and strong. Ask: **When do you go to sleep at night? Where do you sleep?** *¿A qué hora se duermen por la noches? ¿Dónde duermen?*

● Display *Oral Language Development Card 72*. Name what the girl is doing (sleeping) and where she is. Then follow the suggestions on the back of the card.

Oral Language Development Card 72

Phonological Awareness

✓ **Can children blend sounds to form words?**

Blending Phonemes Revisit *Rhymes and Chants Flip Chart* page 33. Have children join in as you sing "A Healthy You!" to the tune of "Head, Shoulders, Knees, and Toes."

● Remind children that words are made up of smaller sounds. Tell children you will say the sounds in a word. You want them to put the sounds together to say the word. Model with the sounds /ē/ /t/ to make *eat*. Say: **What is the girl eating?** *¿Qué esta comiendo la niña? Repitan la palabra* eating.

● Then ask children to find the boy with his arms in the air. Say: **/t/ /ew/. Put these sounds together. What's the word?** *Unan estos sonidos ¿Qué palabra se forma?*

ELL Use the *Rhymes and Chants Flip Chart* to revisit the words *wash, rest, sleep, jump, run, dance, sing,* and *eat.* Use actions and gestures to teach/review the words. Have children repeat as they say the words. Then provide sentence starters for children to complete, such as *I like to eat _____.* or *I can wash my _____.*

For additional suggestions on how to meet the needs of children at the Beginning, Intermediate, Advanced, and Advanced-High levels of English proficiency, see pages 184–187.

Rhymes and Chants Flip Chart, page 33

Center Time

> **Center Rotation** Center Time includes teacher-guided activities and independent activities. Refer to the **Learning Centers** on pages 24–25 for activities in additional centers.

 small group · 60–90 minutes

Writer's Center

Center Tip

✓ **Track children's ability to connect letters to sounds.**

Materials construction paper, crayons, art materials

Hear My Name Have children write their name in large letters at the top of a sheet of construction paper. Children can decorate their names with yarn, glitter, or other art materials.

- Under each letter in their name, have children draw a picture of an object or animal whose name begins with the same letter-sound. Ask: **What sound does this letter stand for? What other words begin with this sound?** *¿Qué sonido tiene esta letra? ¿Qué otras palabras comienzan con este sonido?* Children can also label each picture.

- Have children share their name cards by stating the picture name under each letter. For example: "My name is Ben—bear, egg, nest."

If...children have difficulty thinking of an object or animal whose name begins with a letter in their name, **then...**have them browse through ABC books to look for ideas.

Creativity Center

Center Tip

✓ **Monitor children's ability to describe the importance of healthy habits, such as sleeping.**

Materials construction paper, art supplies, tape

Cozy Quilts Remind children that they should get plenty of sleep each night.

- Ask: **Why do you need to sleep? What do you use when you sleep?** *¿Por qué necesitan dormir? ¿Qué usan cuando duermen?* (bed, pillow, blanket, alarm clock, stuffed animal)

- Have children make a quilt out of construction paper squares.

- Have children cut 9 four-inch squares using a pattern you created. (Or, cut squares in advance for children.) Children should decorate each square with a different design. On one square, they should write their name.

- Children tape together the squares to form a quilt. Display the completed quilts.

If...children have difficulty taping the quilt squares, **then...**turn all the pattern sides facedown, align the quilt pieces, and tape a few pieces together to model how it is done. Children can continue taping pieces.

Learning Goals

Emergent Literacy: Writing
- Child uses scribbles, shapes, pictures, symbols, and letters to represent language.
- Child writes own name or a reasonable approximation of it.

Fine Arts
- Child expresses emotions or ideas through art.

Differentiated Instruction

✋ Extra Support
Creativity Center
If...children have difficulty thinking of different patterns for each square, **then...**suggest less common patterns such as dots or zig-zags.

⭐ Enrichment
Creativity Center
Challenge children to write words on their squares to accompany the designs.

Accommodations for 3's
Creativity Center
If...children have difficulty cutting the squares, **then...**cut them in advance for the children or hold their hands as you cut together.

Focus Question
What are good healthy habits?
¿Cuáles son los hábitos saludables?

Learning Goals

Language and Communication
• Child demonstrates an understanding of oral language by responding appropriately.

Emergent Literacy: Reading
• Child names most upper- and lowercase letters of the alphabet.

• Child identifies the letter that stands for a given sound.

• Child retells or reenacts poems and stories in sequence.

Vocabulary

apple	manzana	bag	bolsa
star	estrella	store	tienda
surprise	sorpresa	town	pueblo

Differentiated Instruction

Extra Support
Read Aloud
If...children have difficulty connecting the shape of the apple seeds to a star, **then**...draw the seed shape on the board and create a star outline around it.

⭐ Enrichment
Learn About Letters and Sounds
Challenge children to write the names of classmates.

Literacy Time

📖 Read Aloud

✓ Can children recall important story details?

Build Background Tell children that you will be reading a story about a healthful food—apples.

● Ask: *What color is an apple? Is an apple a fruit or a vegetable? Does an apple have seeds?* ¿De qué color son las manzanas? ¿La manzana es una fruta o una verdura? ¿Las manzanas tienen semillas?

Listen for Understanding Read aloud "A Special Surprise"/"Una sorpresa especial," *Teacher's Treasure Book* page 269. Follow the drawing and prop directions as you read each reference in the story to help children connect the text to its meaning.

● Ask: *What did Annie get in town? What is inside Annie's bag?* ¿Qué consiguió Annie en el pueblo? ¿Qué hay dentro de la bolsa de Annie?

Respond to the Story Have children name what Annie gave each child. Ask: *What was Annie's special surprise? What shape did you see inside your apple? What are apple seeds used for?* ¿Cuál fue la sorpresa especial de Annie? ¿Qué forma vieron dentro de sus manzanas? ¿Para qué se usan las semillas de manzana?

💡 TIP Help children use the drawings and apple pieces to recall story details. Tell children they can use the drawings during Center Time to retell the story to a friend.

Learn About Letters and Sounds

✓ How many letter-sounds can children identify?

Reviewing the Alphabet Sing the "ABC Song" with children as you page through the *ABC Big Book.* Praise children for all they have learned this year.

● Display the *ABC Picture Cards.* Have two children use the cards to form their names. Display the names side-by-side.

● Have children compare the names. *Are there any letters that are the same? What is the first letter/sound in each name?* ¿Hay letras que son iguales? ¿Cuál es la primera letra y el primer sonido de cada nombre?

● Continue with other pairs.

ELL Review the photos in the *ABC Big Book.* Page through the book as children name the objects and animals they know. Reinforce those picture names they struggle with. Allow them to page through the book during Center Time to practice naming items. Praise them for all they have learned.

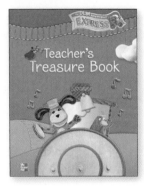
Teacher's Treasure Book, page 269

ABC Big Book

Math Time

Observe and Investigate

☑ **Can children add numbers?**

Hidden Toppings Tell children you are making a "pizza" (paper plate or construction paper circle) with hidden "toppings" (flat, round counters).

- Show three toppings on your pizza, and then cover them with a dark cloth. Add two more toppings one at a time under the cloth. Ask: **How many toppings are there altogether? How did you figure that out?** *¿Cuántos ingredientes hay en total? ¿Cómo llegaron a esa conclusión?* Uncover the toppings to count with children.

- Repeat with new numbers.

- Discuss which toppings are healthier to eat, such as vegetable toppings versus some of the fatty meats.

 Focus on the concepts of *all* and *none*. Hold 5 counters in your hand. Say: **I have all the counters. What do I have?** Then give the counters to a child. Say: **<Child's name> has all the counters. I have none. What do I have?** Hold up your hands to show they are empty. Ask: **Who has all the counters?** Repeat with other counter sets and children.

Building Blocks

Online Math Activity

Children can complete Piece Puzzler 4 and Number Snapshots 3 during computer time or Center Time.

✷✷✷ Social and Emotional Development

Making Good Choices

☑ **Do children regulate their own behavior during classroom activities?**

Managing One's Behavior Display *Making Good Choices Flip Chart*, page 33, "What Happens in Our Classroom?" Discuss with children why it is important to have rules. Ask about rules they have helped to make for the classroom.

- With a Dog Puppet, role-play other common classroom situations that require children to regulate their behavior. For example, explain that the puppet wants to use the materials in the art center, but they are being used by other children. Model what you would say and do to help the puppet.

- After each role-play, ask: **Why is it important to wait your turn? How do classroom rules help us?** *¿Por qué es importante esperar su turno? ¿Cómo nos ayudan las reglas de la clase?*

Making Good Choices Flip Chart, page 33

✓ Learning Goals

Social and Emotional Development
- Child accepts responsibility for and regulates own behavior.

Mathematics
- Child uses concrete objects or makes a verbal word problem to add up to 5 objects.

Science
- Child recognizes and selects healthy foods.

Vocabulary

add	sumar	altogether	en total
count	contar	how many	cuántos
numbers	números		

Differentiated Instruction

✋ **Extra Support**
Observe and Investigate
If...children struggle adding during the hidden activity, **then...**have children keep track of the counters using their fingers. When one is added, for example, they extend one more finger.

⭐ **Enrichment**
Observe and Investigate
Continue the activity, adding to 10 and beyond.

Accommodations for 3's
Observe and Investigate
If...children struggle adding, **then...**focus on adding only one topping. Chorally count the sum, or number of toppings, with children.

Focus Question
What are good healthy habits?
¿Cuáles son los hábitos saludables?

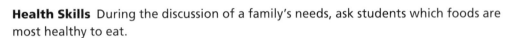

Social Studies Time

large group · 20 minutes

Health Skills During the discussion of a family's needs, ask students which foods are most healthy to eat.

Oral Language and Vocabulary

 Can children identify characteristics and needs of a family?

Talking About Families Ask children to draw a picture of their family and tell about each member.

- Have children compare family characteristics. For example, ask: *How many sisters do you have? How many sisters does _____ have? What does each family member do (e.g., job)?* ¿Cuántas hermanas tienen? ¿Cuántas hermanas tiene (nombre de otro niño) _____? ¿Qué hace cada una?

- Point out that all families are different, but they have some things in common. Ask children what all families need. Be sure they recognize that all families need food, clothing, and shelter to survive.

Understand and Participate

 Can children identify the similarities and differences in families and their needs?

Looking at Family Pictures Display pictures of families from around the world, such as families enjoying a meal at home.

- Describe each picture, such as the names of various foods and types of clothing or homes.

- Point to two pictures. Ask: *How are these families alike? How are they different?* ¿En qué se parecen estas familias? ¿En qué se diferencian?

- Extend the discussion by discussing specific customs of the families pictured (e.g., holidays celebrated, special foods eaten, special clothes worn).

TIP Tell children that they can role-play family members' jobs during the Pretend and Learn Center.

ELL Use the *Photo Library CD-ROM* pictures to teach children words associated with occupations, such as *dentist, farmer, teacher, police officer,* and *cook.* Have children draw a picture of one of their family members on the job and tell about it. Provide language, as needed.

Learning Goals

Language and Communication
- Child names and describes actual or pictured people, places, things, actions, attributes, and events.

Social Studies
- Child identifies similarities and differences in families.
- Child understands basic human needs for food, clothing, shelter.

Vocabulary

clothing	ropa	different	diferente
family	familia	food	comida
needs	necesita	same	igual
shelter	refugio		

Differentiated Instruction

 Extra Support
Understand and Participate
If...children have difficulty comparing and contrasting families, **then...**point to a feature common to each of two pictures. Ask: *Do both families _____?* ¿Las dos familias _____?

Enrichment
Oral Language and Vocabulary
Challenge children to learn more about a family member's job and tell the class about it during sharing time. Children might wish to bring in photos or realia for their explanation.

Special Needs
Behavioral Social/Emotional
If a child is uncomfortable talking about his or her family (which may apply to children with difficult home lives), don't push and just let him or her watch the discussion.

Center Time

Center Rotation Center Time includes teacher-guided activities and independent activities. Refer to the **Learning Centers** on pages 24–25 for activities in additional centers.

 small group · 30 minutes

Refer to the **Learning Centers** on pages 24–25 for activities in additional centers.

Pretend and Learn Center

Center Tip

If... children need help explaining a specific job or identifying job-related tools and tasks, **then...** show a picture of someone performing that job and provide the needed language.

✓ Monitor children's word choices as they describe family members' jobs.

Materials clothing and job-related toys

Role-Play Jobs Tell children they will role-play a family member's job.

- Have children work with a partner. Ask: **What is your job? What do you do on this job?** *¿Cuál es su trabajo? ¿Qué hacen en este trabajo?*

- Have children use clothing and props in their role-play.

Purposeful Play

✓ Observe children as they complete center tasks.

Children choose an open center for free playtime. Encourage children to role-play jobs they learned about as they explore how families are alike and different. Ask questions and provide suggestions to extend the role-play.

Let's Say Good-Bye

 large group · 15 minutes

 Read Aloud Revisit "The Lion's Haircut"/ *"El corte de pelo del león"* for your afternoon Read Aloud. Remind children to listen for things the lion needs.

 Home Connection Refer to the Home Connections activities listed in the Resources and Materials chart on page 21. Remind children to tell families about the things all families need. Sing the "Good-Bye Song"/"Hora de ir a casa" as children prepare to leave.

✓ Learning Goals

Social and Emotional Development
- Child maintains concentration/attention skills until a task is complete

Language and Communication
- Child names and describes actual or pictured people, places, things, actions, attributes, and events.

Social Studies
- Child identifies similarities and differences in families.

Writing

Recap the day. Have children name how families are alike and different. Ask: **What do all families have in common? What makes them different?** *¿Qué tienen todas las familias en común? ¿Qué las hace diferentes?* Record their answers on chart paper. Share the pen by having children write letters and words they know. Ask children to draw a picture to illustrate each sentence.

DAY 4

Focus Question

What are good healthy habits?

¿Cuáles son los hábitos saludables?

 Learning Goals

Social and Emotional Development
• Child maintains concentration/attention skills until a task is complete.

Language and Communication
• Child follows basic rules for conversations (taking turns, staying on topic, listening actively).

Emergent Literacy: Reading
• Child blends two phonemes to form a word.

Vocabulary

dad	papá	family	familia
kittens	gatitos	make-believe	fantasía
mom	mamá	puppies	perritos
real	real		

Differentiated Instruction

 Extra Support

Oral Language and Vocabulary

If...children have difficulty distinguishing real from make-believe, **then...**show pictures of animals from fiction and nonfiction books. Ask: *Does this animal look like a real animal you might see outside? Do animals in real life wear clothes like these? ¿Les parece que este es un animal real que podrían en algún lugar? ¿Los animales de la vida real se visten con este tipo de ropa?*

 Enrichment

Oral Language and Vocabulary

Challenge children to create pretend dialogues between animal family members during Center Time. You might wish to provide a problem the animals have to solve together.

Let's Start the Day

 Opening Routines and Transition Tips

For **Opening Routines** and **Transition Tips** turn to pages 178–181 and visit **DLMExpressOnline.com** for more ideas.

Read **"My Apple"/"Mi manzanita"** from the *Teacher's Treasure Book*, page 128, for your morning Read Aloud.

Language Time

 large group   15 minutes

Social and Emotional Development Praise children's efforts in following directions and completing assigned tasks by naming children and the positive behaviors they are showing. Model completing tasks, as needed.

Oral Language and Vocabulary

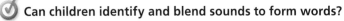 **Can children create a make-believe conversation?**

Animal Families Talk about animal families, real and make-believe, that children have learned or read about. Ask: *How are animal families like people families? Who is in a cat family?* (dad, mom, kittens) *A dog family?* (dad, mom, puppies) *¿En qué se parecen las familias de animales a las familias de personas? ¿Quiénes forman una familia de gatos?* (papá, mamá, gatitos) *¿Y una familia de perros?* (papá, mamá, perritos)

● Discuss how *real* animals, such as cats and dogs, act. Point out, for example, that they meow or bark rather than talk. Only *make-believe* animals can talk like people.

● Ask: *If a cat mom could talk to her kittens, what might she say? Si una gata mamá pudiera hablar con sus gatitos, ¿qué les diría?* Model an animal conversation with a child. Then have partners conduct their own "animal talk."

Phonological Awareness

Can children identify and blend sounds to form words?

Blending Phonemes Display the Dog Puppet and pictures of the following words (as available): *knee, bee, tie, pie, boy, egg, row, shoe, tea, ice, key, toe, two, zoo.* Have a child hold the puppet. Show one of the pictures to the child. Have the child say the word sound by sound to the puppet. Ask the rest of the children: *What word can we make if we blend the sounds together? ¿Qué palabra podemos formar si unimos estos sonidos?* Provide corrective feedback by showing the picture to the class. Repeat with other pairs and words.

ELL Teach the names of the photos used in the Phonological Awareness activity in small groups with English Language Learners prior to using them in the whole group lesson. This will help these children more fully participate in the lesson.

Center Time

▶ **Center Rotation** Center Time includes teacher-guided activities and independent activities. Refer to the **Learning Centers** on pages 24–25 for activities in additional centers.

 small group 60–90 minutes

Learning Goals

Language and Communication
• Child uses newly learned vocabulary daily in multiple contexts.

Emergent Literacy: Reading
• Child enjoys and chooses reading-related activities.
• Child retells or reenacts poems and stories in sequence.

Library and Listening Center

Center Tip

✔ Track children's ability to distinguish real from make-believe.

Materials traditional nursery rhyme books

Browsing Nursery Rhyme Books Have children browse through nursery rhyme books to find rhymes about real and make-believe animal families.

• Say: *Look carefully at the illustrations. Which things could happen in real life? Which things could not happen in real life?* *Observen atentamente las ilustraciones. ¿Qué cosas podrían suceder en la vida real? ¿Cuáles no podrían suceder en la vida real?*

• Prompt children to use the terms *real* and *make-believe* in their responses.

If...children have difficulty using the terms *real* and *make-believe* in their discussions, **then**... provide the sentence frame: *The _____ is make-believe because _____. El/la _____ es de fantasía porque _____.* Model using the frame, then have children repeat.

Pretend and Learn Center

Center Tip

✔ Track how well children can retell stories read aloud to them.

Materials flannel patterns, drawing materials, picture/drawing of an apple slice, sock puppets

Retell and Act Out Stories Explain to children that they will retell the stories you read aloud this week.

• Have children use the drawing materials and picture/drawing of an apple slice as they retell or act out yesterday's story, "A Special Surprise."

• Continue with today's story, "The Three Little Kittens," after it is read. Display the flannel patterns, or have children use or make sock puppets for the retelling.

If...children have difficulty retelling one of the stories, **then**... remind them of specific details, such as what the mother cat said to her kittens. Or, ask questions and provide clues about story details, such as: *Why were the kittens' mittens dirty? Remember, they were eating /p//ĭ/.* *¿Por qué los mitones de los gatitos estaban sucios? Recuerden que estaban comiendo /p//ĭ/.*

Differentiated Instruction

 Extra Support

Pretend and Learn Center
If...children have difficulty retelling "A Special Surprise", **then**...draw the story prompts on a chart. Prompt children to use the drawings in order to tell the story.

 Enrichment

Pretend and Learn Center
Challenge children to make up additional dialogue between story characters. Ask: *What other trouble could the three little kittens get into? What might Mother Cat say?* *¿En qué tipo de problemas se podrían meter los tres gatitos? ¿Qué diría Mamá Gata?*

Accommodations for 3's

Pretend and Learn Center
If...children have difficulty retelling the story, **then**...prompt them by asking what happened first (or at the beginning) and how the story ended.

Focus Question
What are good healthy habits?
¿Cuáles son los hábitos saludables?

Learning Goals

Language and Communication
• Child demonstrates an understanding of oral language by responding appropriately.

Emergent Literacy: Reading
• Child names most upper- and lowercase letters of the alphabet.

• Child identifies the letter that stands for a given sound.

Vocabulary

dirty	sucios	healthy	saludable
kittens	gatitos	mittens	mitones
mother	mamá	wash	lavar

Differentiated Instruction

Extra Support
Learn About Letters and Sounds
If...children have difficulty saying any of the sounds, **then...**show them the correct mouth position (lips, teeth, tongue). Say words beginning with the sound, and have children repeat.

Enrichment
Learn About Letters and Sounds
Once children hop to a letter, have them name other words that begin with the letter-sound.

Special Needs
Cognitive Challenges
Learning the difference between real and make-believe is an important life-long skill. Play a game with the child where you make a sentence and the child holds up a "yes" card if the statement is "real" and a "no" card if it is "not real."

Circle Time

Literacy Time

📖 Read Aloud

✓ **Can children answer questions about story details?**

Build Background Tell children that you will be reading a make-believe story about an animal family.

● Ask: *How might a make-believe cat family be different from a real cat family?* *¿Cómo se diferenciaría una familia de gatos de fantasía de una familia de gatos real?*

Listen for Enjoyment Read aloud *Teacher Treasure Book* page 333, "The Three Little Kittens"/"Los tres gatitos." Use the flannel board patterns (page 437) to act out the story. Highlight all the things the cats do to stay healthy as you read (e.g., eat good foods, wash their paws, clean their clothes, wear proper winter clothing).

● Tell children to listen carefully for the cats' healthy habits and what the mother cat says to her kittens.

Respond to the Story Have children tell why the kittens were in trouble. Ask: *Why were the kittens upset? What did Mother Cat do?* *¿Por qué estaban molestos los gatitos? ¿Qué hizo Mamá Gata?*

💡 **TIP** Use voice inflection to emphasize Mother Cat's feelings regarding the actions of her kittens.

ELL Focus on etiquette words and phrases in "The Three Little Kittens," such as *please* and *thank you*. Role-play with children situations in which each is used. Extend the discussion by modeling the use of common questions children ask adults, such as *May I _____?*

Learn About Letters and Sounds

✓ **How many letter-sounds can children identify?**

Reviewing the Alphabet Sing the "ABC Song" with children as you page through the *ABC Big Book*. Remind children that they have learned all the letter names and sounds.

● Place 3–5 *ABC Picture Cards* in a row on the floor. Make sure there is plenty of space between the cards.

● Have each child, in turn, follow your directions. Say, for example: *Hop to the letter M, Hop to the letter that stands for /s/,* or *Hop to the first letter/sound in David's name.* *Salten hasta la letra M, salten hasta la letra que suena /s/, o salten hasta la primera letra y sonido del nombre de David.*

● Repeat with other *ABC Picture Card* sets. Focus on the sound of each letter.

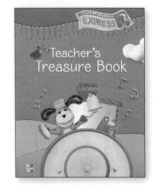

Teacher's Treasure Book, page 333

Mm

moon

ABC Picture Cards

Math Time

large group — *15 minutes*

Observe and Investigate

 Can children add and subtract?

Healthy Kids and Raisins Give each child a paper plate. Tell children they are going to be healthy kids making smart food choices.

- Ask: ***How many raisins do you have on your plates?*** (right now, zero) *¿Cuántas pasas tienen en su plato?* (Ahora mismo, ninguna).

- Distribute some raisins, then have children put a specified number of raisins on their plates.

- Take turns having all children add or subtract raisins, discussing each new amount. For subtraction, children eat their raisins.

- Have children use a word problem to describe what they did. For example, they might say "I had 5 raisins. I ate 2 raisins. How many do I have left?"

- Have children explain why raisins are a healthy food choice.

🏃🏃🏃 Social and Emotional Development

large group — *15 minutes*

Making Good Choices

 Do children regulate their own behavior during classroom activities?

Managing One's Behavior Display the Dog Puppets and some art materials. Act out a scenario in which one of the puppets is using all the art materials, but the other wants to use some of them. Ask: ***What happened? What's the problem?*** *¿Qué sucedió?¿Cuál es el problema?*

- Model a dialogue between the puppets that ends in one puppet choosing another activity until the other puppet is finished with the art materials.

- Ask: ***How did the puppets solve their problem?*** *¿Cómo resolvieron los títeres el problema?*

- Remind children that waiting their turn to use classroom materials shows kindness towards their classmates.

ELL Some children may have difficulties following the conversation between the dog puppets. While role-playing, act out the dogs' actions. Ask yes/no questions to check children's understanding of the dialogue before moving on.

Online Math Activity

Children can complete Piece Puzzler 4 and Number Snapshots 3 during computer time or Center Time.

✓ Learning Goals

Social and Emotional Development
- Child accepts responsibility for and regulates own behavior.

Mathematics
- Child uses concrete objects or makes a verbal word problem to add up to 5 objects.
- Child uses concrete objects or makes a verbal word problem to subtract up to 5 objects from a set.

Science
- Child recognizes and selects healthy foods.

Vocabulary

add	sumar	altogether	total
count	contar	how many	cuántos
subtract	restar		

Differentiated Instruction

 Extra Support

Observe and Investigate
If...children struggle counting their raisins, **then...**have them show the raisin sets using their fingers. Chorally count to the raisin total.

✦ Enrichment

Observe and Investigate
Challenge children to add numbers of raisins that total 10 or more.

Accommodations for 3's

Observe and Investigate
If...children struggle adding raisins, **then...**tell them how many raisins to place on their plates and how many to add using small numbers that add up to no more than 5. Chorally count the total number of raisins. Then ask: ***How many altogether?*** *¿Cuántas son en total?*

Focus Question
What are good healthy habits?
¿Cuáles son los hábitos saludables?

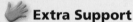

Learning Goals

Language and Communication
• Child speaks in complete sentences of four or more words including a subject, verb, and object.

Mathematics
• Child uses concrete objects or makes a verbal word problem to add up to 5 objects.
• Child uses concrete objects or makes a verbal word problem to subtract up to 5 objects from a set.

Vocabulary

add	sumar	altogether	en total
count	contar	how many	cuántos
problem	problema	subtract	restar

Differentiated Instruction

 Extra Support

Math Time

If...children have difficulty adding items on the chart, **then...**use smaller amounts, guiding children step-by-step.

Enrichment

Math Time

Challenge children to use more sticky notes and cover more objects on the charts.

Math Time

large group   20 minutes

Language and Communication Skills Model for children how to construct their word problem and state it for the class. Also, prompt them with the question: *How many ____ do you have? Answer in a complete sentence. ¿Cuántos ____ tienen? Respondan con una oración completa.*

✓ **Can children add and subtract numbers?**

Making Word Problems Display *Math and Science Flip Chart* page 62, "How Many?" Discuss the animals and objects in the scene.

● Ask: *How many cows are there? How many kittens? How many animals altogether? ¿Cuántas vacas hay? ¿Y gatitos? ¿Cuántos animales hay en total?*

● Continue with other word problems, such as: *How many apples are on this tree? If I pick two apples, how many will be left? ¿Cuántas manzanas hay en este manzano? Si recojo dos manzanas, ¿cuántas quedarán?* Cover the removed apples with self-sticking notes and have children count.

ELL Model stating word problems sentence by sentence for children to respond to or repeat. Say: *I have 4 kittens—1, 2, 3, 4. How many kittens do I have?* (4) *Now it's your turn. Tell me how many kittens you have.* Continue with the rest of the word problem.

For additional suggestions on how to meet the needs of children at the Beginning, Intermediate, Advanced, and Advanced-High levels of English proficiency, see pages 184–187.

✓ **Can children create addition and subtraction word problems?**

Farm Scene Have children draw pictures of animals on sticky notes and place the pictures in the scene on *Math and Science Flip Chart* page 62.

● Children put up to three pictures of one animal and up to three pictures of another animal on the page. Ask: *How many of each animal did you put on the picture? ¿Cuántos dibujos de cada animal colocaron en el dibujo?*

● Children then tell a story about their scene, including the sum of the numbers of pictures.

● Challenge children to create subtraction word problems and model them by removing or covering pictures.

TIP Tell children that they can continue creating word problems in the Math Center on their own or with a friend.

Math and Science Flip Chart, page 62

Center Time

> **Center Rotation** Center Time includes teacher-guided activities and independent activities. Refer to the **Learning Centers** on pages 24–25 for activities in additional centers.

  small group 30 minutes

Math and Science Center

✓ **Track children's ability to add and subtract.**

Materials paper, two-color counters

Place Scenes Tell children that they will create word problems using counters.

- Provide paper and counters. Have children work with partners.

- Have children alternate placing counters on the paper and stating their word problem for their partner to figure out. The counters may represent people, objects, or animals.

Center Tip

If...children need help creating word problems, **then...** model a word problem. Have children put counters on the paper to illustrate the problem, then solve it.

Purposeful Play

✓ **Observe children regulating their behavior during center activities.**

Children choose an open center for free playtime. Encourage children to choose an alternate activity when a desired center is already in use.

Let's Say Good-Bye

  large group 15 minutes

📖 **Read Aloud** Revisit "My Apple"/"Mi manzanita" for your afternoon Read Aloud. Remind children to think about whether an apple is a healthy food.

↩ **Home Connection** Refer to the Home Connections activities listed in the Resources and Materials chart on page 21. Remind children to sing the "ABC Song" and to tell families about the three little kittens and their troubles. Sing the "Good-Bye Song"/"Hora de ir a casa" as children prepare to leave.

 Learning Goals

Social and Emotional Development
- Child accepts responsibility for and regulates own behavior.

Mathematics
- Child uses concrete objects or makes a verbal word problem to add up to 5 objects.
- Child uses concrete objects or makes a verbal word problem to subtract up to 5 objects from a set.

 Writing

Recap the day. Have children tell about a make-believe animal family they have read about. Ask: *What did this make-believe animal do that real animals cannot?* ¿Qué hizo este animal de fantasía que los animales reales no pueden hacer? Record their answers in a list. Read them back as you track the print, and emphasize the spaces between words.

DAY 5

Focus Question
What are good healthy habits?
¿Cuáles son los hábitos saludables?

 Learning Goals

Language and Communication
• Child uses newly learned vocabulary daily in multiple contexts.
• Child understands and uses regular and irregular plural nouns, regular past tense verbs, personal and possessive pronouns, and subject-verb agreement.

Emergent Literacy: Reading
• Child blends two phonemes to form a word.

Vocabulary

mouthwash	enjuague bucal
rinse	enjuagar
teeth	dientes
toothbrush	cepillo de dientes
toothpaste	pasta de dientes

Differentiated Instruction

 Extra Support
Phonological Awareness
If...children have difficulty blending two discrete phonemes to make a word, **then...**focus on blending only words that begin with continuous sounds (e.g., f, l, m, n, r, s, v, z) as they will be easier to blend.

 Enrichment
Phonological Awareness
Show children *Photo Library CD-ROM* pictures of words that contain three sounds (e.g., *sun, dog, coat, red*). Say the sounds that make up one of the photo names. Challenge children to blend the phonemes, and identify the corresponding photo.

Let's Start the Day

 Opening Routines and Transition Tips
For **Opening Routines** and **Transition Tips** turn to pages 178–181 and visit
DLMExpressOnline.com for more ideas.

Read **"The Little Red Hen"/"La gallinita roja"** from the *Teacher's Treasure Book*, page 288, for your morning Read Aloud.

Language Time

large group   15 minutes

Social and Emotional Development Remind children not to shout out answers during the discussion. Rather, they should wait until they are called on, or until it is their turn.

Oral Language and Vocabulary

✓ Can children explain why brushing their teeth is important?

Healthy Habits Talk about the importance of brushing your teeth after meals. Tell children that brushing your teeth several times a day is important to prevent cavities and keep teeth healthy and strong. Ask: **When do you brush your teeth? What do you use?** *¿Cuándo se cepillan los dientes? ¿Qué usan para cepillarlos?*

● Display *Oral Language Development Card 73*. Name what the girl is doing (brushing her teeth) and what she is using. Then follow the suggestions on the back of the card.

● Make sure children understand that *teeth* means "more than one tooth." Review other irregular plurals such as *foot/feet* and *goose/geese*.

● Use the Sequence Card set "Brushing Your Teeth" to demonstrate the steps in the process of brushing teeth.

Oral Language Development Card 73

Phonological Awareness

✓ Can children blend sounds to form words?

Blending Phonemes Using *Rhymes and Chants Flip Chart* page 33, sing "A Healthy You!" once more with children. Have children point out the many ways to stay healthy listed in the poem.

Then review blending the two-phoneme words from the week, including *see, say,* and *two*. Add others (*me, tie, knee, key*). Use pictures or gestures for all the words. Say the two sounds for each pictured word. Ask children to blend the sounds, say the whole word, and identify the corresponding picture.

ELL Use the various Human Body pictures from the *Photo Library CD-ROM*. Name each body part or picture depicting a healthy habit. Ask one-word answer questions about each picture, such as: **Is this an elbow or a knee? How many toes are on the foot? Does an alarm clock ring in the morning or at night?**

Rhymes and Chants Flip Chart, page 33

Center Time

▶ **Center Rotation** Center Time includes teacher-guided activities and independent activities. Refer to the **Learning Centers** on pages 24–25 for activities in additional centers.

 small group 60–90 minutes

Writer's Center

Center Tip

☑ **Track children's ability to identify and write correct letter-sounds.**

Materials magazines, glue, construction paper, crayons, scissors

"I Know My ABCs" Book Have children create an ABC book to display their growing knowledge of the alphabet. Children will make one page for each letter of the alphabet. Suggest they make 2–3 pages a day for the remaining days of school.

- Have children write the upper case and lower case letter on a sheet of construction paper.

- Ask: **What words begin with this letter-sound?** *¿Qué palabras comienzan con esta letra y este sonido?* Have children draw or cut out magazine pictures of objects and animals whose names begin with that letter-sound. Prompt them to label their pictures.

- Bind the pages together to create an "I Know My ABCs" book.

If...children have difficulty identifying items whose names begin with a target letter-sound, **then...** have them browse through ABC books for ideas.

ABC Center

Center Tip

☑ **Track children's ability to match letters and sounds.**

Materials ABC puzzles, assorted ABC books

ABC Puzzles and ABC Books Explain to children that they will practice the letter-sounds they have learned this year using puzzles and ABC books.

- As children place letter pieces in ABC puzzles, ask: **What is this letter's name? What sound does it stand for? What words begin with this sound?** *¿Cuál es esta letra? ¿Qué sonido representa? ¿Qué palabras comienzan con este sonido?*

- As children browse ABC books, have them say the letter-sound for each page and identify as many pictured items as possible.

If...children have difficulty identifying pictured items, **then...**provide the first sound and the picture name, and have them repeat (e.g., **This is /s/ salamander.**)

✓ Learning Goals

Language and Communication
- Child names and describes actual or pictured people, places, things, actions, attributes, and events.

Emergent Literacy: Reading
- Child names most upper- and lowercase letters of the alphabet.
- Child produces the most common sound for a given letter.

Emergent Literacy: Writing
- Child uses scribbles, shapes, pictures, symbols, and letters to represent language.

Differentiated Instruction

Extra Support
Writer's Center
If...children have difficulty recalling letter-sounds, **then...**review the letter-sounds using the *ABC Big Book*. Display the book for children to reference during the activity.

Enrichment
Writer's Center
Challenge children to write additional words known on each page of the ABC books created in Writer's Center. These can include non-pictured words.

Accommodations for 3's
Writer's Center
If...children have difficulty creating a full ABC book, **then...**have them create a book using only the letters in their name.

Learning Goals

Emergent Literacy: Reading
- Child names most upper- and lowercase letters of the alphabet.
- Child identifies the letter that stands for a given sound.
- Child describes, relates to, and uses details and information from books read aloud.

Emergent Literacy: Writing
- Child uses scribbles, shapes, pictures, symbols, and letters to represent language.

Science
- Child practices personal hygiene skills independently (for example, washes hands, blows nose, covers mouth, brushes teeth).

Vocabulary

brushing	cepillarse	check-up	chequeo
habits	hábitos	healthy	sano
strong	fuerte	washing	lavarse

Differentiated Instruction

 Extra Support

Learn About Letters and Sounds
If...children have difficulty writing specific letters, **then...**provide *ABC Picture Cards* for them to trace a letter before writing it. Focus on how the letter is formed (e.g., using lines, curves, or a combination).

Enrichment

Learn About Letters and Sounds
Display a letter-card set of all the letters. Challenge children to name as many as they can as fast as they can. Repeat, having them name each letter's sound.

Literacy Time

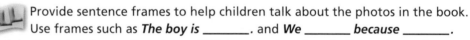

Read Aloud

✓ **Can children describe healthy habits, using information from the book and their own experiences?**

Build Background Tell children that you will be rereading a book about healthy habits.

- Ask: *What did we learn about healthy habits? ¿Qué aprendimos sobre los hábitos saludables?*

Listen for Understanding Display *Concept Big Book 4: Staying Healthy* page 17, and read the title.

- Reread pages 18–21. Stop and have children name and explain the importance of each healthy habit.

- Ask: *Why are healthy habits important? ¿Por qué son importantes los hábitos saludables?*

Respond and Connect Have children connect their new learning to their daily lives. Ask: *What healthy habits do we have at school? At home? When do we wash our hands? Why? ¿Qué hábitos saludables tenemos en la escuela? ¿Y en casa? ¿Cuándo nos lavamos las manos? ¿Por qué?*

TIP Be sure children can relate information in the book to their daily lives.

ELL Provide sentence frames to help children talk about the photos in the book. Use frames such as ***The boy is** _____.* and ***We** _____ **because** _____.* Model using each frame, then have children repeat and apply the sentence frame to the photo.

Learn About Letters and Sounds

✓ **How many letter-sounds can children identify?**

Reviewing the Alphabet Sing the "ABC Song" with children as you page through the *ABC Big Book*. Tell children that they have learned how to write all the letters of the alphabet. Review the upper case and lower case forms of the first letter in their names.

- Then distribute paper and crayons to each child. Have them write their names on paper.

- Ask them to write any other words they know. Assist with letter formation, as needed.

- Teach children how to write a few common words, such as *Mom* and *Dad.* Focus on the sounds in each word and the common letters (e.g., upper case and lower case *Mm* in *Mom*). Have children add these words to their paper.

Staying Healthy
Mantente sano

ABC Big Book

Math Time

Observe and Investigate

✓ **Can children subtract numbers?**

Gone Fishing Tell children they will pretend to be dinosaurs that eat fish. Distribute fish crackers, and have children use paper plates (or blue construction paper) as their "lake" to keep the fish.

- Ask: **How many fish are in your lake right now?** (zero) *¿Cuántos peces hay en el lago en este momento?* (cero) Tell them that 5 fish swam near their "dinosaur," and have them put 5 fish in their lake. Say that the hungry dinosaur ate 2 of the fish. Have children eat 2 fish. Ask: **How many fish are in the lake now?** *¿Cuántos peces quedan ahora en el lago?*

- Continue the story, subtracting and adding various amounts, such as, "You have 6 fish, but the dinosaur wants 3. How many fish will you have left in the lake?"

- Have children create their own word problems for the class to solve.

Online Math Activity

Children can complete Piece Puzzler 4 and Number Snapshots 3 during computer time or Center Time.

ᕮᕮᕮ Social and Emotional Development

Making Good Choices

✓ **Do children regulate their own behavior during classroom activities?**

Managing One's Behavior Display *Making Good Choices Flip Chart* page 33, "What Happens in Our Classroom?"

- Point to the flip chart illustration. Ask: **What did we learn about waiting our turn and following classroom rules?** *¿Qué aprendimos sobre esperar nuestro turno y seguir las reglas de la clase?*

- Have children give examples of when they followed classroom rules. Praise them for their efforts. Ask: **What can you do if you need something, but I am busy?** *¿Qué pueden hacer si necesitan algo pero yo estoy ocupado para ayudarlos?* Discuss and model appropriate responses.

 Continue to focus on the language of classroom etiquette, such as *please, thank you,* and *May I?* Role-play with children situations in which each can be used. Ask questions such as: **What do you say when you need a crayon? What do you say when I give you a crayon?**

Making Good Choices Flip Chart, page 33

Learning Goals

Social and Emotional Development
- Child accepts responsibility for and regulates own behavior.

Mathematics
- Child uses concrete objects or makes a verbal word problem to subtract up to 5 objects from a set.

Vocabulary

add	sumar	count	contar
how many	cuántos	number	número
subtract	restar		

Differentiated Instruction

✋ Extra Support

Observe and Investigate
If...children struggle during Gone Fishing, **then...**use smaller numbers, or state problems one sentence at a time, allowing children to complete each step before proceeding to the next.

⭐ Enrichment

Observe and Investigate
Challenge children during Gone Fishing by using greater numbers. Have children subtract up to 10 or beyond based on their abilities.

Accommodations for 3's

Observe and Investigate
If...children struggle during Gone Fishing, **then...**subtract only one. Then chorally count the remaining fish with children. Increase to subtract two as children are able.

Focus Question

What are good healthy habits?

¿Cuáles son los hábitos saludables?

Learning Goals

Social and Emotional Development
• Child maintains concentration/attention skills until a task is complete.

Science
• Child follows basic health and safety rules.

• Child practices personal hygiene skills independently (for example, washes hands, blows nose, covers mouth, brushes teeth).

Fine Arts
• Child expresses emotions or ideas through art.

Vocabulary

bathroom	lavamanos	brush	cepillarse
habit	hábito	healthy	saludable
teeth	dientes	wash	lavarse

Differentiated Instruction

 Extra Support

Oral Language and Academic Vocabulary
If...children have difficulty remembering details about healthy habits, **then...**display *Staying Healthy* pages 18–21 for children to refer to while painting.

 Enrichment

Explore and Express
Have children add labels to their paintings. Encourage them to write the letters they know.

 Special Needs

Vision Loss
Provide large paper, if the child has a mild vision loss. For a child with severe vision loss, provide an alternative activity such as making a sound recording describing healthy habits.

Art Time

  large group — 20 minutes

Personal Safety Skills Model how to properly use, clean, and store art tools and supplies.

Oral Language and Academic Vocabulary

✓ **Can children describe healthy habits?**

Healthy Habits Remind children that they learned about healthy habits, or ways to prevent disease and help them grow big and strong.

● Ask: *Why do we wash our hands? Where do we wash our hands? How?* ¿Por qué nos lavamos las manos? ¿Dónde nos lavamos las manos? ¿Cómo?

● Ask: *Why do we brush our teeth? Where do we brush our teeth? How?* ¿Por qué nos cepillamos los dientes? ¿Dónde nos cepillamos los dientes? ¿Cómo?

● Have children discuss specific details of healthy habits, including the tools/materials used, such as soap, toothbrush, or warm water.

Explore and Express

✓ **Can children create a healthy habit poster?**

Health Poster Tell children that they will paint a poster showing an important healthy habit.

● Display examples of health and safety posters, such as how to eat properly, how to wash hands, or what to do if someone is choking.

● Ask children to choose a healthy habit to paint. Tell them they should show where this healthy habit takes place (e.g., bathroom sink, bed).

● When completed, say: *Tell me about your poster. What healthy habit are you showing? Where does someone do that?* Cuéntenme sobre sus carteles. ¿Qué hábito saludable están mostrando? ¿Dónde se realiza?

TIP Display children's posters for all to see. Ask children to tell what they like about each painting.

ELL Display the Unit 8 Oral Language Development Card photos (or other available pictures) to provide children with examples of healthy habits. When asking children to consider adding a detail (such as including tools/materials used), point to the detail in one of the displayed photos.

For additional suggestions on how to meet the needs of children at the Beginning, Intermediate, Advanced, and Advanced-High levels of English proficiency, see pages 184–187.

Center Time

  small group   30 minutes

Construction Center

	Center Tip
Monitor children as they make and describe a doctor or dentist office. **Materials** blocks, construction paper, medical toys **Doctor/Dentist Office** Tell children that they will use blocks and other art materials to make a doctor or dentist office. They can use the office to role-play a check-up. ● Have children work with a partner. Ask: *What office will you build? What tools will be found there? What will the doctor/dentist do and say during the check-up?* *¿Qué consultorio construirán? ¿Qué instrumentos hay allí? ¿Qué hará y dirá el doctor/dentista durante la consulta?*	**If...**children need help sharing the materials and working together, **then...**suggest roles for each child. One child might make the large structures using blocks (walls, doors, chair/table) while the other creates the smaller tools from art materials.

Purposeful Play

✓ Observe children role-playing healthy habits.

Children choose an open center for free playtime. Encourage cooperation skills by suggesting they work together to role-play healthy habits. Provide additional props or suggest ideas to extend the activity.

Let's Say Good-Bye

  large group 15 minutes

 Read Aloud Revisit "The Little Red Hen"/ "La gallinita roja" for your afternoon Read Aloud. Remind children to listen for whether or not the animals worked together.

 Home Connection Refer to the Home Connections activities listed in the Resources and Materials chart on page 21. Remind children to tell families what they learned this week about healthy habits. Sing the "Good-Bye Song"/"Hora de ir a casa" as children prepare to leave.

Learning Goals

Language and Communication
• Child names and describes actual or pictured people, places, things, actions, attributes, and events.

Science
• Child practices personal hygiene skills independently (for example, washes hands, blows nose, covers mouth, brushes teeth).

Writing

Recap the day and week. Say: *Tell me one thing you learned about staying healthy.* *Cuéntenme algo que hayan aprendido sobre mantenerse sanos.* Record their answers on chart paper. Share the pen with children as you write. Have each child write his/her name beside their entry.

Week 2

Focus Question

What kinds of foods are healthy?

¿Qué alimentos son saludables?

This week children will differentiate between nutritious, healthy foods and unhealthy foods. They will create graphs of favorite foods, write recipes for healthy foods, categorize foods, keep food journals, and identify the foods they like most and least.

Learning Goals

Social and Emotional Development	1	2	3	4	5
Child accepts responsibility for and regulates own behavior.	✓	✓	✓	✓	✓
Child initiates play scenarios with peers that share a common plan and goal.			✓		

Language and Communication	1	2	3	4	5
Child demonstrates an understanding of oral language by responding appropriately.			✓	✓	
Child begins and ends conversations appropriately.				✓	
Child follows basic rules for conversations (taking turns, staying on topic, listening actively).				✓	
Child names and describes actual or pictured people, places, things, actions, attributes, and events.	✓	✓	✓	✓	✓
Child exhibits an understanding of instructional terms used in the classroom.		✓			
Child understands or knows the meaning of many thousands of words, many more than he or she uses.					✓
Child uses newly learned vocabulary daily in multiple contexts.	✓		✓	✓	
Child understands and uses regular and irregular plural nouns, regular past tense verbs, personal and possessive pronouns, and subject-verb agreement.		✓			

Emergent Literacy: Reading	1	2	3	4	5
Child explores books and other texts to answer questions.		✓			
Child blends two phonemes to form a word.	✓	✓	✓	✓	✓
Child names most upper- and lowercase letters of the alphabet.	✓	✓	✓	✓	✓
Child identifies the letter that stands for a given sound.	✓	✓	✓	✓	✓
Child produces the most common sound for a given letter.	✓		✓		
Child retells or reenacts poems and stories in sequence.				✓	
Child asks and answers questions about books read aloud (such as, "Who?" "What?" "Where?").	✓			✓	✓

Emergent Literacy: Writing	1	2	3	4	5
Child uses scribbles, shapes, pictures, symbols, and letters to represent language.	✓		✓	✓	

Mathematics	1	2	3	4	5
Child collects, organizes, and records data using a graphic representation.	✓	✓	✓	✓	✓

Science	1	2	3	4	5
Child follows basic health and safety rules.					✓
Child recognizes and selects healthy foods.	✓	✓	✓	✓	✓

Social Studies	1	2	3	4	5
Child participates in voting for group decision-making.			✓	✓	

-Fine Arts	1	2	3	4	5
Child uses and experiments with a variety of art materials and tools in various art activities.					✓
Child expresses thoughts, feelings, and energy through music and creative movement.					✓
Child expresses ideas, emotions, and moods through individual and collaborative dramatic play.	✓				

Materials and Resources

DAY 1	DAY 2	DAY 3	DAY 4	DAY 5
Program Materials				
• Teacher's Treasure Book • Oral Language Development Cards 74 and 75 • Rhymes and Chants Flip Chart • *Growing Vegetable Soup* Big Book • ABC Picture Cards • Building Blocks Math Activities • Making Good Choices Flip Chart • Math and Science Flip Chart • Home Connections Resource Guide	• Teacher's Treasure Book • *Growing Vegetable Soup* Big Book • Dog Puppets • Alphabet/Letter Tiles • ABC Picture Cards • Farm Animal Counters • Building Blocks Math Activities • Making Good Choices Flip Chart • Math and Science Flip Chart	• Teacher's Treasure Book • Oral Language Development Card 76 • Sequence Cards: "Making Bee Bim Bop" • Rhymes and Chants Flip Chart • Concept Big Book 4: *Staying Healthy* • ABC Picture Cards • ABC Big Book • Making Good Choices Flip Chart • Dog Puppets • Photo Library CD-ROM	• Teacher's Treasure Book • ABC Picture Cards • Flannel Board Patterns for "Mr. Rabbit and Mr. Bear" • Dog Puppets • Oral Language Development Cards 74 and 75 • Photo Library CD-ROM • Home Connections Resource Guide	• Teacher's Treasure Book • Rhymes and Chants Flip Chart • *Growing Vegetable Soup* Big Book • ABC Picture Cards • Making Good Choices Flip Chart
Other Materials				
• boxes • construction paper • scissors, tape, glue, markers • copies of "To Market, To Market" • signs labeled "yes" and "no" • cut fruit • yogurt and toppings • paper plates • toothpicks	• clips • pictures to match letters (see p. 71) • real restaurant menus • paper plates • crayons • sticky notes • graph on mural paper (see p. 73) • construction paper • name tags and tape • shoe or small boxes	• blocks, boxes and plastic crates • empty food containers and bowls • clay, tape, markers, scissors, glue • paper • cookbooks for children • picture questions (see p. 79) • name cards • magazines • blank books with construction paper covers	• soup pot pattern • drawing paper • magazines • crayons, scissors, glue • graph with names of soups (see p. 85)	• mural paper • magazines, food store ads and restaurant ads • crayons, scissors, glue, tape • salty, sour, and sweet foods • serving utensils and plates • word/picture cards (see p. 90) • healthy snacks • construction and crepe paper • instrumental music
Home Connection				
Encourage children to tell their families what they learned about fruits and vegetables. Send home Weekly Family Letter, Home Connections Resource Guide, pp. 71–72.	Encourage children to tell their families about their graphs of favorite fruits and vegetables.	Encourage children to tell their families what they learned about healthy habits.	Encourage children to tell their families the story of "Mr. Rabbit and Mr. Bear." Send home Story Book 22, Home Connections Resource Guide, pp. 165–168.	Encourage children to tell their families what they learned this week about healthy foods.

Assessment

As you observe children throughout the week, you may fill out an Anecdotal Observational Record Form to document an individual's progress toward a goal or signs indicating the need for developmental or medical evaluation. You may also choose to select work for each child's portfolio. The Anecdotal Observational Record Form and Weekly Assessment rubrics are available in the assessment section of DLMExpressOnline.com.

More Literature Suggestions

- **Gregory, The Terrible Eater** by Mitchell Sharmat
- **Showdown at the Food Pyramid** by Rex Barron
- **Good Enough to Eat: A Kid's Guide to Food and Nutrition** by Lizzy Rockwell
- **Eat Healthy, Feel Great** by William Sears, Martha Sears, and Christie Watts Kelly
- **Ten Apples Up On Top!** by Dr. Seuss
- **Sopa de piedras** por Marcia Brown
- **Caldo, caldo, caldo** por Diane Gonzales Bertrand
- **Gracias a las vacas** por Allan Fowler
- **Martí y el mango** por Daniel Moreton
- **Las tortillas de Magda** por Becky Chavarria-Chairez

Daily Planner

	DAY 1	DAY 2
Let's Start the Day **Language Time** `large group`	**Opening Routines** p. 64 **Morning Read Aloud** p. 64 **Oral Language and Vocabulary** p. 64 Describe Fruit **Phonological Awareness** p.64 Blending Phonemes	**Opening Routines** p. 70 **Morning Read Aloud** p. 70 **Oral Language and Vocabulary** p. 70 Healthy Vegetables **Phonological Awareness** p. 70 Blending Phonemes
Center Time `small group`	**Focus On:** **Pretend and Learn Center** p. 65 **Writer's Center** p. 65	**Focus On:** **ABC Center** p. 71 **Library and Listening Center** p. 71
Circle Time **Literacy Time** `large group`	**Read Aloud** *Growing Vegetable Soup/A sembrar sopa de verduras* p. 66 **Learn About Letters and Sounds:** Review Letters and Sounds p. 66	**Read Aloud** *Growing Vegetable Soup/A sembrar sopa de verduras* p. 72 **Learn About Letters and Sounds:** Review Letters and Sounds p. 72
Math Time `large group`	**People Graphs** p. 67	**Count and Graph** p. 73
Social and Emotional Development `large group`	**Being a Fair Person** p. 67	**Being Responsible** p. 73
Content Connection `large group`	**Science:** **Oral Language and Academic Vocabulary** p. 68 Talking About Healthy Foods **Observe and Investigate** p. 68 What to Eat	**Math:** p. 74 Talk About Graphs p. 74 Making a Graph
Center Time `small group`	**Focus On:** **Math and Science Center** p. 69 **Purposeful Play** p. 69	**Focus On:** **Construction Center** p. 75 **Purposeful Play** p. 75
Let's Say Good-Bye `large group`	**Read Aloud** p. 69 **Writing** p. 69 **Home Connection** p. 69	**Read Aloud** p. 75 **Writing** p. 75 **Home Connection** p. 75

DAY 3

Opening Routines p. 76
Morning Read Aloud p. 76
Oral Language and Vocabulary
p. 76 Cooking Together
Phonological Awareness
p. 76 Blending Phonemes

Focus On:
Construction Center p. 77
Library and Listening Center p. 77

Read Aloud
Staying Healthy/Mantente sano p. 78
Learn About Letters and Sounds:
Review Letters and Sounds p. 78

Picture Questions p. 79

Being Responsible p. 79

Social Studies:
Oral Language and Academic Vocabulary
p. 80 Talking About Healthy Habits
Understand and Participate
p. 80 Cast a Vote

Focus On:
Writer's Center p. 81
Purposeful Play p. 81

Read Aloud p. 81
Writing p. 81
Home Connection p. 81

DAY 4

Opening Routines p. 82
Morning Read Aloud p. 82
Oral Language and Vocabulary
p. 82 Animal Tricks
Phonological Awareness
p. 82 Blending Phonemes

Focus On:
Pretend and Learn Center p. 83
ABC Center p. 83

Read Aloud
"Mr. Rabbit and Mr. Bear"/"El Señor Conejo
y el Señor Oso" p. 84
Learn About Letters and Sounds:
Review Letters and Sounds p. 84

Our Favorite Soup Graph p. 85

Healthy Food Choices p. 85

Math:
p. 86 Talk About Healthy Foods
p. 86 Our Food Graph

Focus On:
Writer's Center p. 87
Purposeful Play p. 87

Read Aloud p. 87
Writing p. 87
Home Connection p. 87

DAY 5

Opening Routines p. 88
Morning Read Aloud p. 88
Oral Language and Vocabulary
p. 88 Healthy Foods
Phonological Awareness
p. 88 Blending Phonemes

Focus On:
Creativity Center p. 89
Math and Science Center p. 89

Read Aloud
*Growing Vegetable Soup/A sembrar
sopa de verduras* p. 90
Learn About Letters and Sounds:
Review Letters and Sounds p. 90

Snack Graph p. 91

Being Responsible p. 91

Music and Movement:
Oral Language and Academic Vocabulary
p. 92 Talking About Vegetables
Explore and Express
p. 92 Streaming Vegetables

Focus On:
Creativity Center p. 93
Purposeful Play p. 93

Read Aloud p. 93
Writing p. 93
Home Connection p. 93

Learning Centers

Math and Science Center

Making Healthy Snacks
Children follow sequential directions to make a healthy fruit snack. See p. 69.

Just a Taste
Children taste foods and describe their properties. See p. 89.

Healthy Food Sources
Children use toy farms and animals to discuss where healthy foods are grown and raised.

Food Vote
Groups of children name healthy foods, draw them, and put counters on pictures of foods to vote for the foods they like most. They count the counters to see which food is the group's favorite.

ABC Center

Letters and Sounds
Children match letter cards with picture cards depicting items that begin with the letter sounds. See p. 71.

Letters and Sounds Soup
Children draw soup pots and fill them with pictures of things that begin with the letters *Nn*, *Vv*, and *Hh*. See p. 83.

Full Body Letters
Children make corresponding letter sounds while lying on the floor to form letters *N, V,* or *H* with their bodies.

Creativity Center

Food Collage
Children clip pictures of foods from magazines and sort them into healthy and unhealthy foods collages. See p. 89.

Making Streamers
Children use tubes and crepe paper to make streamers that match the colors of vegetables. See p. 93.

Handfuls of Healthy Foods
Children trace their fingers and fists and turn the tracings into drawings of healthy foods, such as carrots, potatoes, and apples.

Library and Listening Center

Browsing Food Menus
Children view menus and judge whether listed items are healthy. They draw healthy meals selected from the menus. See p. 71.

Browsing Cookbooks
Children look through cookbooks, choose simple recipes, and draw ingredients. See p. 77.

Healthy Choices
Partners look through books in which characters, such as Goldilocks or Hansel and Gretel, eat food. They discuss whether the foods the characters eat are healthy or not, and why.

Construction Center

Building a Graph
Children construct a graph to show favorite pizza toppings by stacking boxes under labels for toppings they like best. See p. 75.

We're in the Kitchen
Children use blocks, crates, boxes, and food containers to build a kitchen and then role play cooking healthy foods. See p. 77.

Hoe a Row
Partners use blocks and toys to create a garden patch. They pretend to be farmers caring for plants and picking produce.

Writer's Center

To the Market
Children complete the blanks on a written version of the rhyme "To Market, To Market." See p. 65.

My Eating Day
Children use writing, drawings, or clipped pictures of foods to keep a food diary for a day. See p. 81.

Salad Recipe
Children name things that go into salads and then draw each ingredient. They present their recipes to the class. See p. 87.

Tasty Invitation
Children draw healthy snacks they would like to share with classmates. They write classmates' names on the drawings and write or dictate snack names.

Pretend and Learn Center

Healthy Food Stand
Children use art materials to make a produce stand and pretend to be stand owners and customers. See p. 65.

Let's Talk
Children pretend to be animals and people in a make-believe story. They make up the story or retell one that they know. See p. 83.

Good Food
Partners pretend to go to a restaurant and order a healthy meal. Children take turns being the customer and the server.

Healthy Stories
Children relate a true story about eating a delicious, healthy meal, and share what they liked about it and why they think it is healthy.

DAY 1

Let's Start the Day

Focus Question
What kinds of foods are healthy?
¿Qué alimentos son saludables?

Opening Routines and Transition Tips
For **Opening Routines** and **Transition Tips** turn to pages 178–181 and visit DLMExpressOnline.com for more ideas.

Read **"My Father Picks Oranges"**/"Mi papá cosecha naranjas" from the *Teacher's Treasure Book*, page 186, for your morning Read Aloud.

large group **15 minutes**

Language Time

Social and Emotional Development Tell children to wait for their turn to be called on during the group discussion.

Oral Language and Vocabulary
✓ **Can children use descriptive words to tell about fruits?**
Describe Fruit Say: *You just listened to a story about oranges. Acaban de escuchar un cuento sobre las naranjas.* Ask: **What does an orange look like? How does it taste?** *¿A qué se parecen las naranjas? ¿Qué sabor tienen?* Say: **An orange is a fruit. Fruit is a healthy food. You should eat lots of fruit to stay healthy.** *La naranja es una fruta. Las frutas son alimentos saludables. Deben comer muchas frutas para mantenerse saludables.*

* Display *Oral Language Development Card 74*. Name the pictured fruits. Then follow the suggestions on the back of the card.

Oral Language Development Card 74

Phonological Awareness
✓ **Can children blend sounds to say words?**
Blending Phonemes Display *Rhymes and Chants Flip Chart* page 34. Read "The Healthy Food Cheer" several times and have children join in.

* Say: **We can blend sounds together to say a word**. *Podemos combinar sonidos para formar palabras.* Tell children that you will say the sounds that make up a word. They will put the sounds together to say the whole word. Model with /s/ /ē/ to make *see*. Say: **I see many foods in the picture.** *Veo muchos alimentos en la foto.* Repeat with /ē/ /t/ (eat). Ask children to blend the sounds and then find something in the picture that they like to eat.

Rhymes and Chants Flip Chart, page 34

ELL Point to each fruit and vegetable on the *Rhymes and Chants Flip Chart* illustration and name it. Have children repeat. Then say a fruit or a vegetable name and have children point to it on the chart. For additional suggestions on how to meet the needs of children at the Beginning, Intermediate, Advanced, and Advanced-High levels of English proficiency, see pages 184–187.

✓ Learning Goals

Social and Emotional Development
• Child accepts responsibility for and regulates own behavior.

Language and Communication
• Child uses newly learned vocabulary daily in multiple contexts.

Emergent Literacy: Reading
• Child blends two phonemes to form a word.

Vocabulary
bananas	bananas	grapes	uvas
oranges	naranjas	strawberries	fresas
watermelon	sandía		

Differentiated Instruction

 Extra Support
Phonological Awareness
If...children have difficulty blending phonemes, **then**...display pictures illustrating *key* and *bee*. Segment the *key* sounds /k/ /ē/ and help children select the correct picture. Then say: /k/ /ē/, Have children repeat. Use the same process for *bee*.

⭐ **Enrichment**
Phonological Awareness
Say a word, sound by sound. Have children blend the sounds and draw a picture of the word they make. For example, use /m/ /a/ /t/, *mat*; /d/ /o/ /t/, *dot*; /s/ /u/ /n/, *sun*.

 Accommodations for 3's
Phonological Awareness
If...children have difficulty blending phonemes **then**...show a picture of a bee. Say: /b/ /ē/, *bee*. Have children repeat.

Center Time

▶ **Center Rotation** Center Time includes teacher-guided activities and independent activities. Refer to the **Learning Centers** on pages 62–63 for activities in additional centers.

  small group 60–90 minutes

Pretend and Learn Center

	Center Tip

☑ Track the use of fruit and vegetable names and descriptions as children pretend.

☑ Look for examples of children requesting art materials rather than grabbing them.

Materials boxes, construction paper, scissors, tape, glue, markers

Healthy Food Stand Discuss fruit and vegetable stands found on a city street, in a suburban outdoor market, or along a country road. Give children art materials and have them make a fruit and vegetable stand. Remind them to share materials and to wait their turn to talk.

● Have children take turns pretending to be the stand owner and the customers.

● To get the actors started, ask: *What will you tell the customers about your healthy food? What will you buy at the stand?* ¿Qué les dirán a sus clientes sobre los alimentos saludables? ¿Qué comprarán en el puesto?

Center Tip

If...children have difficulty recalling a fruit or vegetable name or a vocabulary word, **then...**give them a clue by segmenting the sounds and having them blend it, for example: /p/ /ē/ /ch/, *peach.*

Writer's Center

	Center Tip

☑ Notice if children demonstrate an interest in writing for a purpose.

Materials copies of "To Market, To Market" (one on chart paper; one per child)

To the Market Copy the familiar nursery rhyme "To Market, To Market" on chart paper. Track the print as you read it aloud several times. Have children join in.

● Put copies of the rhyme in the Center, substituting blanks where children can write replacements for the words "a fat pig" and "jig."

● Have children draw and label names of healthy foods in the first blank. When children are finished writing, hold a "Rhyme Reading" and invite children to share their new versions of the rhyme.

Center Tip

If...children use personal or conventional symbols, such as hearts and stars instead of letters, **then...**encourage them to use letters and ask them what they wrote.

 Learning Goals

Language and Communication
• Child uses newly learned vocabulary daily in multiple contexts.

Emergent Literacy: Writing
• Child uses scribbles, shapes, pictures, symbols, and letters to represent language.

Fine Arts
• Child expresses ideas, emotions, and moods through individual and collaborative dramatic play.

Differentiated Instruction

 Extra Support

Pretend and Learn Center
If...children have difficulty with new vocabulary, **then...**model specific words in conversation with them.

★ **Enrichment**

Pretend and Learn Center
Challenge children to take on the role of farmers delivering fruit and vegetables to the stand.

Accommodations for 3's

Pretend and Learn Center
If...children use single words or phrases as they pretend, **then...**help them expand into simple sentences.

Circle Time

Focus Question
What kinds of foods are healthy?
¿Qué alimentos son saludables?

Learning Goals

Emergent Literacy: Reading
• Child names most upper- and lowercase letters of the alphabet.
• Child identifies the letter that stands for a given sound.
• Child produces the most common sound for a given letter.
• Child asks and answers questions about books read aloud (such as, "Who?" "What?" "Where?").

Science
• Child recognizes and selects healthy foods.

Vocabulary

blossom	flor	bud	capullo
plants	plantas	seeds	semillas
sprouts	retoños	sun	sol
water	agua		

Differentiated Instruction

 Extra Support
Learn About Letters and Sounds
If…children have difficulty with the letter review, **then…**limit the letter choices to three at a time.

Enrichment
Learn About Letters and Sounds
Challenge children to find other food names that begin with the letters reviewed. Have them draw and label pictures in a "Yummy Sounds and Letters" book.

Literacy Time

large group   15 minutes

📖 Read Aloud

✓ Can children identify a sequence of events?

Build Background Tell children that you will be reading a book about vegetables.

● Ask: **What do you know about vegetables? What are your favorites? How do they grow? What would you like to know about vegetables?** *¿Qué saben sobre los vegetales? ¿Cuáles son sus vegetales favoritos? ¿Cómo se cultivan? ¿Qué te gustaría saber sobre los vegetales?*

Listen for Enjoyment Display the Big Book *Growing Vegetable Soup,* and read the title. Conduct a picture walk.

● Browse through the pages. Talk about what is happening to the vegetables from seed to soup. Ask: **What do the vegetables look like now? How did they look before?** *¿Cómo son los vegetales ahora? ¿Cómo eran antes?*

● Read the selection aloud, pausing briefly to read some of the labels. At the end, remind children that vegetables are healthy foods.

Respond to the Story Help children use the illustrations to describe the sequence of events. Then ask: **What did you learn about growing vegetables? What did you learn about making vegetable soup?** *¿Qué aprendieron sobre el cultivo de los vegetales? ¿Qué aprendieron sobre cómo preparar una sopa de vegetales?*

TIP You may want to make a K-W-L chart and record children's responses to what they know about vegetables, what they would like to know, and what they learned.

ELL Point to the pictures as you sequence events in *Growing Vegetable Soup* by rephrasing the text. For example, say: **We get tools. We plant seeds. We see sprouts. We pour water on the plants.**

Learn About Letters and Sounds

✓ Can children identify the sounds and names of *Ss, Mm, Dd,* and *Pp*?

Review Letters and Sounds Distribute *ABC Picture Cards Ss, Mm, Dd,* and *Pp.* Have children name and trace each letter with a finger.

● Recite this rhyme and have children stand and show the letter they hear you name. Encourage them to cheer the letter name.

> *Find the letter* **s,** *here, here, here,*
> *Then stand up and cheer, cheer, cheer!*

● Have children trace each letter with a finger as they say the sound it spells. Then tell children to hold up the *ABC Picture Card* that spells the beginning sound in the food you name. Say: **soup, milk, dates, peas.**

Growing Vegetable Soup
A sembrar sopa de verduras

ABC Picture Cards

large group — 15 minutes

Online Math Activity

Introduce Number Snapshots 4, in which children match a group up to 5 to another corresponding dot arrangement when shown only briefly. Each child should complete the activity this week.

large group — 15 minutes

Math Time

Observe and Investigate

☑ **Can children compare and count people in a graph?**

People Graphs Write "yes" and "no" on signs and display them a couple of feet apart. Ask questions and have children line up in front of the correct sign.

- Possible questions include: *Do you like broccoli? Do you eat fruit on cereal? Do you drink milk every day? Do you snack before bedtime?* *¿Les gusta el brócoli? ¿Comen fruta con el cereal? ¿Toman leche todos los días? ¿Comen algo antes de ir a dormir?*

- After all children have made a choice, help them determine which line has more children. Then guide them to count how many children said "yes" and how many said "no." Repeat the process for other questions.

✗✗✗ Social and Emotional Development

Making Good Choices

☑ **Do children show a desire to be fair with each other?**

Being A Fair Person Discuss times when children have seen people behave unfairly. For example:

- Children are in line to go down a slide. One girl, after taking her turn, runs to the front of the line and slides again before anyone else has a turn.

- A group uses blocks to build a fort. A boy runs across the room and knocks it down.

- A child who starts preschool in the middle of the year is afraid to play with other children because she doesn't know them. Whenever the other children play a game, no one asks her to join them.

- Ask: *Do you think the children are being treated fairly? How do you feel when you are treated unfairly? What does it mean to be fair?* *¿Creen que a estos niños los tratan de forma justa? ¿Cómo se sienten cuando los tratan de modo injusto? ¿Qué significa ser justo?*

- Display the *Making Good Choices Flip Chart,* page 34. Point to the girl with the plate of cookies. Ask: *Is this girl being fair to the children behind her? What could she do to be more fair?* *¿Creen que esta niña es justa con los niños que están detrás? ¿Qué debería hacer para actuar de modo más justo?*

ELL Use simple sentences to describe the scene as you point to the chart. Say: *Who has many cookies? Is that good or fair? Who has no cookies? Is that good or fair? How do you make it fair?*

Making Good Choices Flip Chart, page 34

☑ **Learning Goals**

Social and Emotional Development
- Child accepts responsibility for and regulates own behavior.

Mathematics
- Child collects, organizes, and records data using a graphic representation.

Vocabulary

fair   justo   graph   grafica

unfair   injusto

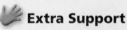

Differentiated Instruction

✋ **Extra Support**

Making Good Choices

If...children do not recognize why it is important to be fair, **then...**ask them how they would feel if someone took more than what was fair and left them with nothing.

⭐ **Enrichment**

Making Good Choices

Ask children what the boy who was left with no cookies should say to the children that took more than was fair. Ask what his classmates should say to them.

Accommodations for 3's

Observe and Investigate

If...children struggle comparing the lines, **then...**organize small groups to answer each question.

Focus Question
What kinds of foods are healthy?
¿Qué alimentos son saludables?

Learning Goals

Language and Communication
• Child names and describes actual or pictured people, places, things, actions, attributes, and events.

Science
• Child recognizes and selects healthy foods.

Vocabulary

choice   elegir

grocery store   tienda de alimentos

meal   comida   vegetables   vegetales

Differentiated Instruction

 Extra Support

Observe and Investigate

If...children have difficulty categorizing foods, **then...**ask them if cake or milk is a healthier choice. Repeat with potato chips and chicken.

 Enrichment

Observe and Investigate

Challenge children to cut out food pictures from magazine and grocery store ads. Have them categorize the foods as "go" and "whoa."

 Special Needs

Vision Loss

It may be easier for students with vision loss to follow this week's lessons if you use real fruits, vegetables, and food packages in addition to pictures.

Science Time

large group   20 minutes

Oral Language and Academic Vocabulary

☑ **Can children use words to describe healthy foods?**

Talking About Healthy Foods Point to the family on the *Math and Science Flip Chart* page 63. Say: ***This family is shopping for food at the grocery store. Let's look at the foods they can choose.*** *Esta familia está comprando alimentos en la tienda de alimentos. Observemos los alimentos que eligen.*

● Focus on the dairy foods in the second circle. Ask: ***What is a healthy food here? Which foods should the family choose?*** *¿Qué alimento es saludable? ¿Qué alimento debe elegir la familia?* Point to the whipped cream. Say: ***Whipped cream tastes good, but you should eat only a little bit and not too often.*** *La crema batida es muy rica, pero sólo deben comer un poco y no con mucha frecuencia.* Discuss the foods in each circle, comparing healthy and not so healthy choices.

● Discuss the importance of choosing a variety of foods to stay healthy. We get different nutrients from different foods. We need nutrients to help us stay healthy and grow. We should eat fruits, vegetables, and grains (bread). We also need foods that have protein, like meat, shrimp, and tofu.

● Display *Oral Language Development Card 75*. Say: ***These are vegetables. Vegetables are healthy foods.*** *Estos son vegetales. Los vegetales son alimentos saludables.* Work with children to name the vegetables. Then follow the suggestions on the back of the card.

Observe and Investigate

☑ **Can children recognize that foods can be grouped according to health benefits?**

What to Eat Tell children that you will point to a food on the *Math and Science Flip Chart*. Explain: ***If the food is healthy, say, "Go." That means it has nutrients our body needs. It is healthy for us to eat. If the food is not healthy, say, "Whoa." That means we should stop and think about that food. We can eat it sometimes, but not too often and in small portions.*** *Si el alimento es saludable, digan "Vamos". Esto significa que tiene los nutrientes que nuestro cuerpo necesita y es saludable. Si el alimento no es saludable, digan "Basta". Eso significa que debemos dejar de comer y tomar esos alimentos. Podemos comerlos a veces, pero no muy a menudo y siempre en pequeñas porciones.*

● Model first and then point to foods on the chart and have children say "go" or "whoa." Allow time for children to explain their responses.

TIP Recognize that some foods could be difficult to categorize with "go" and "whoa" as they fall somewhere in between.

ELL Use facial expressions and gestures to reflect "go" and "whoa" foods. Lick lips and show thumbs up for "go." Turn up nose and put hands up to stop for "whoa."

Math and Science Flip Chart, page 63

Oral Language Development Card 75

Center Time

▶ **Center Rotation** Center Time includes teacher-guided activities and independent activities. Refer to the **Learning Centers** on pages 62–63 for activities in additional centers.

 small group 30 minutes

Math and Science Center

| | Center Tip |

✓ **Encourage children make healthy food choices.**

Materials Bite-sized pieces of fruit; plain or vanilla yogurt; toppings, such as chopped nuts, raisins, and granola; paper plates, toothpicks.

Making Healthy Snacks Display fruit, yogurt and toppings. Say: *These are healthy foods. Éstos son alimentos saludables.* Tell children that you will make a healthy snack. On a chart, write the steps in sequence and then demonstrate:

1. Stick a toothpick in a piece of fruit.
2. Dip the fruit in yogurt
3. Dip the fruit in a topping.

- Have children talk about the steps in the process and describe the foods as they make their snacks. Encourage children to taste several fruits and talk about which ones they like best.

Center Tip

If...children have a difficult time accepting new foods, **then**...encourage gently but don't force children to eat the snack they make.

Learning Goals

Social and Emotional Development
• Child accepts responsibility for and regulates own behavior.

Language and Communication
• Child names and describes actual or pictured people, places, things, actions, attributes, and events.

Science
• Child recognizes and selects healthy foods.

Writing

Recap the day. Have children help you write a grocery list. Ask: *What foods should we write on our list? ¿Qué alimentos debemos anotar en nuestra lista?* Have children suggest foods to add to the grocery list. Read the completed list and talk about which foods are healthy and which are not.

Purposeful Play

✓ **Observe children appropriately handling classroom materials.**

Children choose an open center for free playtime. Encourage cooperation skills by suggesting they work together to create a skit about bringing healthy foods to a school picnic.

Let's Say Good-Bye

  large group 15 minutes

 Read Aloud Revisit "My Father Picks Oranges"/"Mi papá cosecha naranjas" for your afternoon Read Aloud. Remind children to listen for letter sounds they learned.

 Home Connection Refer to the Home Connections activities listed in the Resources and Materials chart on page 59. Remind children to tell families what they have learned about fruits and vegetables. Sing the "Good-Bye Song"/"Hora de ir a casa" as children prepare to leave.

Focus Question
What kinds of foods are healthy?
¿Qué alimentos son saludables?

▶ **Opening Routines and Transition Tips**
For **Opening Routines** and **Transition Tips** turn to pages 178–181 and visit **DLMExpressOnline.com** for more ideas.

📖 Read **"The Great Big Pumpkin"**/"La calabaza gigante" from the *Teacher's Treasure Book*, page 292, for your morning Read Aloud.

✓ Learning Goals

Language and Communication
• Child names and describes actual or pictured people, places, things, actions, attributes, and events.

• Child understands and uses regular and irregular plural nouns, regular past tense verbs, personal and possessive pronouns, and subject-verb agreement.

Emergent Literacy: Reading
• Child blends two phonemes to form a word.

Vocabulary

cabbage	col	corn	maíz
green beans	guisantes	potato	papa
squash	calabaza	tomato	tomate
zucchini	calabacín		

Differentiated Instruction

 Extra Support

Oral Language and Vocabulary
If...children have difficulty describing the vegetable, **then...**ask questions about the illustration. For example, ask: *What color is cabbage? Does it have leaves? What shape does cabbage remind you of? ¿De qué color es la col? ¿Tiene hojas? ¿A qué figura les recuerda la col?*

 Enrichment

Oral Language and Vocabulary
Challenge children to describe vegetables as they grow and change from seed, to sprout, to plant with flowers, and finally vegetables ready for harvest.

Language Time
Oral Language and Vocabulary

✓ **Can children describe vegetables?**

Healthy Vegetables Revisit the book *Growing Vegetable Soup*. Talk about the labeled vegetables in the illustrations. Ask: *Which vegetables did you see? Which vegetables did you eat? ¿Qué vegetales ven? ¿Qué vegetales comen?* Model how to use the correct tense: *I saw a tomato. I ate a carrot. Yo vi un tomate. Yo comí una zanahoria.* Have children do the same in their responses.

● Have children describe in detail what the grown vegetables look like. Then ask: *Which new vegetables would you like to try? What do you think they might taste like? ¿Qué nuevos vegetales les gustaría probar? ¿Qué sabor piensan que podrían tener?*

ELL Whenever possible, give children opportunities to handle the vegetables before and after you describe them.

For additional suggestions on how to meet the needs of children at the Beginning, Intermediate, Advanced, and Advanced-High levels of English proficiency, see pages 184–187.

Phonological Awareness

✓ **Can children blend sounds to say words?**

Blending Phonemes Display a Dog Puppet and pictures illustrating *bee, egg, key,* and *pie.* Say: *This puppet is tired today. The dog wants to find a picture, but is speaking slowly. Let's help the dog find the picture. We can blend the sounds to say the picture name. El títere está cansado hoy. Quiere encontrar una ilustración, pero no puede hablar muy rápido. Ayudémoslo a encontrarla. Podemos combinar los sonidos para formar el nombre de la ilustración.* Model and then have children blend sounds to say words. Have them select the matching picture. For example, the dog says: /p/ /ī/; children say: /p/ /ī/, *pie*.

Repeat with /k/ /ē/, *key; /e/ /g/,egg; /b/ /ē/, bee.*

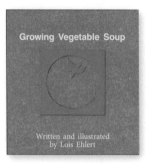
Growing Vegetable Soup
A sembrar sopa de verduras

Center Time

▶ **Center Rotation** Center Time includes teacher-guided activities and independent activities. Refer to the **Learning Centers** on pages 62–63 for activities in additional centers.

 small group 60–90 minutes

Learning Goals

Emergent Literacy: Reading
- Child names most upper- and lowercase letters of the alphabet.
- Child identifies the letter that stands for a given sound.

Science
- Child recognizes and selects healthy foods.

ABC Center

 Keep track of the letter-sounds children are mastering.

Materials clips, five or six Alphabet/Letter Tiles and matching pictures for letters children have learned (for example, a-apple, s-sun, m-moon, d-dog, p-pig)

Letters and Sounds In advance, display the Alphabet/Letter Tiles. Have children name the letters shown.

- Display the pictures. Have children say each picture name and identify the beginning sound. Model how to use a clip to attach the picture to the tile that spells the beginning sound.

- Model a few times and then have children continue on their own.

- Repeat with the rest of the alphabet in groups of five or six letters at a time.

Center Tip
If...children have difficulty identifying beginning sounds, **then**...give them a clue by isolating the beginning sound: /s/ /s/ /s/ sun.

Differentiated Instruction

🖐 Extra Support
ABC Center
If...children have difficulty remembering the sound of a letter, **then**...have them trace or write the letter in a layer of sunflower seeds in a pie tin as they say its sound. Invite them to eat the healthy seeds when they are finished.

⭐ Enrichment
ABC Center
Challenge children to draw on cards pictures of other words that have beginning sounds spelled with the letters on the Alphabet/Letter Tiles. Have them clip the picture cards to the tiles.

Accommodations for 3's
Library and Listening Center
If...children have difficulty comparing foods, **then**...ask yes/no questions, such as: *Does milk help you to grow big and strong? Is milk good for you? Is milk a healthy food? Does a cupcake help you grow big and strong? Is a cupcake good for you? Is a cupcake a healthy food? ¿Los ayuda la leche a crecer fuertes y saludables? ¿Les hace bien la leche? ¿Es la leche un alimento saludable? ¿Los ayuda un bizcocho a crecer fuertes y saludables? ¿Les hacen bien los bizcochos? ¿Son los bizcochos un alimento saludable?*

Library and Listening Center

 Listen for words children use to describe healthy foods.

Materials real restaurant menus for children, preferably with pictures, or sample menus with drawings that you create; paper plates; crayons

Browsing Food Menus Provide a variety of children's menus. Help children compare the foods offered and determine which are healthy. Have them name the vegetables on the menus.

- Distribute paper plates. Have children order healthy foods from menus. Have them draw and label the foods they select on the plate.

- Say: *Tell me about your order. Why did you choose these foods?*
  Hablen sobre su orden. ¿Por qué escogieron esos alimentos?

Center Tip
If...children have difficulty selecting healthy foods, **then**...remind them that fruits and vegetables are healthy foods.

Focus Question

What kinds of foods are healthy?

¿Qué alimentos son saludables?

Learning Goals

Emergent Literacy: Reading

• Child explores books and other texts to answer questions.

• Child names most upper- and lowercase letters of the alphabet.

• Child identifies the letter that stands for a given sound.

Vocabulary

cooked	cocinado	dig up	arrancar
raw	crudo	weed	mala hierba

Differentiated Instruction

Extra Support
Read Aloud

If...children have difficulty using pictures to identify a sequence of events, **then...**put sticky notes on the pages labeled 1, 2, and 3 and rephrase what happens. For example:
1. We pick vegetables. 2. We wash vegetables. 3. We cut up vegetables.

★ Enrichment
Read Aloud

Challenge children to draw conclusions about the illustrator. Ask: *Why do you think the illustrator choose to show a picture of a tomato on the front cover?* *¿Por qué piensan que el ilustrador decidió mostrar la ilustración de un tomate en la cubierta?*

♥ Special Needs
Speech/Language Delays

Even if the child does not correctly say or pronounce a letter, don't stop him or her. Repeat the letter or sound correctly, and encourage the child to repeat it after you.

Literacy Time

large group · 15 minutes

📖 Read Aloud

✓ **Can children identify a sequence of events?**

Build Background Ask children about the different ways they have eaten vegetables.

● Ask: *Did you ever eat raw, or uncooked, vegetables? Did you eat them with dip or peanut butter? How did you eat cooked vegetables—in a stew? On a pizza? in vegetable soup?* *¿Han comido alguna vez vegetales crudos? ¿Los han comido con salsa o con mantequilla de cacahuate? ¿Cómo han comido los vegetales cocidos: guisados, en una pizza o en una sopa de vegetales?*

Listen for Understanding Display the cover of *Growing Vegetable Soup*. Say: *This is the front cover. Ésta es la cubierta.* Read the title, the author's name, and the illustrator. Point out that in this book, the author is also the illustrator. Say: *The person who makes the pictures is the illustrator. La persona que hace las ilustraciones es el ilustrador.* Ask: *Which vegetable did the illustrator show on the front cover? ¿Qué vegetal muestra el ilustrador en la cubierta?*

● Reread the selection. Help children focus on sequence of events, by pausing to ask: *What happens first? next? last? What can you tell from the pictures? ¿Qué sucedió primero, después y por último? ¿Qué pueden decir a partir de las ilustraciones?*

Respond to the Story Ask: *What if the picture of sprouts was the first picture in the book? Would this make sense? Why? ¿Y si la primera ilustración del cuento hubiera sido la de los brotes? ¿Tendría esto sentido? ¿Por qué?* Guide children to recognize that when events are in the right order, or sequence, it helps readers understand what is happening. Then have children tell which picture they liked best and why.

💡 **TIP** Be sure children can use picture details to describe events in order. Point to specific happenings in the illustration for children to talk about.

Learn About Letters and Sounds

✓ **Can children identify the sounds and names of *Ff, Ll, Tt,* and *Hh*?**

Review Letters and Sounds Distribute *ABC Picture Cards* Ff, Ll, Tt, Hh. Have children name and trace each letter with a finger.

● Have children trace each letter again with a finger as they say the sound it spells. Then have children play school. Ask one child to be the teacher and hold up a picture of a fish, a lion, a turtle, or a horse for children to name.

● Have children say the beginning sound of the picture name and hold up the *ABC Picture Card* that spells the beginning sound.

● Have children take turns being the teacher. As children participate, notice if they are able to wait patiently for their turn as teacher.

 Invite children to share the names of the items pictured in their native languages. Discuss what letters might begin the word.

Growing Vegetable Soup
A sembrar sopa de verduras

ABC Picture Cards

Math Time

Observe and Investigate

✓ **Can children classify and count objects for a graphing activity?**

Count and Graph In advance, make a four-column, ten-row graph on mural paper. In a big pile, display 4 types of Farm Animal Counters that can be organized into groups of 3, 7, 9, and 10. Ask children to count the number of each type of animal. Guide them to discover that it will be easier to count the objects if they are grouped. Have children classify the animals into four piles by type of animal.

- Ask children which pile they think has the most animals in it. Then have them count the number of animals in each pile. Record the numbers.

- Display the graph on a table or on the floor. Help children take one animal from the first pile and place it in a box in the first column of the graph. Continue placing the animals from the first pile in the first column. Then do the same with the second, third, and fourth piles.

- Have children study the finished graph to determine which column has the most animals. Have them identify the column with the fewest animals. Then count the animals on the graph together to confirm the recorded numbers.

✕✕✕ Social and Emotional Development

Making Good Choices

✓ **Do children show a desire to be responsible?**

Being Responsible Revisit the *Making Good Choices Flip Chart* page 34, "Making Fair Choices."

- Display a Dog Puppet. Say: *Tell the dog what this girl is doing. Explain how she can make good choices. Díganle al perrito qué hace la niña. Expliquen cómo podría ser más responsable.*

- Provide each child a turn to tell the puppet what would be a good choice.

ELL Children may be more comfortable using the other Dog Puppet to talk to the Dog Puppet.

Making Good Choices Flip Chart, page 34

Building Blocks

Online Math Activity

Introduce Countdown Crazy, in which children click numerals in a backward sequence to count down from 10 to 0. Each child should complete the activity this week.

✓ Learning Goals

Social and Emotional Development
- Child accepts responsibility for and regulates own behavior.

Mathematics
- Child collects, organizes, and records data using a graphic representation.

Vocabulary

column	columna	graph	gráfica
group	grupo	responsible	responsable

Differentiated Instruction

✋ Extra Support

Making Good Choices

If...children need support talking to the puppet, **then...**prompt with questions and comments: *Do you think the girl likes cookies? How do you know? The girl has lots of cookies. How many cookies are left? Is it the right thing to do? ¿Piensan que a la niña le gustan las galletitas? ¿Cómo lo saben? Las niña tiene muchas galletitas. ¿Cuántas galletitas le quedan? ¿Está haciendo lo correcto?*

⭐ Enrichment

Observe and Investigate

Challenge children to classify, count, and graph other items such as counters, Pattern Blocks, or crayons.

Focus Question
What kinds of foods are healthy?
¿Qué alimentos son saludables?

Learning Goals

Language and Communication
• Child exhibits an understanding of instructional terms used in the classroom.

Mathematics
• Child collects, organizes, and records data using a graphic representation

Vocabulary

count	*contar*
vote	*voto*

graph	*gráfica*

Differentiated Instruction

 Extra Support

Math Time

If...children have difficulty recognizing that the chart shows that children used name tags to record votes, **then...**point to the graph and say, for example: *Patti voted for peas. Erik voted for corn. Which vegetable did Mike vote for?* *Patti votó por los guisantes. Erik votó por el maíz. ¿Por qué vegetal votó Mike?*

Enrichment

Math Time

Challenge children to think of other ways the children's votes might have been recorded on the graph.

Math Time

 Can children use words to talk about data displayed on a graph?

Talk About Graphs Display *Math and Science Flip Chart,* page 64: "How Many Children?" Review that this is a graph. Explain that a graph is one way to show how many.

• Tell children that each child in this class voted for their favorite vegetable. Explain that then the children made a graph to show what they found out.

• Have children examine how the data on the graph is organized. Ask them what vegetables the children voted for.

• Discuss how the data is recorded on the graph. Ask children how the students showed each vote on the graph.

• Discuss which vegetable is the class favorite.

• Help children count how many children chose each vegetable and use sticky notes to label each column with the correct number.

 Can children organize and record data?

Making a Graph Help children make a graph to show their favorite fruit. Have them use *Math and Science Flip Chart* page 64 as a model.

• Work with children to organize pictures of four fruits at the top of a large four-column graph.

• Distribute sticky notes. Have children use the notes to make a name tag.

• Ask them to answer questions: *Which fruit is your favorite? How will you show your vote? Which fruit do you think the most children will choose?* *¿Cuál es su fruta favorita? ¿Cómo mostrarán su voto? ¿Qué fruta creen que elegirá la mayoría de los niños?* Guide children to place their name tag in the correct column on the graph.

• Guide children to count how many children chose each fruit and to label each column with the correct number.

• Discuss which fruit is the class favorite. Ask: *If we were going to choose a fruit to have for snack today, which fruit should we choose? Why?* *Si tuviéramos que elegir una fruta para nuestro refrigerio de hoy, ¿qué fruta deberíamos elegir? ¿Por qué?*

 Tell children they will have another opportunity to make a graph—this time in the Construction Center.

ELL Point to the pictures and name the vegetables and fruit on the graphs. Have children repeat. Say a fruit or vegetable name and have children draw a picture of the food you name.

Math and Science Flip Chart, page 64

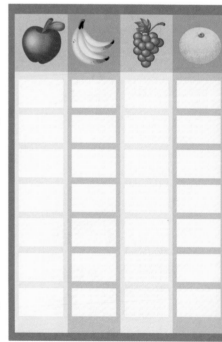

Center Time

 small group • 30 minutes

Construction Center | Center Tip

✓ **Observe children as they use boxes to build a graph.**

Materials construction paper, name tags, crayons, tape, shoe boxes or other small boxes (all the same size)

Building a Graph Distribute one box to each child. Talk about pizza toppings children like. Tell children they are going to build a graph to find out how many children like certain kinds of pizza toppings.

- Have children personalize the box with drawings. Have them write their name on a name tag and tape it to one side of the box.

- Tape to a wall a row of pictures of different healthy pizza toppings. Have children build a graph by stacking their boxes with the names showing below the topping they like best.

- Have children use the graph to discuss which topping is the class favorite. Ask: *How many children chose each topping? ¿Cuántos niños eligieron cada ingrediente?*

Center Tip

If... children knock over boxes and don't put them back in the same place on the graph, **then...** have children replace the boxes. If children need assistance, help them.

Learning Goals

Social and Emotional Development
• Child accepts responsibility for and regulates own behavior.

Mathematics
• Child collects, organizes, and records data using a graphic representation.

Writing

Recap the day. Have children begin a "Munching Journal" where they can write about what they learn about healthy foods. Today have children draw and label pictures of their favorite fruits and vegetables in the journal.

Purposeful Play

✓ **Observe children sharing classroom materials and working cooperatively.**

Children choose an open center for free playtime. Encourage cooperation skills by suggesting they work together to create a skit about ordering healthy food in a restaurant, using the menus from the Library and Listening Center.

Let's Say Good-Bye

   large group • 15 minutes

 Read Aloud Revisit "The Great Big Pumpkin"/"La calabaza gigante" for your afternoon Read Aloud. Have children listen for the order of events.

 Home Connection Refer to the Home Connections activities listed in the Resources and Materials chart on page 59. Remind children to tell families about their graphs of favorite fruits. Sing the "Good-Bye Song"/ "Hora de ir a casa" as children prepare to leave.

DAY 3

Focus Question

What kinds of foods are healthy?

¿Qué alimentos son saludables?

Language and Communication
• Child uses newly learned vocabulary daily in multiple contexts.

Emergent Literacy: Reading
• Child blends two phonemes to form a word.

Science
• Child recognizes and selects healthy foods.

Vocabulary

bowl	tazón	cook	cocinar
kitchen	cocina	measure	medir
mix	mezclar	stove	estufa

Differentiated Instruction

 Extra Support

Phonological Awareness
If...children have difficulty blending phonemes, **then...**provide more practice with two-phoneme words. Point to a boy and say, /h/ /ē/, he. Have children repeat. Wave hi and say, /h/ /ī/, hi. Have children repeat.

⭐ **Enrichment**

Phonological Awareness
Challenge children to take turns segmenting and blending three-phoneme words, using *ABC Picture Cards* dog, pig, leaf, moon, and nose.

Accommodations for 3's

Oral Language and Vocabulary
If...children have difficulty naming kitchen utensils, **then...**provide real utensils and encourage children to use the names as they play with them. Be sure the utensils are safe with no sharp edges.

Let's Start the Day

▶ **Opening Routines and Transition Tips**

For **Opening Routines** and **Transition Tips** turn to pages 178–181 and visit **DLMExpressOnline.com** for more ideas.

 Read **"The Great Big Turnip"/"El nabo gigante"** from the *Teacher's Treasure Book*, page 243, for your morning Read Aloud.

Language Time

 large group 15 minutes

🚸 **Social and Emotional Development** Tell children that when they cook they should always be with a grown up and never use a stove on their own.

Oral Language and Vocabulary

✓ **Can children use descriptive words to talk about cooking?**

Cooking Together Have children talk about their experiences with cooking. Ask: *What did you cook? Who did you cook with? How did you help? ¿Qué han cocinado? ¿Con quién han cocinado? ¿Cómo ayudaron en la cocina?*

• Display *Oral Language Development Card 76*, "Let's Get Cooking." Point out and name the kitchen equipment and utensils. Then follow the suggestions on the back of the card.

• Display and discuss the Sequence Card set "Making Bee Bim Bop" to show another example of food being prepared.

 Display Oral Language Development Card 76. Say: *This family cooks.* Then, ask: *What do families do?* Have children complete this sentence frame: *They _____ together.*

Phonological Awareness

✓ **Can children blend sounds to say words?**

Blending Phonemes Display picture cards of key, pie, and bow. Name each picture.

• Revisit *Rhymes and Chants Flip Chart*, page 34, "The Healthy Food Cheer" and cheer together. Then cheer a new version. Segment the picture names and have children blend them.

> *Words, words, give a cheer!*
> *We're so glad a /k/ /ē/ key is here.*

Repeat with /p/ /ī/, pie; /b/ /ō/, bow.

Oral Language Development Card 76

The Healthy Food Cheer

Carrots, carrots, give a cheer!
We're so glad for carrots here.
Broccoli is good for you,
And it makes you healthy, too!

Apples, apples, give a cheer!
We're so glad for apples here.
Lettuce is so good for you.
And it makes you healthy, too!

Rhymes and Chants Flip Chart, page 34

Center Time

▶ **Center Rotation** Center Time includes teacher-guided activities and independent activities. Refer to the **Learning Centers** on pages 62–63 for activities in additional centers.

small group   60–90 minutes

Construction Center

☑ **Listen for the use of oral vocabulary that you focus on.**

Materials large blocks, boxes, plastic crates, empty food containers, bowls, modeling clay, construction paper, tape, markers, scissors

We're in the Kitchen Have children talk about times they work together with a family member in the kitchen. To help them understand the words *appliances* and *utensils*, ask: **What appliances did you use? Did you use a stove? a refrigerator? a microwave oven? What utensils did you need? Did you use a spoon? a fork? a ladle? a spatula?** *¿Qué aparatos usaron? ¿Usaron una cocina? ¿Un refrigerador? ¿Un horno a microondas? ¿Qué utensilios necesitaron? ¿Usaron una cuchara? ¿Un tenedor? ¿Un cucharón? ¿Una espátula?*

- Have children use building materials and art supplies to work together to build a kitchen. Remind them to ask for materials in a polite way instead of just grabbing them.

- When the kitchen is finished, have children pretend to cook some healthy foods in the kitchen. Encourage children to discuss the foods as they prepare them.

Center Tip

If...children forget to ask politely for building materials, **then...**remind them to use words like "please" and "thank you." Comment on those who do act responsibly.

Library and Listening Center

☑ **Track the use of food names as children share favorite recipes.**

Materials cookbooks for children that feature healthy foods, drawing paper, crayons

Browsing Cookbooks Point to the ingredients for a recipe and say: **These are ingredients. You use them to make [food name].** *Éstos son ingredientes. Los usamos para preparar [nombre del alimento].* Have children browse cookbooks that have simple, healthy recipes. Have them choose a favorite recipe. Read the ingredients list, providing explanations of terms if necessary. Have students draw the ingredients.

- Have children share their drawings. Ask: **What food can you make with these ingredients?** *¿Qué comida pueden preparar con estos ingredientes?*

Center Tip

If...children have difficulty recognizing that the ingredients make up the food, **then...**draw a picture of the food next to the children's drawing of ingredients. Draw a line from each ingredient to the food. Say, for example: *Bread is in the sandwich. Jam is in the sandwich.*

 Learning Goals

Social and Emotional Development
- Child accepts responsibility for and regulates own behavior.

Language and Communication
- Child uses newly learned vocabulary daily in multiple contexts.

Science
- Child recognizes and selects healthy foods.

Differentiated Instruction

 Extra Support
Construction Center
If...children have difficulty getting started, **then...**show them pictures of a kitchen and appliances in the Home section of the *Photo Library CD-ROM.*

⭐ **Enrichment**
Construction Center
Challenge children to role play a family making dinner together in the kitchen.

Accommodations for 3's
Construction Center
If...children struggle to discuss foods as they cook, **then...**offer prompts. For example: *What are you making? It looks yummy. What did you put in it? May I have a taste, please? ¿Qué están preparando? Se ve delicioso. ¿Qué le pusieron? ¿Puedo probarlo, por favor?*

 Special Needs
Delayed Motor Development
As children are building a kitchen in the Construction Center, get a construction hat and let the child be the engineer or foreman. She or he can suggest to the other children where and how to place the materials.

Focus Question
What kinds of foods are healthy?
¿Qué alimentos son saludables?

Circle Time

Literacy Time

 Read Aloud

✓ **Can children identify good habits of nutrition and exercise?**

Build Background Tell children that you will read about ways to stay healthy.

- Say: *Remember healthy habits are things you do regularly to stay healthy, like washing your hands before you eat. What are some of your healthy habits? Recuerden que los hábitos saludables son cosas que hacemos regularmente, como lavarnos las manos antes de comer. ¿Cuáles son algunos de sus hábitos saludables?*

Listen for Understanding Display *Concept Big Book 4: Staying Healthy* and read the title. Tell children to listen to find out about healthy habits.

- Read pages 21–23 aloud. Then point to the photos and read the labels.

- Say: *Getting exercise is a healthy habit. How are the children getting exercise? Hacer ejercicio es un hábito saludable. ¿Cómo hacen ejercicio los niños?*

- Say: *Eating healthy food is a healthy habit. Name some healthy foods you see in the photos. Comer alimentos saludables es un hábito saludable. Nombre algunos de los alimentos saludables que ven en las ilustraciones.*

Respond to the Selection Have children use the photos on page 23 to identify the sequence of events. Say: *First the child buys food at the market. What happens next? What happens last? Primero el niño compra alimentos en el mercado. ¿Qué sucede después? ¿Qué sucede por último?* Then, ask: *What did you learn about staying healthy? ¿Qué han aprendido sobre mantenerse sano?*

TIP Be sure children recognize that labels are helpful in telling what something is or what someone is doing.

ELL One at a time, point to the photos in the book and read the labels *swim, build, eat, buy, pack*. Act out the words. Then have children say the words as you pantomime the actions again. Finally say a word and have children act it out.

Learn About Letters and Sounds

✓ **Can children identify the sounds and names of *Gg, Rr, Bb,* and *Jj*?**

Review Letters and Sounds Distribute *ABC Picture Cards* Gg, Rr, Bb, and Jj. Have children name and trace each letter with a finger. Then have children point to a letter card and say the sound it spells.

- Display the *ABC Big Book*. Say the beginning sound /g/, /r/, /b/, or /j/ and have children repeat. Then page through the book and have children say the sound when they see a picture whose name begins with the sound and the letter that spells the sound.

Staying Healthy
Mantente sano

ABC Big Book

Learning Goals

Language and Communication
- Child demonstrates an understanding of oral language by responding appropriately.

Emergent Literacy: Reading
- Child names most upper- and lowercase letters of the alphabet.
- Child identifies the letter that stands for a given sound.
- Child produces the most common sound for a given letter.

Science
- Child recognizes and selects healthy foods.

Vocabulary

check-up	chequeo	energy	energía
exercise	ejercicio	grains	cereales
healthy habits	hábitos	market	mercado

Differentiated Instruction

 Extra Support
Read Aloud
If...children have difficulty identifying the sequence of events, **then...**use self-stick notes to label the photos in order 1, 2, 3.

 Enrichment
Read Aloud
Have children revisit the photos on page 21 of *Staying Healthy*. Have them discuss why getting a check-up is a healthy habit.

Math Time

large group
15 minutes

Observe and Investigate

✓ **Can children create a simple graph?**

Picture Questions Create picture questions on the board. As you introduce each question, ask children to predict which choice describes more children in the class.

- Have children write their names on cards, then put their name cards under the correct answer based on their clothing for the day.

  - Zipper?/No zipper?

  - Sneakers?/Shoes?

  - Velcro Tabs?/ Shoelaces?

  - Buttons? /No Buttons?

- Guide children to count how many names are in each column and label the columns with the correct numbers. Help children to compare the two columns. Repeat with other questions.

large group
15 minutes

☆☆☆ Social and Emotional Development

Making Good Choices

✓ **Do children show a desire to be responsible?**

Being Responsible Display *Making Good Choices Flip Chart* page 34, "Making Fair Choices." Review with children what is fair to do when they get to put food on their plates and who they should be thinking about.

- With the Dog Puppets, role play other situations to model children being responsible. For example, show that the puppets drink milk at a party and then have empty milk cartons. Ask children what the puppets should do.

- After the role play, ask: ***What should I do with my milk carton? What would happen if other children leave their milk cartons around the room? What is the right thing to do?*** *¿Qué debo hacer con la caja de leche vacía? ¿Y si otros niños dejan cajas de leche vacías por todo el salón? ¿Qué es lo correcto?*

ELL Distribute clean, empty individual milk cartons and a recycling bin (or a wastebasket if milk cartons are not recyclable in your area). Model first and then have children act out how they would be responsible.

Making Good Choices Flip Chart, page 34

✓ Learning Goals

Social and Emotional Development
• Child accepts responsibility for and regulates own behavior.

Mathematics
• Child collects, organizes, and records data using a graphic representation.

Vocabulary

column	columna	compare	comparar
picture	ilustración	question	pregunta

Differentiated Instruction

✋ Extra Support

Observe and Investigate

If...children have difficulty remembering the question using the picture, **then**...ask the question as they approach the graph with their name tag. For example, point to the pictures and ask: ***Are you wearing sneakers? Are you wearing shoes?*** *¿Estás usando zapatillas deportivas? ¿Estás usando zapatos?*

⭐ Enrichment

Observe and Investigate

Challenge children to draw other picture questions. Display their picture questions for the group to graph.

Accommodations for 3's

Observe and Investigate

If...children struggle with the picture questions, **then**...find children who reflect each picture question. Bring them up to the graph, point to the example, and have them stand beside the picture question. Help them add their name tags below the question.

Focus Question
What kinds of foods are healthy?
¿Qué alimentos son saludables?

Social Studies Time

 large group / 20 minutes

Oral Language and Academic Vocabulary

 Can children use words to describe types of exercise and healthy foods?

Talking About Healthy Habits Ask children what they learned about exercise and healthy foods from the Concept Big Book *Staying Healthy*. Remind them that they need exercise and healthy foods to stay healthy.

• Ask: *What kinds of exercise do you do at school? after school? ¿Qué ejercicios hacen en la escuela? ¿Y después de la escuela?*

• Ask: *What kinds of healthy foods do you eat for breakfast? for lunch? for dinner? ¿Qué alimentos saludables comen en el desayuno? ¿Y en el almuerzo? ¿Y en la cena?* Record children's responses on a "My Eating Day" chart and place the chart in the Writing Center.

ELL Use the Food section of the *Photo Library CD-ROM* to teach children food names, such as *cereal, bagel, soup, salad, chicken,* and *spaghetti*.

For additional suggestions on how to meet the needs of children at the Beginning, Intermediate, Advanced, and Advanced-High levels of English proficiency, see pages 184–187.

Understand and Participate

 Can children make group decisions by voting?

Cast a Vote Discuss voting and the function it has in electing local leaders that you name. Explain that children can vote too. Say: *Your vote can decide what happens in our classroom. Su voto puede decidir lo que ocurre en el salón de clases.* Then have children vote to decide which exercise they will do.

• Ask: *Would you rather do jumping jacks or run in place? ¿Quieren saltar en el lugar abriendo las piernas y las manos o quieren correr en el lugar?* Have children discuss reasons why they might choose one exercise or the other. Then have children vote, either by a show of hands or by holding up a name tag.

• Guide children to tally the votes by counting or creating a graph. Have the class do the exercise that received more votes.

Center Time

> **Center Rotation** Center Time includes teacher-guided activities and independent activities. Refer to the **Learning Centers** on pages 62–63 for activities in additional centers.

 small group 30 minutes

Writer's Center

Center Tip

✓ **Notice if children use letters or symbols to make words.**

Materials blank books with construction paper covers and three blank pages, crayons or recycled magazines, scissors, glue

My Eating Day Distribute blank books. Have children copy the title "My Eating Day" on the cover of their book.

- Tell children they will write to tell what they eat during the day. Explain that the first page of the book is for foods they eat for breakfast, the second is for lunch, and the third is for dinner.

- Have children vote on whether they want to draw pictures of food or cut out pictures from magazines. Tally the votes and, depending on the results, provide crayons or magazines, scissors, and glue.

- When books are finished, have children share them with the group.

If...children label a picture with shapes which are letter-like in form, **then**...model how to write the word as you talk about the features of the letters.

Purposeful Play

✓ **Observe children as they work in pairs or small groups.**

Children choose an open center for free playtime. Encourage cooperation skills by suggesting they work together to create a TV cooking show using the cookbooks for children in the kitchen they constructed.

Let's Say Good-Bye

  large group 15 minutes

 Read Aloud Revisit "The Great Big Turnip"/ "El nabo gigante" for your afternoon Read Aloud. Ask children to think about how this story is like "The Great Big Pumpkin," which they heard on Day 2.

 Home Connection Refer to the Home Connections activities listed in the Resources and Materials chart on page 59. Remind children to tell families about healthy habits. Sing the "Good-Bye Song"/ "Hora de ir a casa" as children prepare to leave.

 Learning Goals

Social and Emotional Development
- Child initiates play scenarios with peers that share a common plan and goal.

Emergent Literacy: Writing
- Child uses scribbles, shapes, pictures, symbols, and letters to represent language.

Science
- Child recognizes and selects healthy foods.

Social Studies
- Child participates in voting for group decision-making.

Writing

Recap the day. Have children name healthy habits. Ask: *What can children do to stay healthy?* ¿Qué podemos hacer para mantenernos sanos? Record their answers on chart paper. Share the pen by having children write letters and words they know. Ask children to draw a picture to illustrate each sentence.

Focus Question
What kinds of foods are healthy?
¿Qué alimentos son saludables?

Learning Goals

Emergent Literacy: Reading
• Child blends two phonemes to form a word.
• Child asks and answers questions about books read aloud (such as, "Who?" "What?" "Where?").

Vocabulary

make-believe	fantasía	real	real
tricks	trampas	tricky	tramposo

Differentiated Instruction

 Extra Support

Oral Language and Vocabulary
If...children have difficulty recognizing features of folktales, **then...**as you reread familiar tales, stop and point them out. For example, say: *This goat talks. Can a real goat talk? This little goat plays a trick on the troll. Can real goats play tricks? Este chivo habla. ¿Pueden hablar los chivos reales? Este chivito engaña al ogro. ¿Pueden los chivitos hacer trucos?*

 Enrichment

Oral Language and Vocabulary
Challenge children to act out scenes from familiar make-believe stories in which animals play tricks. Have the rest of the group guess the title of the story.

Let's Start the Day

Opening Routines and Transition Tips
For **Opening Routines** and **Transition Tips** turn to pages 178–181 and visit DLMExpressOnline.com for more ideas.

Read **"Once I Ate an Orange"/**"Mi naranjo" from the *Teacher's Treasure Book*, page 114, for your morning Read Aloud.

Language Time

 large group — **15 minutes**

 Social and Emotional Development As children discuss previously read folktales, remind them of characters who acted responsibly.

Oral Language and Vocabulary

 Can children recognize features of folktales?

Animal Tricks Talk about previously read folktales. Ask: *How do you know that "The Three Little Pigs" is a make-believe story? What makes "The Three Billy Goats Gruff" a make-believe story?* ¿Cómo saben que "Los tres cerditos" es un cuento de fantasía? ¿Qué es lo que hace que "Los tres chivitos Gruff" sea un cuento de fantasía?

● Guide children to recall that animals talk and act like people in these make-believe stories.

● Then talk about folktales previously read in which animals try to play tricks. Ask: *What animal was in the story? Who did the animal try to trick? Did the trick work? What happens to the tricky animal?* ¿Qué animal aparecía en el cuento? ¿A quién trató de engañar el animal? ¿Funcionó el truco? ¿Qué le pasó al animal tramposo?

ELL As you discuss features of make-believe stories, have the books you mention on display so that children can use the illustrations for support. For additional suggestions on how to meet the needs of children at the Beginning, Intermediate, Advanced, and Advanced-High levels of English proficiency, see pages 184–187.

Phonological Awareness

 Can children blend sounds to say a word?

Blending Phonemes Have partners stand near each other. Display *ABC Picture Card* Ee. Show children how to move apart as you segment the sounds in the picture name: /e/ /g/. Then have children come together and hold hands as they blend the sounds to say the word: /e/ /g/, *egg*. Repeat with pictures from the *ABC Take-Home Book* showing *ape, pie, key,* and *bee* until everyone has had a turn.

Ee

egg   eagle

ABC Picture Card

Center Time

▶ **Center Rotation** Center Time includes teacher-guided activities and independent activities. Refer to the **Learning Centers** on pages 62–63 for activities in additional centers.

small group   60–90 minutes

Pretend and Learn Center

✓ **Track children's ability to create conversation between animals and people.**

Let's Talk Have children pretend to be animal and people characters in a make-believe story.

- Say: *Remember the animals talk and act like real people. Often the animals try to trick others. Recuerden que los animales hablan y actúan como personas reales. A veces los animales tratan de engañar a otros.*

- Tell children they can play characters from a story they know, such as Little Red Riding Hood and the wolf.

- Explain that they can also make up stories. Prompt children with an example: a pig wants to eat all the apples at a farmer's fruit stand so the pig tries to trick the farmer.

- After reading "Mr. Rabbit and Mr. Bear" encourage children to act out a conversation between the girl and Mr. Rabbit or the farmer and Mr. Rabbit.

Center Tip

If...children try to participate even though the Pretend and Learn Center is crowded, **then...** remind them that the responsible thing to do would be to select another center.

ABC Center

✓ **Keep track of the letter-sounds children are beginning to master.**

Materials soup pot pattern, drawing paper, recycled magazines, crayons, scissors, glue

Letters and Sounds Soup Have children trace around the pattern to draw three soup pots.

- Have children write three letters, one per pot, *Nn, Vv, Hh*. Then have them fill the pots with pictures of things that have names that begin with /n/, /v/, and /h/. They can draw the pictures or cut them out of magazines.

- In groups of three letters at a time, repeat with other consonant letters and sounds children have learned.

Center Tip

If...children have difficulty with picture examples, **then...** provide alphabet books that show a single picture for each letter and letter sound. Ask children to tell the name of the picture, the sound they hear at the beginning of the name, and the letter that spells that sound.

 Learning Goals

Language and Communication
- Child begins and ends conversations appropriately.
- Child follows basic rules for conversations (taking turns, staying on topic, listening actively).

Emergent Literacy: Reading
- Child produces the most common sound for a given letter.

 Differentiated Instruction

✋ **Extra Support**

ABC Center

If...children struggle with picture examples, **then...**give them several magazine pictures whose names have the featured beginning sounds. Have them sort and then glue the pictures in their pots.

 Enrichment

Pretend and Learn Center

To help children recall characters and plots, provide them with familiar folktales. Have children select one story to extend by having the characters take part in one more conversation.

Accommodations for 3's

Pretend and Learn Center

If...children have difficulty participating in a conversation, **then...**take the part of the person or animal. Offer questions and prompts to keep the conversation going.

Focus Question

What kinds of foods are healthy?

¿Qué alimentos son saludables?

Learning Goals

Language and Communication
• Child demonstrates an understanding of oral language by responding appropriately.

Emergent Literacy: Reading
• Child names most upper- and lowercase letters of the alphabet.
• Child identifies the letter that stands for a given sound.

Vocabulary

fence gate	portón	lock	cerrado
naughty	tramposo	nice	amable
truth	verdad	unlocked	abierto

Differentiated Instruction

 Extra Support

Read Aloud

If...children have difficulty retelling the story, **then...**reread each section of the story and then stop to ask questions. For the beginning, ask: *What does Mr. Rabbit want? How does he get it? The next day, Mr. Rabbit wants lettuce again. How does he get it? Mr. Rabbit eats the farmer's lettuce. What happens when the farmer finds out? ¿Qué quiere Señor Conejo? ¿Cómo lo consigue? Al otro día, Señor Conejo quiere lechuga otra vez, ¿cómo la consigue? Señor Conejo come la lechuga del granjero. ¿Qué pasa cuando el granjero se da cuenta?*

Enrichment

Read Aloud

Challenge children to act out the scene between the farmer and Mr. Rabbit when Mr. Rabbit asks the farmer for a healthy snack.

Special Needs

Delayed Motor Development

Enlarge the flannel board cutouts provided in the *Teacher's Treasure Book* and mount them on thick paper, so the child can see and use them on his or her wheelchair tray.

Literacy Time

📖 Read Aloud

✓ Can children answer questions about information read aloud, such as identifying a sequence of events?

Build Background Tell children that you will be reading a make-believe story about a tricky animal.

● Ask: *What do animals do in make-believe stories? ¿Qué hacen los animales en los cuentos de fantasía?*

Listen for Enjoyment Read aloud *Teacher's Treasure Book* page 335, "Mr. Rabbit and Mr. Bear"/"El Señor Conejo y el Señor Oso." Use flannel board cutouts (page 438) to act out the story.

● Tell children to listen carefully to find out how Mr. Rabbit plays tricks.

● Ask: *How does Mr. Rabbit trick the girl? How does Mr. Rabbit trick Mr. Bear? ¿Cómo Señor Conejo engaña a la niña? ¿Cómo Señor Conejo engaña al oso?*

Respond to the Story Have children retell what happened at the beginning, middle, and end of the story. Ask: *Do you think Mr. Rabbit was being responsible at the beginning of the story? Tell why you think this. Do you think Mr. Rabbit did the right thing at the end of the story? Explain. ¿Piensan que Señor Conejo fue responsable al principio del cuento? Expliquen por qué piensan así. ¿Piensan que Señor Conejo hizo lo correcto al final del cuento? Expliquen su respuesta.*

TIP To help children make a connection to the unit theme, ask: *What healthy snacks might the farmer give to Mr. Rabbit? ¿Qué alimento saludable puede dar el granjero a Señor Conejo?*

ELL Tell children what the farmer means when he says, "I'll teach him a lesson."

Learn About Letters and Sounds

✓ Can children identify the sounds and names of *Nn, Cc, Xx*, and *Vv*?

Review Letters and Sounds Distribute *ABC Picture Cards* Nn, Cc, Xx, and Vv. Have children name each letter as they trace it with a finger.

● Have children trace each letter with a finger as they say the sound it spells. Then tell children to hold up the *ABC Picture Card* that spells the beginning sounds (or final sound for *Xx*) in phrases you say. Say:

● *nine nifty nuts*

● *cut carrot cake*

● *vroom, vroom, van*

● *mix, Max, mix*

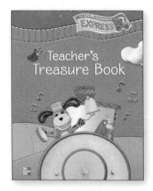

Teacher's Treasure Book, page 335

ABC Picture Cards

large group | 15 minutes

Math Time

Observe and Investigate

✓ **Can children organize, record, and analyze data on a graph?**

Our Favorite Soup Graph Show children a horizontal graph with the names of various soups, including vegetable soup, at the beginning of each row. Have children talk about the soups they have tasted.

- Ask children to predict what will be the favorite soup in the class.

- Have children tape a plastic spoon in the row for the soup they like best.

- Look at the chart. Discuss which soup is the class favorite.

- Ask children how they can tell which soup is the class favorite without counting.

Online Math Activity

Have children complete Number Snapshots 4 or Countdown Crazy during computer time or Center Time

large group | 15 minutes

✗✗✗ Social and Emotional Development

Making Good Choices

✓ **Do children understand healthy food choices?**

Healthy Food Choices Display the Dog Puppets. Tell children that the puppets are in the car at a drive-through restaurant. They are trying to decide whether to order junk food or healthy food. Model a dialogue between the puppets that ends with them ordering a grilled chicken sandwich and a cup of yogurt with granola topping.

- Ask: *Did the dogs make healthy food choices? ¿Eligieron los perritos alimentos saludables?*

- Discuss ways in which the dogs made a healthy choice. You may need to point out to children that meats (such as chicken), dairy products (such as yogurt) and grains (such as granola) provide important nutrients. Ask: *Did the dogs choose different kinds of healthy foods? Why is it important to eat many different kinds of foods? ¿Eligieron los perritos diferentes alimentos saludables? ¿Por qué es importante comer diferentes tipos de comida?* Say: *You know some healthy foods. You can pick these healthy foods when you have a choice. Ustedes conocen algunos alimentos saludables. Pueden elegir un alimento saludable cuando tienen la opción.*

ELL Use photos or drawings of the healthy foods and junk foods the Dog Puppets talk about in the modeling. Hold the picture up when you name it during the dialogue. Afterwards, have children identify the food pictured.

 Learning Goals

Social and Emotional Development
- Child accepts responsibility for and regulates own behavior.

Mathematics
- Child collects, organizes, and records data using a graphic representation.

Science
- Child recognizes and selects healthy foods.

Vocabulary

favorite	favorito	graph	gráfica
label	etiqueta	row	fila

Differentiated Instruction

 Extra Support

Observe and Investigate
If...children have difficulty analyzing the data by studying the graph, **then...**guide them to count and label how many children chose each soup.

 Enrichment

Observe and Investigate
Challenge children to create a graph with cereal box tops. Have them collect and analyze the data and then report on their findings.

Accommodations for 3's

Observe and Investigate
If...children struggle analyzing data using spoons, **then...**tape soup labels along the board and have them use the picture/name blocks they constructed to build a graph.

Focus Question
What kinds of foods are healthy?
¿Qué alimentos son saludables?

Math Time

 large group 20 minutes

✅ **Can children name healthy foods to include on a food graph?**

Talking about Healthy Foods Have children talk about their experiences with salad bars. Display *Oral Language Development Cards 74* and *75* ("Fruit Salad" and "Vegetable Bonanza") and have children browse the Food section of the *Photo Library CD-ROM* for ideas of foods they might see on a salad bar.

● Use a large sheet of chart paper to make a graph. Have children discuss which salad foods to show on the graph. Draw simple pictures of the foods children suggest along the bottom of the graph.

● Ask children to predict the favorite salad food for the class.

● Guide children to look at the graph pictures and name salad foods they like to eat. Record their votes on the graph, using squares of green construction paper. Encourage children to name more than one food.

ELL Go on an outing to a restaurant that has a salad bar, or show children a photo of a salad bar. Point out and name the salad foods and have children repeat. Encourage children to draw pictures of salad foods they like. Have them share the pictures, using a sentence frame: *I like to eat _____.*

✅ **Can children compare and analyze information on a graph?**

Our Food Graph Work with children to compare and analyze the salad graph.

● Compare information on the graph using terms such as *least* and *most*.

● Ask children which salad foods the most children like to eat. Ask them which salad foods the fewest children like.

● Tell children to suppose they are going to set up a salad bar in the classroom. Help them use the information on the graph to determine which foods they should have the most of and which the least. Guide them to notice if there are some foods that should not be served on the salad bar.

TIP Tell children that they can use what they learned about salad foods to write a recipe for a salad in the Writer's Center.

Oral Language Development Cards 74 and 75

Center Time

> **Center Rotation** Center Time includes teacher-guided activities and independent activities. Refer to the **Learning Centers** on pages 62–63 for activities in additional centers.

 small group · 30 minutes

Writer's Center

☑ **Track children's ability to write words that name healthy foods.**

Materials crayons, drawing paper

Salad Recipe Have children name some salad foods. Ask: *Which foods would you put in a salad? ¿Qué alimentos pondrían en una ensalada?* Explain that they will write salad recipes.

- Provide children with paper strips. Have them draw foods they want in a salad in a row on the paper strip.

- Have children write the name of the food below each picture to compose a recipe.

- When the recipes are finished, have children use them to tell the class how to make a salad.

Center Tip

If...children need help labeling the pictures, **then**...have them write the first letter of the picture name. You can then complete the word.

Learning Goals

Social and Emotional Development
- Child accepts responsibility for and regulates own behavior.

Emergent Literacy: Writing
- Child uses scribbles, shapes, pictures, symbols, and letters to represent language.

Writing

Recap the day. Have children talk about make-believe stories that have tricky animals that talk. Ask: *What make-believe stories do you know? ¿Qué cuentos de fantasía conocen?* Record their answers. Point out that important words in story titles begin with capital letters. Call on children to name and circle capital letters in the titles.

Purposeful Play

☑ **Observe children appropriately handling classroom materials.**

Children choose an open center for free playtime. Encourage cooperation skills by suggesting they work together to create a skit about Mr. Bear, a girl, and a honey pot.

Let's Say Good-Bye

 large group · 15 minutes

 Read Aloud Revisit "Once I Ate an Orange"/"Mi naranjo" for your afternoon Read Aloud. Remind children to listen for the steps in a seed becoming a tree.

 Home Connection Refer to the Home Connections activities listed in the Resources and Materials chart on page 59. Remind children to tell families the story of "Mr. Rabbit and Mr. Bear." Sing the "Good-Bye Song"/ "Hora de ir a casa" as children prepare to leave.

Week 2 Healthy Foods

DAY 5

Let's Start the Day

Focus Question

What kinds of foods are healthy?

¿Qué alimentos son saludables?

Learning Goals

Language and Communication
• Child demonstrates an understanding of oral language by responding appropriately.

Emergent Literacy: Reading
• Child blends two phonemes to form a word.

Science
• Child recognizes and selects healthy foods.

Vocabulary

| apples | manzanas | carrots | zanahorias |
| food | alimentos | healthy | saludables |

Differentiated Instruction

 Extra Support

Oral Language and Vocabulary
If...children have difficulty blending sounds, **then...**show pictures and then segment and blend two-syllable words. Have children echo. For example: */b/ /ē/, bee* and */ŏ/ /ks/, ox.*

 Enrichment

Oral Language and Vocabulary
Show pictures and name less familiar fruits and vegetables, such as pomegranates and artichokes. Have children describe the foods and talk about how they might feel and taste.

▶ **Opening Routines and Transition Tips**
For **Opening Routines** and **Transition Tips** turn to pages 178–181 and visit DLMExpressOnline.com for more ideas.

📖 Read **"Let's Pretend to Make Tortillas"/**"Hagamos que estamos haciendo tortillas" from the *Teacher's Treasure Book*, page 245, for your morning Read Aloud.

Language Time

large group | 15 minutes

👪 **Social and Emotional Development** When children have a choice, note whether they select healthy foods.

Oral Language and Vocabulary

✓ **Can children share what they know about healthy foods?**

Healthy Foods Talk about what children have learned this week about healthy foods. Ask: *What do you know about healthy foods? ¿Qué saben acerca de los alimentos saludables?*

• Display *Rhymes and Chants Flip Chart* page 34. Cheer "The Healthy Food Cheer" with children. Talk about apples, carrots, and other healthy foods pictured on the chart.

• Then, one at a time, hold up pictures of healthy foods and a few not so healthy foods. Ask, for example: *What is this food? Is [food name] a healthy food? Should we cheer for [food name]? ¿Qué es este alimento? ¿Es saludable? ¿Deberíamos dale un aplauso a [nombre del alimento]?*

• Cheer for the foods children correctly identify as healthy foods.

Phonological Awareness

✓ **Can children blend sounds to say words?**

Blending Phonemes Display the *Rhymes and Chants Flip Chart,* page 34. Write the numerals 8 and 2 on the board.

• Tell children to blend the sounds in the word you say to find out how many times they can cheer for healthy foods.

Then say: */ā/ /t/.* Have children blend the sounds to say: */ā/ /t/, eight.* Then cheer eight times. Repeat with */t/ /o͞o/, two* and have children cheer two times.

ELL Have children point to a food pictured on the *Rhymes and Chants Flip Chart* and name it. Then have them use sentence frames to talk about the food. *I eat _____ for _____. I eat _____ with a _____. I like to eat _____.* For additional suggestions on how to meet the needs of children at the Beginning, Intermediate, Advanced, and Advanced-High levels of English proficiency, see pages 184–187.

Rhymes and Chants Flip Chart, page 34

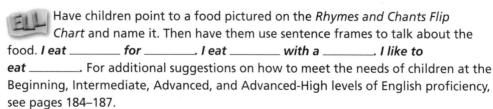

Center Time

▶ **Center Rotation** Center Time includes teacher-guided activities and independent activities. Refer to the **Learning Centers** on pages 62–63 for activities in additional centers.

small group — 60–90 minutes

Learning Goals

Language and Communication
• Child understands or knows the meaning of many thousands of words, many more than he or she uses.

Science
• Child recognizes and selects healthy foods.

Creativity Center

✓ Look for examples of children being responsible by contributing to the decision-making.

Materials two sheets of mural paper, food magazines, supermarket and restaurant ads, scissors, glue, crayons

Food Collage Have children work together to make food collages.

● Title one mural "Healthy Foods" and another "Not-So-Healthy Foods."

● Have children cut out pictures of foods from magazines and food ads. Have them work together to decide whether a food is healthy or not so healthy. Have children glue the pictures to the appropriate mural.

● Display the two collages. Ask: *How can the murals help us make healthy food choices? ¿Cómo nos ayudan los murales a tomar decisiones saludables?*

Center Tip

If...children have difficulty deciding where food pictures should be grouped, **then...**offer comments and ask questions. For example, remind children that fruits and vegetables are healthy foods. Ask whether a picture shows a fruit or vegetable, and whether they will grow strong and stay healthy if they eat lots of that food.

Differentiated Instruction

🖐 Extra Support
Math and Science Center
If...children struggle making choices, **then...** limit the food samples to three or four.

⭐ Enrichment
Math and Science Center
Challenge children to describe foods by texture or feel, for example, crunchy crackers, squishy pickles, or chewy raisins.

Accommodations for 3's
Math and Science Center
If...children resist tasting, **then...**have them watch and listen as you taste and describe foods.

Math and Science Center

✓ Track children's ability to use their senses to describe foods.

Materials salty foods: pretzels, crackers; sour foods: lemon wedges, dill pickles; sweet foods: grapes, raisins; serving utensils

In advance, select a few different kinds of finger food for each serving time. Have enough samples so that each child can have a small taste of each food. Place samples on paper plates. Make sure everyone washes his or her hands before tasting.

Just a Taste Display several different kinds of food. Name or ask children to name each food. Encourage children to taste the foods and talk about the tastes, using descriptive words *salty, sour,* and *sweet.*

● Ask for example: *How does the pretzel taste? Does it taste salty? ¿Qué sabor tienen los pretzels? ¿Son salados?*

● Have children draw a food they tasted and write two words to tell about it, for example, *sweet raisin, sour lemon,* or *salty cracker.*

Center Tip

If...some children have food allergies **then...**be sure to check individual student medical forms and the food's ingredient statement carefully. Provide separate plates if necessary..

Learning Goals

Emergent Literacy: Reading

• Child names most upper- and lowercase letters of the alphabet.

• Child identifies the letter that stands for a given sound.

• Child asks and answers questions about books read aloud (such as, "Who?" "What?" "Where?").

Vocabulary

carry	cargar	cook	cocinar
cut	cortar	eat	comer
wash	lavar		

Differentiated Instruction

 Extra Support

Read Aloud

If...children have difficulty ordering the cards, **then**...point to and discuss the illustrations in the book. Then reread and have children act out washing, cutting, cooking vegetables and eating vegetable soup.

 Enrichment

Learn About Letters and Sounds

Have children name and write the letters they learned this year. Have them say the beginning sound that each letter spells. Challenge children to draw a picture whose name begins with the sound the letter spells.

Literacy Time

 large group · 15 minutes

📖 Read Aloud

✓ **Can children identify a sequence of events?**

Build Background Tell children that you will be rereading *Growing Vegetable Soup*. Ask: *How does your family eat vegetables? ¿Comen vegetales sus familias?*

Listen for Understanding Reread *Growing Vegetable Soup*.

• Stop and have children name vegetables and tell what they look like.

• Ask: *What color is this vegetable? What shape does it remind you of? What else do you notice about this vegetable? ¿De qué color es este vegetal? ¿A qué figura se parece? ¿Qué más notan de este vegetal?*

• Pause to have children tell what happens after the vegetables are grown. Say: *Next we pick the vegetables or dig them up. What happens last?* (We carry them home.) *Después cosechamos, o recogemos, los vegetales. ¿Qué pasa al final?* (Los llevamos a casa.)

• Point out the three ordered steps in the vegetable soup recipe at the end of the book.

Respond and Connect Write the following words on cards with related pictures and display them in random order: *wash, cut, cook, eat*. Have children put the words in order and then use them in sentences to tell how to make vegetable soup. Ask: *How do you know that this is a healthy food? ¿Cómo saben que ésta es una comida saludable?*

TIP Be sure children understand what is meant by "and we can grow it again next year"/"y podemos sembrarla otra vez el año que viene."

ELL Pantomime as you say: *I wash vegetables. I cut vegetables. I cook vegetables. I eat vegetable soup!* Have children repeat the sentences as you act them out again. Then have children act out the sentences as they repeat them.

Learn About Letters and Sounds

✓ **Can children identify the sounds and names of *Kk, Hh, Yy, Ww,* and *Zz*?**

Review Letters and Sounds Distribute *ABC Picture Cards* Kk, Hh, Yy, Ww, and Zz. Have children name and trace each letter with a finger. Have children trace each letter again as they say the sound it spells.

• Label five paper plates with Kk, Hh, Yy, Ww, and Zz. Display pictures of *kite, key, hand, hat, yarn, yawn, wagon, wallet, zipper,* and *zebra*. Tell children that they are going to fill the paper plates—but this time not with food.

• Say a picture name. Have children repeat the beginning sound. Have children place the picture on the paper plate with the letter that spells the beginning sound.

Growing Vegetable Soup
A sembrar sopa de verduras

ABC Picture Cards

large group | 15 minutes

Math Time

Observe and Investigate

☑ **Can children display data on a graph?**

Snack Graph Use mural paper to create a graph. List children's names down the left side of the graph and attach a sample of healthy snacks along the bottom. Some snacks you might use are popcorn, nuts, raisins, oyster crackers, tiny pretzels, and small cheese cubes.

● Serve samples of snacks on paper plates.

● Encourage children to taste each snack and talk about how it tastes. Then give each child two smiley face stickers. Have them place the stickers on the graph to show which snacks they like best.

● Discuss which snack is the class favorite.

ELL Name snacks children taste and have them repeat one of these sentences: *I like to eat _____. I don't like to eat _____.* Give them a sticker for each food they like and have them place the sticker on the graph.

large group

⅄⅄⅄ Social and Emotional Development

Making Good Choices

☑ **Do children show a desire to be fair?**

Being Responsible Display *Making Good Choices Flip Chart* page 34, "Making Fair Choices."

● Point to the flip chart illustration. Ask: **What have we learned about being fair?** *¿Qué hemos aprendido sobre ser justos?*

● Point to the boy with the empty plate. Ask: **How do you think this boy feels? What could happen that would make him feel better?** *¿Cómo creen que se siente este niño? ¿Qué podría pasar para que se sintiera mejor?*

● Have children discuss a fair way for classmates to take plates of food.

● Play the song "Excuse Me"/"Permiso" from the Making Good Choices Audio CD. Ask children what the song says about polite ways to ask to share.

Making Good Choices Flip Chart, page 34

 Building Blocks

Online Math Activity

Have children complete Number Snapshots 4 or Countdown Crazy during computer time or Center Time.

☑ **Learning Goals**

Social and Emotional Development
● Child accepts responsibility for and regulates own behavior.

Mathematics
● Child collects, organizes, and records data using a graphic representation.

Vocabulary

favorite favorito   graph gráfica

vote votar

Differentiated Instruction

✋ **Extra Support**

Making Good Choices

If...children have difficulty understanding fairness **then...**present them with scenarios. Say: *Suppose the Library and Listening Center has 10 books. You and two other children sit down and the first person takes 9 books. Is this right? What can you do to make it right? Imaginen que en el Centro de libros y audio hay diez libros. Además de ustedes hay dos niños más, y la primera persona toma 9 libros. ¿Es correcto eso? ¿Qué deben hacer para hacer lo correcto?*

★ **Enrichment**

Observe and Investigate

Challenge children to make a healthy snack graph with pictures of snacks they like. Have them collect and record data by tallying classmates' votes.

Learning Goals

Language and Communication
• Child names and describes actual or pictured people, places, things, actions, attributes, and events.

Science
• Child follows basic health and safety rules.

Fine Arts
• Child expresses thoughts, feelings, and energy through music and creative movement.

Vocabulary

fast	rápido	move	moverse
slow	lento	soup	sopa
water	agua		

Differentiated Instruction

 Extra Support

Explore and Express
If...children are reluctant to move to the music, **then**...invite them to be partners with you.

 Enrichment

Explore and Express
Have children pretend to be vegetables growing from tiny seeds to full grown plants as they move with streamers to music.

Special Needs

Hearing Impairment
Even children who cannot hear can feel vibrations. Encourage children to move their streamers to the rhythm they feel.

Music and Movement Time

large group   20 minutes

Personal Safety Skills Model how to move safely in the open space available.

Oral Language and Academic Vocabulary

 Can children use words to describe vegetables and vegetable soup?

Talking About Vegetables Remind children that they learned about healthy foods like vegetables. Say: *Healthy foods like vegetables are very colorful. Los alimentos saludables, como los vegetales, son muy coloridos.*

● Ask: *What color is a carrot? What color is a tomato? Which vegetables are green? ¿De qué color es la zanahoria? ¿De qué color es el tomate? ¿Qué vegetales son verdes?*

● Discuss times children have seen soup cooking on a stove. Ask: *What happens when the water gets hot? ¿Qué pasa cuando el agua se calienta?* Say: *The water moves and bubbles. The vegetables move too. El agua empieza a moverse burbujea. Los vegetales también se mueven.*

● Talk about eating vegetable soup. Say: *What happens to the vegetables when you stir the soup? What happens when you blow on it? ¿Qué les pasa a los vegetales cuando revuelven la sopa? ¿Qué pasa cuando la soplan?*

Explore and Express

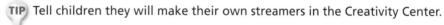 **Can children create movements to music?**

Streaming Vegetables Give each child a crepe paper streamer. Tell children to pretend to be colorful vegetables moving in vegetable soup.

● Play instrumental music that changes tempo often. Have children move their bodies to the music. Encourage them to move their streamers in the same ways vegetables move in soup— spinning, swirling, popping up and down.

● Have them move fast when the tempo is fast and slow when it slows down. Say: *When the music stops, you can gently fall to the bottom of the pot. Cuando se detenga la música, deben caer suavemente al fondo de la olla.*

TIP Tell children they will make their own streamers in the Creativity Center.

ELL If children are comfortable moving to the music, use this as an opportunity to let them shine. Say, for example: *Look at Anna. She is swirling fast. Now she is moving up and down.*

Center Time

> **Center Rotation** Center Time includes teacher-guided activities and independent activities. Refer to the **Learning Centers** on pages 62–63 for activities in additional centers.

  small group 30 minutes

Creativity Center

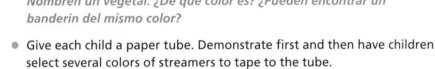

> ✓ Monitor children as they make streamers.

Materials construction paper rolled into a tube and taped to hold it together; red, green, yellow, orange, brown crepe paper strips; tape

Making Streamers Tell children that they will use crepe paper to make colorful streamers.

- Display several different colors of streamers. Say: **Name a vegetable. What color is it? Can you find a streamer that matches the color?** *Nombren un vegetal. ¿De qué color es? ¿Pueden encontrar un banderín del mismo color?*

- Give each child a paper tube. Demonstrate first and then have children select several colors of streamers to tape to the tube.

- Have children use their streamers to continue the Streaming Vegetables movement to music.

Center Tip

If...children need help commenting on vegetable colors, **then...**have them revisit the illustrations in *Growing Vegetable Soup.*

 Learning Goals

Social and Emotional Development
- Child accepts responsibility for and regulates own behavior.

Science
- Child recognizes and selects healthy foods.

Fine Arts
- Child uses and experiments with a variety of art materials and tools in various art activities.

Writing

Recap the day and week. Then say: **Let's write riddles about healthy foods.** Model with: *It is a green vegetable. It starts with the letter* b. *What is this healthy food?* (possible answers: broccoli or brussels sprouts) *Es un vegetal verde. Comienza con la letra* b. *¿Qué alimento saludable es?* Record children's riddles on chart paper. Share the pen with children as you write. Encourage children to write letters that spell sounds they know.

Purposeful Play

> ✓ Observe children sharing classroom materials and working cooperatively.

Children choose an open center for free playtime. Encourage cooperation skills by suggesting they work together to create a skit about children helping a grown-up who eats only not so healthy foods.

Let's Say Good-Bye

 large group 15 minutes

 Read Aloud Revisit "Let's Pretend to Make Tortillas"/"Hagamos que estamos haciendo tortillas" for your afternoon Read Aloud. Remind children to listen for the steps it takes to make tortillas.

 Home Connection Refer to the Home Connections activities listed in the Resources and Materials chart on page 59. Remind children to tell families what they learned this week about healthy foods. Sing the "Good-Bye Song"/"Hora de ir a casa" as children prepare to leave.

Focus Question

Why is exercise important?
¿Por qué es importante hacer ejercicio?

This week children will learn about healthy physical activities. They will discuss exercise at home and school, demonstrate balance and coordination, use ordinal numbers to describe and perform a sequence of movements, name parts of the body that move, and describe how exercise helps bodies grow and be strong.

Learning Goals

Social and Emotional Development	1	2	3	4	5
Child is aware of self in terms of abilities, characteristics and preferences, and respects personal boundaries.	✓	✓			✓
Child describes personal interests and competencies positively (such as, "I can hop.").		✓	✓		
Child initiates interactions with others in work and play situations.	✓	✓	✓	✓	✓
Child initiates play scenarios with peers that share a common plan and goal.	✓		✓		✓

Language and Communication	1	2	3	4	5
Child demonstrates an understanding of oral language by responding appropriately.			✓		
Child follows two- and three-step oral directions.				✓	✓
Child uses oral language for a variety of purposes.		✓			✓
Child begins and ends conversations appropriately.			✓		
Child communicates relevant information for the situation (for example, introduces herself; requests assistance).				✓	
Child follows basic rules for conversations (taking turns, staying on topic, listening actively).	✓	✓	✓		
Child names and describes actual or pictured people, places, things, actions, attributes, and events.	✓	✓	✓	✓	✓
Child uses newly learned vocabulary daily in multiple contexts.	✓		✓	✓	
Child understands and uses regular and irregular plural nouns, regular past tense verbs, personal and possessive pronouns, and subject-verb agreement.	✓	✓			

Emergent Literacy: Reading	1	2	3	4	5
Child enjoys and chooses reading-related activities.			✓		
Child blends onset and rime to form a word without pictoral support.		✓			
Child blends two phonemes to form a word.	✓	✓	✓	✓	✓
Child names most upper- and lowercase letters of the alphabet.	✓	✓	✓	✓	✓
Child identifies the letter that stands for a given sound.	✓	✓	✓	✓	✓
Child produces the most common sound for a given letter.		✓	✓		✓
Child describes, relates to, and uses details and information from books read aloud.	✓	✓	✓	✓	✓
Child asks and answers questions about books read aloud (such as, "Who?" "What?" "Where?").	✓	✓		✓	

Emergent Literacy: Writing	1	2	3	4	5
Child uses scribbles, shapes, pictures, symbols, and letters to represent language.					✓

Mathematics	1	2	3	4	5
Child recites number words in sequence from one to thirty.		✓			✓
Child understands and uses ordinal numbers (such as first, second, third) to identify position in a series.				✓	
Child recognizes and names numerals 0 through 9.	✓				
Child uses concrete objects or makes a verbal word problem to add up to 5 objects.	✓	✓	✓	✓	✓
Child uses concrete objects or makes a verbal word problem to subtract up to 5 objects from a set.	✓		✓	✓	✓
Child measures the length and height of people or objects using standard or non-standard tools or objects.		✓			

Science	1	2	3	4	5
Child follows basic health and safety rules.	✓				
Child identifies and participates in exercises and activities to enhance physical fitness.	✓	✓	✓	✓	✓

Social Studies	1	2	3	4	5
Child understands and discusses roles, responsibilities, and services provided by community workers.		✓			

Fine Arts	1	2	3	4	5
Child expresses thoughts, feelings, and energy through music and creative movement.					✓
Child expresses ideas, emotions, and moods through individual and collaborative dramatic play.				✓	✓

Physical Development	1	2	3	4	5
Child coordinates body movements in a variety of locomotive activities (such as walking, jumping, running, hopping, skipping, climbing).				✓	✓
Child engages in a sequence of movements to perform a task.		✓		✓	

Materials and Resources

DAY 1	DAY 2	DAY 3	DAY 4	DAY 5

Program Materials

• Teacher's Treasure Book • Oral Language Development Card 77 • Rhymes and Chants Flip Chart • *Rise and Exercise!* Big Book • Building Blocks Math Activities • Making Good Choices Flip Chart • Math and Science Flip Chart • Magnetic Wands and Counters • Home Connections Resource Guide	• Teacher's Treasure Book • Dog Puppets • *Rise and Exercise!* Big Book • Counting Cards and Numeral Cards • Building Blocks Math Activities • Making Good Choices Flip Chart • Math and Science Flip Chart • Connecting Cubes	• Teacher's Treasure Book • Oral Language Development Card 78 • Rhymes and Chants Flip Chart • Concept Big Book 4: *Staying Healthy* • ABC Picture Cards • Dog Puppets • Making Good Choices Flip Chart • Photo Library CD-ROM	• Teacher's Treasure Book • Sequence Cards: "Building a Snowman" • Dog Puppets • Flannel Board Patterns for "The Llama's Warning" • Alphabet/Letter Tiles • Two-Color Counters • Numeral Cards 0-3 • Home Connections Resource Guide	• Teacher's Treasure Book • Rhymes and Chants Flip Chart • *Rise and Exercise!* Big Book • ABC Picture Cards • Making Good Choices Flip Chart • Flannel Board Patterns for "The Llama's Warning"

Other Materials

• books showing outdoor activities • paper • crayons • fish crackers • paper plates • washtub or trash can • paper fish • paper clips	• playground slide outlines • color-coded letter cutouts (see p. 109) • masking tape • picture cards of exercises (see p. 109) • copies of sentence frame • pencils and crayons • onset/rime cards (see p. 110)	• student photos • magnetic strip • magnetic letters • magnetic whiteboard • books about the Olympics • paper and crayons • books about community workers • butcher paper • toy action figures or stuffed animals • objects for toy obstacle course (see p. 119)	• paper finger puppet outlines • cardstock • colored pencils • butcher paper • yardstick • large red, green, blue, and yellow circles • spinners • markers, glue • masking tape • beanbags	• paper doll outlines • pictures of objects whose names have two phonemes (see p. 126) • pencils, glue, crayons • construction paper • instrumental music and action songs • raisins and paper plates • paper doll parts on cardstock • hole punch • brad fasteners • decorative supplies

Home Connection

Encourage children to tell their families about exercising. Send home Weekly Family Letter, Home Connections Resource Guide, pp. 73–74.	Encourage children to tell their families ways to exercise.	Encourage children to tell their families about healthy habits.	Encourage children to retell their families why it is important to exercise. Send home Story Book 23, Home Connections Resource Guide, pp. 169–172.	Encourage children to tell their families what they learned this week about exercising.

Assessment

As you observe children throughout the week, you may fill out an Anecdotal Observational Record Form to document an individual's progress toward a goal or signs indicating the need for developmental or medical evaluation. You may also choose to select work for each child's portfolio. The Anecdotal Observational Record Form and Weekly Assessment rubrics are available in the assessment section of DLMExpressOnline.com.

More Literature Suggestions

- **I Love to Exercise** by Phoenix Brown
- **Oscar & Otis: Fat Fighters** by Alicia Kirschenheiter
- **My Amazing Body: A First Look at Health and Fitness** by Pat Thomas
- **E is for Exercise** by Symone LaDeane
- **On The Stairs** by Julie Hofstrand Larios and Mary Hofstrand
- **Un partido de fútbol** por Grace Maccarone
- **Pedro aprende a nadar** por Sara Gerson
- **Jugamos bajo la lluvia** por Angela Shelf Medearis
- **Fiebre de béisbol** por Sindy McKay
- **De la A a la Z con los deportes** por Rafael Cruz-Contarini

Daily Planner

	DAY 1	DAY 2
Let's Start the Day **Language Time** `large group`	Opening Routines p. 102 Morning Read Aloud p. 102 Oral Language and Vocabulary p. 102 Outdoor Activities Phonological Awareness p. 102 Blending Phonemes	Opening Routines p. 108 Morning Read Aloud p. 108 Oral Language and Vocabulary p. 108 Parts That Move Phonological Awareness p. 108 Blending Phonemes
Center Time `small group`	Focus On: Library and Listening Center p. 103 Pretend and Learn Center p. 103	Focus On: ABC Center p. 109 Writer's Center p. 109
Circle Time **Literacy Time** `large group`	Read Aloud *Rise and Exercise!! A ejercitarse, ¡uno, dos, tres!* p. 104 Learn About Letters and Sounds: "I Spy" Letter Match p. 104	Read Aloud *Rise and Exercise!! A ejercitarse, ¡uno, dos, tres!* p. 110 Learn About Letters and Sounds: What's the Missing Letter? p. 110
Math Time `large group`	Gone Fishing 2 p. 105	Compare Game (Adding) p. 111
Social and Emotional Development `large group`	Working Together p. 105	Working Together p. 111
Content Connection `large group`	Science: Oral Language and Academic Vocabulary p. 106 Talking About Body Movement Observe and Investigate p. 106 Exploring Body Movement	Math: p. 112 I'm Thinking of a Number p. 112 Towers of Numbers
Center Time `small group`	Focus On: Math and Science Center p. 107 Purposeful Play p. 107	Focus On: Math and Science Center p. 113 Purposeful Play p. 113
Let's Say Good-Bye `large group`	Read Aloud p. 107 Writing p. 107 Home Connection p. 107	Read Aloud p. 113 Writing p. 113 Home Connection p. 113

Focus Question

Why is exercise important?

¿Por qué es importante hacer ejercicio?

DAY 3

Opening Routines p. 114
Morning Read Aloud p. 114
Oral Language and Vocabulary
p. 114 Riding a Bicycle
Phonological Awareness
p. 114 Blending Phonemes

Focus On:
ABC Center p. 115
Library and Listening Center p. 115

Read Aloud *Staying Healthy/Mantente sano* p. 116
Learn About Letters and Sounds:
Say, See, Show p. 116

Finger Games p. 117

Working Together p. 117

Social Studies:
Oral Language and Academic Vocabulary
p. 118 Talking About Jobs
Understand and Participate
p. 118 Looking at Community Jobs

Focus On:
Pretend and Learn Center p. 119
Purposeful Play p. 119

Read Aloud p. 119
Writing p. 119
Home Connection p. 119

DAY 4

Opening Routines p. 120
Morning Read Aloud p. 120
Oral Language and Vocabulary
p. 120 First, Second, Third
Phonological Awareness
p. 120 Blending Phonemes

Focus On:
Creativity Center p. 121
Construction Center p. 121

Read Aloud "The Llama's Warning"/"La advertencia de la llama" p. 122
Learn About Letters and Sounds:
Folktale Letters p. 122

Snapshots (Adding) p. 123

Working Together p. 123

Math:
p. 124 Talk About Making Numbers
p. 124 Finger Games

Focus On:
Math and Science Center p. 125
Purposeful Play p. 125

Read Aloud p. 125
Writing p. 125
Home Connection p. 125

DAY 5

Opening Routines p. 126
Morning Read Aloud p. 126
Oral Language and Vocabulary
p. 126 Listen and Play
Phonological Awareness
p. 126 Blending Phonemes

Focus On:
Writer's Center p. 127
Creativity Center p. 127

Read Aloud *Rise and Exercise!/A ejercitarse, ¡uno, dos, tres!* p. 128
Learn About Letters and Sounds:
Review and Practice Letters p. 128

Monsters and Raisins p. 129

Working Together p. 129

Dramatic Play:
Oral Language and Academic Vocabulary
p. 130 Recalling Story Details
Explore and Express
p. 130 Dramatizing the Folktale

Focus On:
Construction Center p. 131
Purposeful Play p. 131

Read Aloud p. 131
Writing p. 131
Home Connection p. 131

Learning Centers

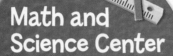

Math and Science Center

Fishing for Numbers
Children use magnets to "catch" numbered fish. They compare numbers on the fish they catch to determine which is greater. See p. 107.

Walking the Line
Children walk on a line to collect colored cubes at the end. They make a tower with the cubes and compare the number of cubes in their towers. See p. 113.

Number Toss
Children toss bean bags onto a numbered grid and add the numbers on which the bags land. They count to the sum number as they perform repetitions of an exercise. See p. 125.

Exercise Count
Children perform a physical activity, such as hopping or skipping. They count each exercise repetition until they are tired or not able to count to the next number.

ABC Center

Slide Together
Children put letters together to form two-letter words. Children blend, say, and write the words. See p. 109.

Name Sort
Children sort photographs of classmates by the initial letters and letter sounds of their names. See p. 115.

Sing to a Letter
Children tell their partner a letter. The partner sings the alphabet song up to that letter and stops. Then they switch roles.

Creativity Center

Finger Puppet Stories
Children decorate and cut out finger puppets. They use the puppets to tell stories about exercising. See p. 121.

Music and Movement
Children perform exercises and stretches to music. They mimic animal movements and name the body parts they use. See p. 127.

Safety Ahead
Children use paper plates to cut out pretend safety helmets. They discuss with partners which activities they should do while wearing safety helmets, such as biking or playing football, and draw pictures to represent those activities on the helmets. Then they can pose the helmets on a "Safety Ahead" wall.

Sports Gear
Children choose a sport and draw pictures of themselves wearing the proper protective gear, such as knee pads or helmets, used to play that sport safely.

Library and Listening Center

Browsing Outdoor Activity Books
Children look through books and identify an outdoor activity they would most like to do. They draw the activity and describe it. See p. 103.

Books About the Olympics
Children look through books about Olympic sports, choose their favorite events, and draw them. They describe why they like the sports and which parts of the body are used to play them. See p. 115.

Activity Song
Children sing songs about movements and act them out. For example, they pretend to row while singing "Row, Row, Row Your Boat" or march while singing "The Ants Go Marching."

Construction Center

Flexibility Game
Children create a floor game board on which they place their hands and feet. They use colored spinners to indicate where their hands and feet should go. See p. 121.

Paper Dolls in Motion
Children assemble moveable paper dolls, identify the parts of their bodies, and describe how doll parts move. See p. 131.

Sport Models
Partners work together to create models of places where sporting events take place. They use blocks and toy figures to make a skating rink, gymnasium, basketball court, baseball diamond, or hiking mountain.

Writer's Center

My Exercise Book
Partners complete sentence frames about exercises, perform the exercises, illustrate the sentence, and compile the pages into books. See p. 109.

A Happy Healthy Me
Children label body parts on paper dolls. They attach the doll to paper, copy a sentence, and draw pictures of healthy activities around the doll. See p. 127.

Athletic Rewards
Children identify an athlete or superhero they admire and draw an award certificate to honor them. As they draw, they explain how the athlete or hero benefits from exercise. Children write or dictate the purpose of the award and sign it.

Sports Medals
Children draw medals for athletes to receive. They copy the phrase "1st Place" or write their own words. Children cut out the medals and string them on yarn. They hold athletic contests and award medals.

Pretend and Learn Center

Calling All Superheroes
Children draw pictures or comic strips showing themselves as a superhero with unusual athletic skills. They pretend to be superheroes and discuss habits that help them maintain their strength. See p. 103.

The Great Race
Children create an obstacle course for toy figures. They plan and describe what will happen during the race and then act it out. See p. 119.

Head Coach
Children pretend to take an exercise or sports class together in groups. One child acts as the instructor or coach and the others are participants or players. Children switch roles so each child gets a turn as instructor or coach.

DAY 1

Let's Start the Day

Focus Question
Why is exercise important?
¿Por qué es importante hacer ejercicio?

✓ Learning Goals

Language and Communication
• Child uses newly learned vocabulary daily in multiple contexts.

Emergent Literacy: Reading
• Child blends two phonemes to form a word.

Science
• Child identifies and participates in exercises and activities to enhance physical fitness.

Vocabulary

elbow pads	coderas	exercise	ejercicio
helmet	casco	knee pads	rodilleras
roller skate	patines	sidewalk	acera

Differentiated Instruction

✋ Extra Support

Phonological Awareness
If...children have difficulty blending phonemes to say a word, **then...**give them two connecting cubes to put together as they blend and say a two-phoneme word. For example, hold a green cube in your left hand as you say /o/; pick up a red cube in your right hand as you say /n/. Then put the cubes together as you say: /o/ /n/, on.

★ Enrichment

Phonological Awareness
Challenge children to blend and say three-phoneme action words such as *sit, hop,* and *run.*

Accommodations for 3's

Phonological Awareness
If...children have difficulty recognizing and blending two-phoneme words, **then...**have them move a teddy bear, leg by leg, on and off the play rug, as they blend and say /o/ /n/, /aw/ /f/.

▶ Opening Routines and Transition Tips

For **Opening Routines** and **Transition Tips** turn to pages 178–181 and visit **DLMExpressOnline.com** for more ideas.

📖 Read **"Going for a Swim"/"Voy a nadar"** from the *Teacher's Treasure Book,* page 193, for your morning Read Aloud.

Language Time

large group 15 minutes

👥 **Social and Emotional Development** Remind children to take turns sharing ideas and to listen respectfully to each other without interrupting.

Oral Language and Vocabulary

✓ **Can children use descriptive words to tell about outdoor activities?**

Outdoor Activities Talk about outdoor activities children do for fun and exercise. Ask: **What do you do for playtime outside? What are some ways you exercise after school?** *¿Qué hacen para divertirse al aire libre? ¿Cómo hacen ejercicio después de clases?*

● Display *Oral Language Development Card 77.* Point to and name the roller skates and protective gear. Then follow the suggestions on the back of the card.

Oral Language Development Card 77

Phonological Awareness

✓ **Can children blend two-phoneme words?**

Blending Phonemes Display *Rhymes and Chants Flip Chart,* p. 35. Tell children to listen carefully as you say a word slowly.

● Say: */o/ /n/.* Have children repeat after you. Ask: **What's the word?** *¿Cuál es la palabra?* Confirm: */o/ /n/, on.*

● Then point to the child on the swing and say: **This child is "on" the swing.** *El niño está en el columpio.* Say again: **Where is the child?** *¿Dónde está el niño?* (on the swing) Then point to the child on the slide. Ask: **Where is this child?** *¿Dónde está el niño?* (on the slide).

● Follow the same procedure for *off* and *up.*

ELL Demonstrate opposites *on/off* by moving an object on and off the table as you say */o/ /n/, on.../aw/ /f/, off.* Have children repeat after you. Then have children do the actions themselves as they say the words. Have them also turn on and off the lights as they say the words. Follow the same approach for opposites *up/down.*

For additional suggestions on how to meet the needs of children at the Beginning, Intermediate, Advanced, and Advanced-High levels of English proficiency, see pages 184–187.

Rhymes and Chants Flip Chart, page 35

Center Time

▶ **Center Rotation** Center Time includes teacher-guided activities and independent activities. Refer to the **Learning Centers** on pages 100–101 for independent activity ideas.

 small group 60–90 minutes

Library and Listening Center

✓ **Track children's understanding of exercise, names of body parts, and use of action words as children tell about their drawings.**

Materials fiction and nonfiction books showing outdoor activities (including seasonal sports), paper, crayons

Browsing Outdoor Activity Books Have children browse through books about outdoor activities and then choose the activity they'd like to do the most. Help them name and describe the activity.

● Have children draw their favorite activity and share their drawings. Encourage them to include labels.

● Ask: *What do you like about this activity? Do you think it's a good way to exercise? Why? ¿Por qué les gusta esta actividad? ¿Es una buena manera de hacer ejercicio? ¿Por qué?*

Center Tip
If...children have difficulty recalling an activity name or a vocabulary word, **then...**give them a clue by starting to sound out the name for them, or show them the first letter of the name.

Pretend and Learn Center

✓ **Track the use of descriptive words as children tell about superhero strength and abilities.**

Materials drawing paper, crayons

Calling All Superheroes Tell children to pretend they are a superhero with super strength or other special athletic abilities.

● Have children draw a series of pictures or comic strips showing how they use their special abilities to help others. Ask: *What parts of your body have super strength or ability? What can you do? ¿Qué parte del cuerpo tiene el poder especial? ¿Qué puedes hacer?*

● Have children role-play being a superhero as they share their stories and pictures. Invite classmates to ask the superhero questions about healthy habits. For example, ask: *What do you do to keep your body healthy and strong? ¿Qué hacen para mantener su cuerpo sano y fuerte?*

Center Tip
If...children have difficulty thinking of superhero abilities, **then...**prompt them to think about what cartoon superheroes can do, such as jump over tall buildings, lift huge things, and run extremely fast

Learning Goals

Social and Emotional Development
● Child is aware of self in terms of abilities, characteristics and preferences, and respects personal boundaries.

● Child initiates play scenarios with peers that share a common plan and goal.

Language and Communication
● Child follows basic rules for conversations (taking turns, staying on topic, listening actively).

● Child uses newly learned vocabulary daily in multiple contexts.

Emergent Literacy: Reading
● Child describes, relates to, and uses details and information from books read aloud.

Differentiated Instruction

 Extra Support

Library and Listening Center
If...children have difficulty drawing favorite activity pictures, **then...**give them tracing paper to trace and color the picture from the book.

 Enrichment

Library and Listening Center
Challenge children to take turns saying descriptive words and phrases about the activities shown in the pictures. Tell them to say words that would help someone draw or visualize that exact same picture.

Circle Time

Literacy Time

 large group · 15 minutes

Read Aloud

 Can children describe, compare, and relate to information in the story?

Build Background Tell children that you will be reading a book about different ways to exercise.

- Ask: *Why is it important to exercise? What are some ways that you run and play to keep your body healthy and strong?* *¿Por qué es importante hacer ejercicio? ¿En qué actividades corren? ¿Cómo se mantiene el cuerpo saludable y fuerte?*

Listen for Enjoyment Display the front cover of the Big Book *Rise and Exercise!* and read the title aloud. Then conduct a picture walk.

- Browse through the pages. Name and describe the picture details, including actions and attire.

- Ask: *What is this child doing? What are the other children doing?* *¿Qué hace este niño? ¿Qué hacen los otros niños?*

Respond to the Story Point to each picture. Have children tell about the exercises or activities. Ask: *Which picture shows children stretching (spinning, jumping, dancing)?* *¿En cuál de las imágenes trepa (baila, salta, corre) un niño o una niña?*

 TIP Have children compare the exercises shown in the pictures. Ask: *How is this exercise different from the last one? What do you notice about their arms? legs? feet?* *¿En qués se diferencian estos ejercicios? ¿Qué notan sobre los brazos (piernas, pies) del niño(a)?*

Learn About Letters and Sounds

 Can children match letter sounds to corresponding letters in words?

"I Spy" Letter Match After children describe and compare pictures from the book, play a phonetic game of "I Spy" with the picture names.

- Display the first letters of the picture names on separate self-stick notes.

- Turn to the illustration on page 4. Say: *I spy something that begins with /b/.* *Veo, veo, algo para que empieza con /b/.* Model how to take the letter *Bb* and stick it onto the picture of the bed. Say: *Bed begins with /b/.../b/ for* **b**. *Bed empieza con /b/... /b/ la letra b.*

- Continue with other picture names, having children stick letters onto matching pictures and explaining their choices. Have other children confirm whether the answer is correct. Explain that there may be more than one possible answer, such as *Gg* for *girl* or *ground*.

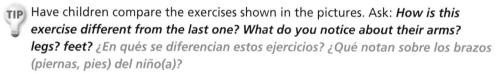 **ELL** As you browse *Rise and Exercise!* point to specific things in the illustrations as you say the corresponding name. Encourage children to point to the pictures and name things they know.

Rise and Exercise!
A ejercitarse, ¡uno, dos, tres!

Math Time

Observe and Investigate

✓ **Can children compare amounts?**

Gone Fishing 2 Tell children they are going to pretend to be dinosaurs that eat fish. Distribute fish crackers, and have children use paper plates (or blue construction paper) as their "lake" to eventually keep the fish.

- Ask children how many fish are in their lake right now (0). Tell them four fish swam near the "dinosaur," and have them put four fish in their lake. Ask: *How many fish are in your lake? ¿Cuántos peces hay en el lago?* (4)

- Tell children that the dinosaur is so happy to have four fish that he or she eats them all! (Children eat the crackers.) Ask: *How many fish are now in the lake? ¿Cuántos peces hay en el lago ahora?* (0)

- Continue the story, adding or subtracting various amounts. For example: *You have 4 but want 6. How many do you need to add? Tienes 4 peces pero quieres 6. ¿Cuántos necesitas sumar?* For subtraction, have children eat only some of their crackers, and then ask how many are still left in the lake.

- Invite children to create their own addition and subtraction word problems for their classmates to act out.

ELL Use the following sentence frames while you demonstrate adding and comparing amounts. First put fish crackers in your hand, then show how many more you're going to add, and then count to show how many fish you have altogether. Have children do the same as they repeat the sentences.
I have ____. I add ____ more. Now I have ____.

👥 Social and Emotional Development

Making Good Choices

✓ **Do children show a desire to work together?**

Working Together Discuss children's prior experiences with teams. Ask: *What makes a good team member? ¿Qué hace que alguien sea un buen miembro de un equipo?* Display *Making Good Choices Flip Chart* page 35. Point to the solitary girl watching the others.

- Ask: *Do you think the girl wants to play with the other children? What do you think the other children should do about it? ¿Creen que la niña quiere jugar con los otros niños? ¿Qué creen que deberían hacer los otros niños?*

- Then discuss working together and showing good teamwork.

Making Good Choices Flip Chart, page 35

Building Blocks

Online Math Activity

Introduce Number Compare 2: Dots to 7, in which children compare two cards with varied dot arrangements and choose the card with the greater value. Each child should complete the activity this week.

Learning Goals

Social and Emotional Development
- Child initiates interactions with others in work and play situations.

Mathematics
- Child uses concrete objects or makes a verbal word problem to add up to 5 objects.
- Child uses concrete objects or makes a verbal word problem to subtract up to 5 objects from a set.

Vocabulary

adding	sumar	dinosaur	dinosaurio
fish	pescar	lake	lago
share	compartir	subtracting	restar
together	juntos		

Differentiated Instruction

✋ **Extra Support**
Observe and Investigate
If... children have difficulty comparing amounts, **then...** use smaller numbers, or state problems one sentence at a time.

⭐ **Enrichment**
Observe and Investigate
To make the fishing activity more challenging, increase the first number and then the second. You might also extend the activity by having children complete a number sentence to show the addition or subtraction, such as $4 - 4 = 0$.

Focus Question
Why is exercise important?
¿Por qué es importante hacer ejercicio?

 Learning Goals

Social and Emotional Development
• Child is aware of self in terms of abilities, characteristics and preferences, and respects personal boundaries.

Language and Communication
• Child names and describes actual or pictured people, places, things, actions, attributes, and events.

• Child understands and uses regular and irregular plural nouns, regular past tense verbs, personal and possessive pronouns, and subject-verb agreement.

Science
• Child follows basic health and safety rules.

• Child identifies and participates in exercises and activities to enhance physical fitness.

Vocabulary

arms	brazos	body	cuerpo
feet	pie	foot	piernas
hands	manos	legs	rodillas

Differentiated Instruction

 Extra Support

Science
If...children have difficulty recalling the names of different body parts, **then...**use self-stick notes to label the parts on the flip chart.

 Enrichment

Science
Challenge children to learn the names, locations, and functions of other parts of the body used for movement, such as the neck, shoulders, waist, and joints (elbows, wrists, knees, ankles).

 Special Needs

Vision Loss
As each part of the body is discussed, allow the child an opportunity to "see and understand" the body part, by touching and feeling it on themselves.

Science Time

  large group 20 minutes

Personal Safety Skills Demonstrate ways to stretch the body before performing any kind of exercise or strenuous activity. Be sure children have enough space around them for freedom of movement while exercising. Remind children to be careful and respectful of people around them.

Oral Language and Academic Vocabulary

Can children use words to name different parts of the body used for movement?
Talking About Body Movement Point to the soccer player on the Math and Science Flip Chart page 65. Say: *This soccer player has a healthy body. He uses different parts of his body to play the game. Este jugador tiene un cuerpo saludable. Usa muchas partes de su cuerpo para jugar.*

• Point to different parts of the body on the chart as you name each part. Have children repeat after you. Explain that the plural form of *foot* is *feet*. Say: *one hand, two hands; one foot, two feet.* Have children repeat the words after you.

Observe and Investigate

Can children describe how they use different parts of their body to move?
Exploring Body Movement Tell children they will explore how their body moves.

• Lead children through a variety of movement exercises (bends, stretches, leg lifts, sidesteps, beanbag toss/balance). You can also go outside to get more space to exercise.

• As children perform each action, ask questions such as: *What part of your body did you use to grab? to lift? to kick? to jump? ¿Qué parte del cuerpo usan para agarrar algo? ¿Para levantarse? ¿Para patear? ¿Para brincar?*

• Have individual children show their favorite exercise. Have other children identify the body parts the child is using. Have everyone do the exercise.

• After you've exercised, have children feel and describe their heartbeats.

• To summarize the activity, work with children to complete sentence frames about how their bodies move. For example: *I used my <u>hands</u> to _____. (grab, catch, throw, hold) Yo uso mis manos para _____. (agarrar, atajar, lanzar, atrapar)* and *When I kicked, I used my _____.(leg, knee, foot) Cuando pateo, uso mi _____. (piernas, rodillas, pies)*

ELL Have children lie on butcher paper as you trace around them to make a life-size body outline. Help children label the parts of their body. Point to each part as you say the name, and have children repeat after you.

A Healthy Body
Cuerpo sano

Math and Science Flip Chart, page 65

Center Time

▶ **Center Rotation** Center Time includes teacher-guided activities and independent activities. Refer to the **Learning Centers** on pages 100–101 for independent activity ideas.

small group | 30 minutes

Math and Science Center

✓ **Check that children are counting and adding numbers correctly.**

Materials washtub or small trashcan; 24 paper fish in three different sizes labeled 1, 2, and 3; paper clips; Magnetic Wand; counters

Fishing for Numbers Invite children to go fishing for numbers.

● Attach a paper clip "mouth" to each paper fish. Put all the fish into a container representing the pond.

● Demonstrate how players catch fish with the magnet. Compare the numbers on the fish. Ask: **Which fish shows more?** *¿Qué pez tiene el número más alto?* The player who catches the greater number gets to keep both fish. If the numbers are equal, both children keep their catch. If players catch more than one fish at a time, they may either keep one and put the rest back, or try to add the numbers. If their sum is correct, they can keep the fish. If not, they put all the fish back.

● The player with the most fish at the end of the game wins.

Center Tip

If...children have difficulty comparing numerals or adding them mentally, **then...**have them use counters to count, compare, and add the amounts.

✓ Learning Goals

Language and Communication
• Child names and describes actual or pictured people, places, things, actions, attributes, and events.

Mathematics
• Child recognizes and names numerals 0 through 9.
• Child uses concrete objects or makes a verbal word problem to add up to 5 objects.

Science
• Child identifies and participates in exercises and activities to enhance physical fitness.

✎ Writing

Recap the day. Have children name exercises and parts of the body used for movement. Ask: **What is your favorite way to get exercise?** *¿Cuál es su forma preferida de hacer ejercicio?* Record their answers. Read them back as you track the print, and emphasize the correspondence between speech and print.

Purposeful Play

✓ **Observe children appropriately handling classroom materials.**

Children choose an open center for free playtime. Encourage cooperation skills by suggesting they work together to think of and play other number games with the fish.

Let's Say Good-Bye

large group | 15 minutes

 Read Aloud Revisit "Going for a Swim"/"Voy a nadar" for your afternoon Read Aloud. Ask children to listen for words that tell about exercise and other kinds of movement.

 Home Connection Refer to the Home Connections activities listed in the Resources and Materials chart on page 97. Remind children to tell families about the exercises they did. Sing the "Good-Bye Song"/ "Hora de ir a casa" as children prepare to leave.

DAY 2

Let's Start the Day

Focus Question

Why is exercise important?
¿Por qué es importante hacer ejercicio?

Opening Routines and Transition Tips
For **Opening Routines** and **Transition Tips** turn to pages 178–181 and visit DLMExpressOnline.com for more ideas.

Read **"Miguel and Maribel: Dance of Opposites"/**"Miguel y Maribel: Un baile de opuestos" from the *Teacher's Treasure Book*, page 258, for your morning Read Aloud.

✓ Learning Goals

Language and Communication
• Child understands and uses regular and irregular plural nouns, regular past tense verbs, personal and possessive pronouns, and subject-verb agreement.

Emergent Literacy: Reading
• Child blends two phonemes to form a word.

Physical Development
• Child engages in a sequence of movements to perform a task.

Vocabulary

arms	brazos	demonstrate	demostrar
exercise	ejercicio	knees	rodillas
legs	piernas	watch	observar

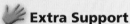

Differentiated Instruction

✋ Extra Support
Oral Language and Vocabulary
If...children have difficulty recalling the names of body parts, **then...**give them verbal and visual cues to help them, such as: *lift* for *leg*, *waving "hello"* for *hand*, or pointing out that the letter *r* looks like an arm.

⭐ Enrichment
Oral Language and Vocabulary
Expand children's vocabulary during the discussion and movement activity by including the names of other body parts that move, such as *neck, elbow, wrist, hand, fingers, ankle, foot, feet, toes*. Point to and move each body part as you say the name. Have children repeat after you.

Language Time

large group   15 minutes

👫 Social and Emotional Development Remind children to stay within their own space and to be careful when doing movement activities together.

Oral Language and Vocabulary

✓ **Can children identify parts of the body that move during exercise?**

Parts That Move Name different body parts that move during exercise, such as *arms*, *legs* and *feet*. Have children repeat the name as they move or tap that part of their body. For example: **Show me your feet...What are these called?** *Muéstrenme los pies... ¿Cómo se llama esta parte?*

● Practice word recognition and body movement by doing the "Hokey Pokey" or another movement activity with children. Tell them to first watch closely as you demonstrate each movement, and then follow along with you. After the activity, have children name the body parts that moved.

Phonological Awareness

✓ **Can children blend two-phoneme words?**

Blending Phonemes Display a Dog Puppet. Tell children that the dog needs their help blending sounds to say a word. Tell them to listen carefully and then say the word. For example, the dog says: /n/ /ē/. Children reply: **knee**. Have children blend and say the word again: /n/ /ē/, **knee**. Use two-phoneme words from the book *Rise and Exercise!*, including illustrated words *two, up, all, on, he*, and *she*.

ELL Display pictures or use classroom examples to go with each word that children blend. For example, point to your knee as you say /n/ /ē/, **knee**. Have children repeat after you.

For additional suggestions on how to meet the needs of children at the Beginning, Intermediate, Advanced, and Advanced-High levels of English proficiency, see pages 184–187.

Center Time

▶ **Center Rotation** Center Time includes teacher-guided activities and independent activities. Refer to the **Learning Centers** on pages 100–101 for independent activity ideas.

small group 60–90 minutes

ABC Center

Center Tip

☑ **Track children's ability to blend and say words.**

Materials playground slide outlines, color-coded letter cutouts of *d, g, h, m, n, p, t, a, e, i, o,* and *u*

Slide Together Explain to children that they will be sliding letters together to form words. Review the name and sound of each letter.

- Model how to slide *g* down, followed by *o*, to form the word *go* at the bottom of the slide. As you slide each letter, say the letter sound: **/g/.../o/**. Blend and say the word as you put the letters together at the bottom: **/g/ /o/, go**. Have children copy you.

- Tell children to form words that begin with a consonant, such as *go, no, he, do,* and *me,* and words that begin with a vowel, such as *in, it, up, an,* and *at.* Have them say and write the words they form.

If...children have difficulty recalling a letter's sound, **then...**have them trace the letter with their finger and repeat the sound you say before continuing with the activity.

Writer's Center

Center Tip

☑ **Track children's use of numbers and action words**

Materials number cards 1–5, labeled picture cards of exercises (jumping jacks, sit-ups, knee-bends, toe-touches, push-ups, leg lifts), photocopies of sentence frames, pencils and crayons

My Exercise Book Have children make their own exercise book. Use these sentence frames: Can I do _____? Yes, I can!

- Model how to choose a number card and an exercise card for the blank. Read the completed sentence. Demonstrate how to do that many repetitions of the chosen exercise (for example, two sit-ups).

- Tell children to trace the sentence "Yes, I can!" and draw a picture of the exercise after they succeed.

- Have pairs or trios of children work together, choosing different cards for each page. Invite children to share their completed book.

If...children have difficulty completing the chosen exercise or number of repetitions, **then...**have them choose another number card or exercise card.

 Learning Goals

Emergent Literacy: Reading
- Child blends two phonemes to form a word.
- Child names most upper- and lowercase letters of the alphabet.
- Child identifies the letter that stands for a given sound.
- Child produces the most common sound for a given letter.

Science
- Child identifies and participates in exercises and activities to enhance physical fitness.

Differentiated Instruction

⭐ Enrichment

ABC Center
Challenge children to slide together three-letter words by using a consonant at the beginning and end of the word, such as *not, hot, dot, dig, wig, wet, pit, pan, pat.* Suggest that they form rhyming words.

Accommodations for 3's

Writer's Center
If...children have difficulty writing the number words and exercise names, **then...**have them write numerals, and give them sticker labels showing pictures of the exercises to put into their frames.

Circle Time

Literacy Time

 large group · 15 minutes

📖 Read Aloud

✓ **Can children describe, compare, and relate to information in the story?**

Build Background Tell children that you will read about children doing fun exercises. Ask: *What do you do for exercise? ¿Qué hacen para hacer ejercicio?*

Listen for Understanding Display the cover of *Rise and Exercise!* and read the title aloud.

- Turn to the first picture and have children describe what they see. Then read aloud the print. Ask: *What time of day is it? What are the people in the pictures doing? ¿Qué hora del día es? ¿Qué están haciendo las personas de las ilustraciones?*

- Turn to the next picture. Ask: *What are the people doing now? ¿Ahora que sucede?* Continue for the rest of the book.

Respond to the Story Have children recall the different exercises and activities that the people in the book do. Ask: *What exercises can you do? ¿Qué ejercicios pueden hacer ustedes?* Then revisit each picture, and have children do each exercise. Say: *Show me how to stretch (bend, jump, stand, kneel) like the people in this picture. Muéstrenme como estirarse (saltar, girar, correr) como las personas de esta ilustración.*

Rise and Exercise!
A ejercitarse, ¡uno, dos, tres!

💡 **TIP** Be sure children can use picture details to describe each exercise or activity. Remind children to be careful as they demonstrate each exercise shown in the book.

Learn About Letters and Sounds

✓ **Can children identify the first letter of a word?**

What's the Missing Letter? Prepare separate onset and rime cards for each of these words from the book: *m-ove, r-ise, f-eet, b-ike, h-op, j-ump, s-it, g-ood.* Tell children you need their help putting together words from the book.

- Display the initial letters at the top of a pocket chart, and review each letter and sound. For example, say: *This is M...M for /m/...say /m/. Ésta es la M...M para /m/...digan /m/.* Have children repeat after you.

- Display the rime **-un.** Say: *I want to make the word fun. I'm missing the first letter. It makes the /f/ sound. What letter makes the /f/ sound? Quiero formar la palabra fun, pero me falta la primera letra, la que tiene el sonido /f/. ¿Qué letra tiene el sonido /f/?* Have children say which letter to choose from the pocket chart. Put the word parts together as you blend and say the word: */f/-un, fun.* Have children repeat after you.

- Continue with other word parts, having children help you form and blend words.

ELL Make color-coded word cards for different color names. As you read the book, point to specific colors in the pictures as you say the name. Show and say the matching word card for children to repeat after you.

Social and Emotional Development
• Child describes personal interests and competencies positively (such as, "I can hop.").

Language and Communication
• Child follows basic rules for conversations (taking turns, staying on topic, listening actively).

• Child uses newly learned vocabulary daily in multiple contexts.

Emergent Literacy: Reading
• Child blends onset and rime to form a word without pictoral support.

• Child describes, relates to, and uses details and information from books read aloud.

• Child asks and answers questions about books read aloud (such as, "Who?" "What?" "Where?").

Science
• Child identifies and participates in exercises and activities to enhance physical fitness.

Vocabulary

bend	doblar	climb	girar
exercise	ejercicio	jump	saltar
kneel	arrodillarse	stand	pararse
stretch	estirarse		

🖐 Extra Support

Learn About Letters and Sounds

If...children have difficulty identifying and blending onsets and rimes, **then...**color-code the different parts, using green for the onset and red for the rime. Have children use their finger to trace the letters as they blend and say the word. You might also use fewer words for the activity.

⭐ Enrichment

Learn About Letters and Sounds

Give children copies of the word parts to put together themselves during the activity. Have them trace the letters as they say the word.

large group — 15 minutes

Math Time

Observe and Investigate

☑ **Can children compare sums of numbers?**

Compare Game (Adding) For each pair of children, use two or more sets of Counting Cards 1–10 (*Teacher's Treasure Book,* pages 506–507). Mix the cards, and deal them equally, facedown, to each player.

● Players simultaneously flip two cards to add and then compare which sum is greater. The player with more says "I have more!" and takes the opponent's cards. If sums are equal, each player flips another card to break the tie.

● Observe children's strategies to assess and evaluate: Do they subitize (recognize how many without counting) or count from 1? How do they determine sums? Do they compose numbers (e.g., 2 and 2 is 4)?

● The winner is the player with more cards when all cards have been played. Or, play without a winner by not allowing players to collect cards.

large group — 15 minutes

✗✗✗ Social and Emotional Development

Making Good Choices

☑ **Do children show a desire to work together?**

Working Together Revisit *Making Good Choices Flip Chart* page 35, "How Can I Show Good Teamwork?"

● Display a Dog Puppet. Say: ***Tell the puppet how this girl is feeling and what the other children do to make her feel better.*** *Expliquen al títere cómo se siente esta niña y qué pueden hacer los otros niños para hacer que se sienta mejor.*

● Provide several children a turn to tell the puppet why the girl is sitting by herself and what the other children can do to help her feel like part of their group. Remind children to show good teamwork when they work together during Center Time.

● Play the song "I'm Going to Play, Too"/"Yo, tambien, jugare" from the Making Good Choices Audio CD. Ask children how the song might help the girl who is sitting by herself.

ELL Provide sentence frames to help during the conversation with the dog puppet. Use these and others: ***The girl is _____. She wants _____. The other children tell her _____.*** Model the use of each frame. Have children repeat, then apply using their own words. Some children may feel more comfortable just repeating the completed frame you provided.

Making Good Choices Flip Chart, page 35

Building Blocks

Online Math Activity

Introduce Number Snapshots 5, in which children match scrambled arrangements up to 5 to their corresponding numerals when shown only briefly. All students should complete the activity this week.

☑ Learning Goals

Social and Emotional Development
● Child initiates interactions with others in work and play situations.

Mathematics
● Child uses concrete objects or makes a verbal word problem to add up to 5 objects.

Vocabulary

add	sumar	compare	comparar
equal	igual	greater	más que
help	ayudar	polite	educado(a)
share	compartir		

Differentiated Instruction

 Extra Support

Observe and Investigate

If...children struggle to compare numbers, **then...**use fewer cards and/or cards of smaller amounts.

 Enrichment

Observe and Investigate

Challenge children by having them use counting cards greater than 10. You might also have children play in trios instead of pairs, challenging them to compare three amounts simultaneously.

 Special Needs

Cognitive Challenges

When playing the "Compare Game" begin with only numbers 1 and 2 rather than sums to 10.

Learning Goals

Language and Communication
• Child uses oral language for a variety of purposes.

Mathematics
• Child recites number words in sequence from one to thirty.
• Child uses concrete objects or makes a verbal word problem to add up to 5 objects.
• Child measures the length and height of people or objects using standard or non-standard tools.

Vocabulary

compare	comparar	count	contar
equal to	iguales	less than	menos de
more than	más de	the most	más grande
number	número		

 Differentiated Instruction

 Extra Support

Math Time

If...children have difficulty comparing numbers using counting cards or cubes, **then...**have them use a number line to compare numbers. Review number sequence, and remind them that the greater numbers are further down the line.

Enrichment

Math Time

Challenge children to make their own bar graph showing classmates' favorite exercises. Tell them to use the same three choices as the flip chart. Tell them to ask only 10 classmates. Have them share and compare their results.

Math Time

  large group 20 minutes

Language and Communication Skills Use comparative words and phrases while discussing numbers and amounts with children, and check their understanding. Model as needed.

Can children compare numbers?

I'm Thinking of a Number Hide a Counting Card (*Teacher's Treasure Book*, pages 506–507). Tell children that you hid "a secret number."

● Explain to children that you hid a card with a number on it. Say: *Guess my number. Adivinen mi número.*

● Tell children only whether a guess is more or less than the secret number. When a child guesses correctly, excitedly reveal the card.

● Repeat several times, hiding other cards. As children become comfortable, ask for explanations of why they made their guess, such as "I knew 4 was more than the secret number and 2 was less, so I guessed 3." Also include more clues, such as: *Your guess is two more than my number. El número que dijeron es dos más que mi número.*

Can children use concrete models to compare numbers?

Towers of Numbers Tell children they will be using cube towers to compare numbers.

● Display *Math and Science Flip Chart* page 66, "Our Favorite Exercise." Explain that the towers show how many children like each exercise. Ask: *Without counting, how do you know which exercise children like most? Sin contar, ¿cómo saben cuál es el ejercicio preferido de los niños?* Explain: *The blue tower is tallest, so children like bicycling the most. La torre azul es la más grande, entonces a los niños les gusta más hacer ese ejercicio.*

● Build a green 4-cube tower, a blue 2-cube tower, and a red 6-cube tower. Tell children the green tower has 4 cubes. Ask: *Which tower has more than 4 cubes? Which tower has less than 4 cubes? How do you know? ¿Cuál de las torres tiene más de 4 cubos? ¿Cual tiene menos de 4 cubos? ¿Cómo saben?*

● Attach the green and blue towers together, and put it next to the red tower. Say: *Compare these two towers. Comparen estas dos torres.* (The red tower is the same height as the blue and green towers together.)

● Continue comparing with other cube towers. Have children make their own towers to compare.

ELL Have children put a 4-cube tower and a 6-cube tower side by side. Say *more than* as you point to the taller tower. Have children repeat after you. Pull off the two extra cubes to show to children as you repeat *more than*. Then count them...*1, 2.* Say: *two more.* Have children repeat after you. Repeat several times with other towers.

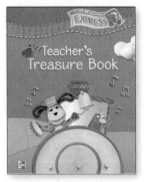

Teacher's Treasure Book p. 506

Math and Science Flip Chart, page 66

Center Time

Center Rotation Center Time includes teacher-guided activities and independent activities. Refer to the **Learning Centers** on pages 100–101 for independent activity ideas.

  small group · 30 minutes

Refer to the **Learning Centers** on pages 100–101 for independent activity ideas.

Math and Science Center

☑ **Check that children are comparing and adding numbers correctly.**

Materials masking tape, tubs of red and blue connecting cubes

Walking the Line Have children practice movement and balance as they collect cubes for addition.

- Use masking tape to make a walk-on line for each pair or group of children. Put containers of red cubes and of blue cubes at the end.

- Have children take turns walking on the line, grabbing a handful of blue and a handful of red cubes at the end, and then walking back. Tell them to stay on the line, like a balance beam.

- Have them make a cube tower with the red and blue cubes. When all group members have finished, have pairs of players compare their towers. Ask: *Who has more cubes? How do you know? ¿Quién tiene más cubos? ¿Cómo lo saben?*

Center Tip

If...children have difficulty comparing towers, **then...** have them stand the towers next to each other. Help them recognize that the taller tower has more cubes.

Purposeful Play

☑ **Observe children sharing classroom materials and working cooperatively.**

Children choose an open center for free playtime. Encourage cooperation skills by suggesting that they work together to demonstrate a set of exercises.

Let's Say Good-Bye

 large group · 15 minutes

 Read Aloud Revisit "Miguel and Maribel: Dance of Opposites"/ "Miguel y Maribel: Un baile de opuestos" for your afternoon Read Aloud. Remind children to listen for ways in which the two characters move.

 Home Connection Refer to the Home Connections activities listed in the Resources and Materials chart on page 97. Remind children to tell families about ways to exercise. Sing the "Good-Bye Song"/"Hora de ir a casa" as children prepare to leave.

☑ Learning Goals

Social and Emotional Development
- Child is aware of self in terms of abilities, characteristics and preferences, and respects personal boundaries.

Language and Communication
- Child names and describes actual or pictured people, places, things, actions, attributes, and events.

Mathematics
- Child uses concrete objects or makes a verbal word problem to add up to 5 objects.
- Child measures the length and height of people or objects using standard or non-standard tools.

Writing

Recap the day. Have children tell what they learned about keeping their body healthy and strong. Ask: *What is your favorite exercise? ¿Cuál es tu ejercicio favorito?* Ask them to draw a picture showing themselves exercising.

Week 3 Healthy Fun

DAY 3

Let's Start the Day

Focus Question

Why is exercise important? ¿Por qué es importante hacer ejercicio?

 Learning Goals

Language and Communication
• Child follows basic rules for conversations (taking turns, staying on topic, listening actively).

• Child uses newly learned vocabulary daily in multiple contexts.

Emergent Literacy: Reading
• Child blends two phonemes to form a word.

Vocabulary

bicycle	bicicleta	helmet	casco
pedal	pedalear	pedals	pedales
wheels	ruedas		

Differentiated Instruction

 Extra Support

Phonological Awareness

If...children have difficulty blending phonemes to say a word, **then...**have them use their hands as a visual cue for putting together words. For example, for the word *on*: put your left hand up as you say */o/*, put your right hand up as you say */n/*, then clap your hands together as you say **on.** Have children repeat after you: */o/ /n/,* **on.**

Enrichment

Phonological Awareness

Challenge children to think of rhyming words for each two-phoneme word, such as *go, no, low.* Ask: **Did you change the first sound or the second sound? Say the new sound.** *¿Cambiaron el primero o el segundo sonido? Digan el nuevo sonido.*

▶ **Opening Routines and Transition Tips**

For **Opening Routines** and **Transition Tips** turn to pages 178–181 and visit DLMExpressOnline.com for more ideas.

📖 Read **"I Can, You Can!"/**"¡Yo puedo, tú puedes!" from the *Teacher's Treasure Book,* page 248, for your morning Read Aloud.

Language Time

🧍🧍🧍 **Social and Emotional Development** Ask children why it is important to listen attentively to each other as they share their knowledge and experience. Acknowledge children who listen appropriately and respond positively by naming them and the behavior they are showing.

Oral Language and Vocabulary

✅ **Can children use descriptive words to tell about riding a bicycle?**

Riding a Bicycle Have children share what they know about bicycles. Ask: **What is a bicycle? What is a shorter name for "bicycle"? Why do people ride a bike? How do you ride it?** *¿Qué es una bicicleta? ¿Cuál es el nombre más corto que usamos para "bicicleta"? ¿Por qué es que a la gente le gusta andar en bici? ¿Cómo se maneja?*

● Display *Oral Language Development Card 78.* Point to and name the bicycle and protective gear. Then follow the suggestions on the back of the card.

Phonological Awareness

✅ **Can children blend two-phoneme words?**

Blending Phonemes Revisit *Rhymes and Chants Flip Chart,* p. 35. Tell children you need their help blending sounds to say words. Say the chant to children, stopping at every two-phoneme word and saying the letter sounds for children to blend. For example: **"Sing /i/ /n/...(in)...a swing."**

ELL Have children blend and say the words *up, down, on, off* as you all stand up, sit down, step on a rug, and step off a rug. Do the action as you say the final blended word. For example, **stand /u/ /p/... up!** (everyone stands up when they say "up"). Repeat several times.

Oral Language Development Card 78

Rhymes and Chants Flip Chart, page 35

Center Time

▶ **Center Rotation** Center Time includes teacher-guided activities and independent activities. Refer to the **Learning Centers** on pages 100–101 for independent activity ideas.

 small group 60–90 minutes

ABC Center

✓ **Track children's ability to sort names beginning with the same letter.**

Materials sets of student photos taped onto magnetic strip, magnetic letters, magnetic whiteboard

Name Sort Tell children they will be sorting pictures of their classmates by the first letter of their name.

- Model how to sound out a student's name and predict the first letter of his or her name. Say: **This is a picture of Sam. The first sound I hear is /s/.../s/ am. I know letter S makes that sound, /s/. So I put the picture of Sam with the letter S on the board.** *Ésta es una foto de Sam. El primer sonido que escucho es /s/... /s/ am. Sé que la letra S suena así, /s/. Entonces, pongo la foto de Sam con la letra S en el pizarrón.*

- Have pairs or trios work together to sort a set of student photos. If a name has an unusual spelling, write the initial letter on the photo.

Center Tip

If...children have difficulty identifying the initial letter of a name,
then...write the letter on the back of the photo, and tell children to find the matching magnetic letter for sorting.

Library and Listening Center

✓ **Track children's ability to describe and compare Olympic events.**

Materials picture books about the Olympic Games, paper and crayons

Books About the Olympics Have children browse through books about the Olympic Games. Tell them to choose their favorite summer and winter events. Help them name, describe, and compare them.

- Ask: **How do you think the athletes prepare for the Olympic Games? What do you think they do to keep their body healthy and strong?** *¿Cómo creen que se preparan los atletas para las Olimpíadas? ¿Qué harán para mantenerse sanos y fuertes?*

- Have children draw pictures of their favorite Olympic events. Encourage them to draw themselves competing in the activity.

- Ask: **Why do you like this event? What parts of your body need to be strong to do it?** *¿Qué les gusta de este deporte? ¿Qué parte del cuerpo debe ser fuerte para hacer esto?*

Center Tip

If...children have difficulty recalling healthy habits or naming parts of the body,
then...remind them of the exercises and vocabulary words included in this week's literature selections.

 Learning Goals

Language and Communication
- Child uses newly learned vocabulary daily in multiple contexts.

Emergent Literacy: Reading
- Child names most upper- and lowercase letters of the alphabet.
- Child identifies the letter that stands for a given sound.

Differentiated Instruction

 Extra Support

Library and Listening Center
If...children have difficulty describing and comparing pictures of Olympic events,
then...help them by pointing out different sports equipment used, parts of the body used, and seasonal details.

 Enrichment

Library and Listening Center
Challenge children to tell an imaginative story about competing in the Olympic Games. Have children tell a tale together, taking turns adding parts of the story.

 Special Needs

Delayed Motor Development
By working in a pair or trio, a child who cannot move the photos to sort them can direct a partner where to place them.

Focus Question
**Why is exercise important?
¿Por qué es importante hacer ejercicio?**

Circle Time

Literacy Time

📖 Read Aloud

✅ **Can children recall important story details about exercising for good health?**

Build Background Tell children that you will be reading about staying healthy.

● Ask: *What are some ways you stay healthy? ¿Cómo se mantienen sanos?*

Listen for Understanding Read aloud *Concept Big Book 4: Staying Healthy.* Refer children to the pictures as you read aloud the text, pointing out details that help convey meaning. Focus on facts about exercise.

● After page 24, ask: *What kinds of exercise are mentioned in the book? What kinds of exercise do you see in the pictures? ¿Qué ejercicios se mencionan en el libro? ¿Cuáles de esos ejercicios ven en las fotos?*

● After page 25, ask: *What are the people doing? ¿Qué están haciendo estas personas?* Have the class do ten jumping jacks too. Then ask: *How does your body feel different after you have been exercising? ¿Cómo les dice su cuerpo que han hecho ejercicio?*

Respond to the Story Have children share what they learned about exercising and staying healthy. Ask: *How does exercise help you stay healthy? Why is exercise a good habit? ¿De qué manera los ayuda el ejercicio a mantenerse sanos? ¿Por qué es un hábito saludable?*

TIP Have children help you read the book by having them say the word *healthy* every time you pause at that word in the book.

ELL Display the labeled pictures on page 24 of the book. Say the word as you point to the label, and have children repeat after you. Say the word again as you point to the corresponding picture, and have children repeat after you. Then demonstrate the action as you say the word, and have children repeat after you.

*Staying Healthy
Mantente sano*

Learn About Letters and Sounds

✅ **Can children identify and match initial letters and letter sounds?**

Say, See, Show Give children the following *ABC Picture Cards* to put in front of them on the play rug: *Dd, Gg, Hh, Mm, Ss, Ww.* Tell children they will do some fun exercises while they practice their letters.

● Say: *Listen and repeat after me…/w/, /w/, walk. Escuchen y repitan conmigo…/w/, /w/, walk.* After they reply, ask: *What is the first letter to spell "walk"? Listen carefully to the sound …/w/. Show me the letter for /w/. ¿Cuál es la primera letra de "walk"? Escuchen atentamente el sonido... /w/. Muéstrenme la letra que tiene el sonido /w/.*

● Have children use their finger to trace the letter on the card.

● Say: *Show the action. Walk around the rug…say "walk, walk, walk." Representemos la acción. Caminemos alrededor de la alfombra y digan "walk, walk, walk."*

● Continue with other action words, such as: *march, skip, gallop, hop, dance.*

Math Time

Observe and Investigate

✓ **Can children compare and compose numbers?**

Finger Games Tell children they will show numbers with their fingers. Before you begin, remind children to listen carefully and to keep their hands to themselves.

● Tell children to show 5 with their fingers. Discuss the different responses: Ask: *How many did you show on one hand? How many did you show on the other? How many fingers are showing altogether?* ¿Cuántos dedos mostraron de una mano? ¿Cuántos mostraron de la otra? ¿Cuántos son en total?

● Ask them to show another way to make 5, using both hands if they have not yet, and repeat the questions.

● Repeat, always asking children to describe their actions. Alternate directives as follows: show 4 on both hands; show 4 a different way; show 4 with the same number on each hand; show 4 with more on one hand than the other. Repeat with other numbers, adjusting finger combinations as needed.

Online Math Activity

Children can complete Number Compare 2 and Number Snapshots 5 during computer time or Center Time.

👫 Social and Emotional Development

Making Good Choices

✓ **Do children show a desire to work together?**

Working Together Display *Making Good Choices Flip Chart* page 35, "How Can I Show Good Teamwork?" Ask the children what happened when the boys and girls stacked the blocks.

● With the two Dog Puppets, role play other situations to model working together and showing good teamwork. For example, explain that the puppets have been given the job of cleaning up the class library. Have students make suggestions about what you would say and do to help the puppets work together to complete that task.

● After each role play, ask: *How did I help the puppets? What did I say?* ¿Cómo ayudé a los títeres? ¿Qué dije?

 While role playing with the dogs, point to the objects being mentioned, and repeat key words and phrases to help children follow what is happening. For example: *Dogs clean. Get books. No fights. Be friends.*

Making Good Choices Flip Chart, page 35

 Learning Goals

Social and Emotional Development
• Child initiates interactions with others in work and play situations.

Language and Communication
• Child begins and ends conversations appropriately.

Mathematics
• Child uses concrete objects or makes a verbal word problem to add up to 5 objects.
• Child uses concrete objects or makes a verbal word problem to subtract up to 5 objects from a set.

Vocabulary

altogether	en total	fingers	dedos
help	ayudar	how many	cuántos
numbers	números	share	compartir
show	mostrar		

 Differentiated Instruction

✋ **Extra Support**

Observe and Investigate

If...children have difficulty making numbers with their fingers, **then...**show them one way, and ask: *How many fingers do I show on each hand? How many altogether?* ¿Cuántos dedos muestro en cada mano? ¿Cuántos son en total? Then ask: *How can I show the same number another way?* ¿Cómo puedo mostrar el mismo número de otra forma?

⭐ **Enrichment**

Observe and Investigate

Challenge children to draw and label stick hands to show different ways to make the same number.

Accommodations for 3's

Observe and Investigate

If...children have difficulty making numbers with their fingers, **then...**reduce the number of times they show different combinations, or have them use your hands to show different combinations (pulling up or folding down your fingers).

Focus Question
Why is exercise important?
¿Por qué es importante hacer ejercicio?

Learning Goals

Social and Emotional Development
• Child describes personal interests and competencies positively (such as, "I can hop.").

Language and Communication
• Child names and describes actual or pictured people, places, things, actions, attributes, and events.

Emergent Literacy: Reading
• Child describes, relates to, and uses details and information from books read aloud.

Social Studies
• Child understands and discusses roles, responsibilities, and services provided by community workers.

Vocabulary

build	construir	carry	llevar
climb	trepar	healthy	sano
lift	levantar	muscles	músculos
strong	fuerte		

Differentiated Instruction

 Extra Support

Understand and Participate
If...children have difficulty naming different jobs in their community, **then...**suggest that they think of people in their family or people they have seen working in stores, parks, playgrounds, and other places they have visited.

 Enrichment

Understand and Participate
Challenge children to use play objects to show a community of people doing different jobs. Have them show and tell how people in their community work together.

Social Studies Time

Health Skills During the discussion about community workers, discuss how being physically fit helps people perform their job better.

Oral Language and Academic Vocabulary

✓ **Can children identify jobs that require physical strength and endurance?**

Talking About Jobs Ask children to recall what they learned about healthy habits from *Concept Big Book 4: Staying Healthy.* Remind them that it's important to exercise to keep their bodies healthy and strong.

● Ask: **Why do firefighters need to keep their bodies healthy and strong?** *¿Por qué es importante que los bomberos se mantengan sanos y fuertes?*

● Explain that many workers in their community have jobs that involve using their muscles to lift, climb, build, and carry things. Having a healthy, strong body helps them do their job.

Understand and Participate

✓ **Can children describe how a healthy body helps people do their job?**

Looking at Community Jobs Display books that show different community workers, such as firefighters, construction workers, gardeners, trash collectors, and movers.

● Page through the books with children, pointing to people doing their job in the community.

● Ask: **What is their job? How do they use their body to do their job? Why do they need a strong and healthy body to do it?** *¿Cuál es su trabajo? ¿Cómo usa su cuerpo para hacer ese trabajo? ¿Por qué necesitan un cuerpo sano y fuerte para hacerlo?*

● Ask children to think about their own chores and responsibilities at home and at school. Ask: **How does having a strong and healthy body help you do your work?** *¿Cómo les ayuda un cuerpo sano y fuerte a hacer sus tareas?*

● Have children draw a picture of a job they would like to do when they grow up, or have children work together to draw and label a wall mural. Ask: **What job would you like to do?** *¿Qué oficio les te gustaría tener?*

ELL Use the *Photo Library CD-ROM* and other labeled picture cards to teach children the names of different jobs and professions. Have children use play objects to show people doing their job.

For additional suggestions on how to meet the needs of children at the Beginning, Intermediate, Advanced, and Advanced-High levels of English proficiency, see pages 184–187.

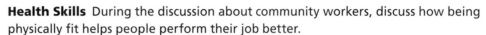

Center Time

▶ **Center Rotation** Center Time includes teacher-guided activities and independent activities. Refer to the **Learning Centers** on pages 100–101 for independent activity ideas.

 small group 30 minutes

Refer to the **Learning Centers** on pages 100–101 for independent activity ideas.

 ✓ **Learning Goals**

Social and Emotional Development
• Child initiates play scenarios with peers that share a common plan and goal.

Science
• Child identifies and participates in exercises and activities to enhance physical fitness.

Pretend and Learn Center

	Center Tip

✓ **Track the use of descriptive words as children role-play the race.**

Materials butcher paper strips, toy action figures or stuffed animals, assorted objects for a toy obstacle course (cardboard tubes, straws, blocks, paper cups, table tennis balls), crayons

The Great Race Explain that an obstacle course has things that participants must go over, under, through, or around as they race to the finish line. Tell children to pretend their toy figures are racing through an obstacle course.

• Tell children to set up an obstacle course for their toy figures. Have them draw the path on butcher paper, including a start and finish line. Give them a variety of small objects to set up as obstacles.

• Have children plan their race before they role-play what happens. Ask: *How are the runners preparing for the race? What will they be doing in the race? Who will win the race? ¿Cómo se preparan los participantes? ¿Qué harán en la carrera? ¿Quién ganará?*

Center Tip

If...children have difficulty deciding how to set up their toy obstacle course, **then...**provide pictures of obstacle courses they can use for reference.

Writing

Recap the day. Have children tell what they learned about healthy living. Ask: **Why do people need to exercise?** *¿Por qué las personas necesitan hacer ejercicio?* Record their answers on chart paper. Share the pen by having children write letters and words they know. Ask children to draw a picture to illustrate each sentence.

Purposeful Play

✓ **Observe children as they work in pairs or small groups.**

Children choose an open center for free playtime. Encourage cooperation skills by suggesting they work together to create and show a skit about a community of animals working together.

Let's Say Good-Bye

 large group 15 minutes

Read Aloud Revisit "I Can, You Can!"/"¡Yo puedo, tú puedes!" for your afternoon Read Aloud. Remind children to listen for words that describe movements.

 Home Connection Refer to the Home Connections activities listed in the Resources and Materials chart on page 97. Remind children to tell families about healthy habits. Sing the "Good-Bye Song"/"Hora de ir a casa" as children prepare to leave.

DAY 4

Let's Start the Day

Focus Question
Why is exercise important?
¿Por qué es importante hacer ejercicio?

 Learning Goals

Language and Communication
• Child follows two- and three-step oral directions.

Emergent Literacy: Reading
• Child blends two phonemes to form a word.

Mathematics
• Child understands and uses ordinal numbers (such as first, second, third) to identify position in a series.

Physical Development
• Child engages in a sequence of movements to perform a task.

Vocabulary

fifth	quinto(a)	first	primer(o/a)
fourth	cuarto(a)	healthy	sano
second	segundo(a)	third	tercer(o/a)

Differentiated Instruction

 Extra Support

Oral Language and Vocabulary
If...children have difficulty recalling the movements, **then...**use only two types of movements (such as steps and claps).

 Enrichment

Oral Language and Vocabulary
Have children explain how to play an outdoor game or activity, such as riding a bike, playing T-ball, or playing hide-and-go-seek. Have them use sequential words (*first, second, third; first, next, last*). Then have classmates retell the steps.

▶ **Opening Routines and Transition Tips**
For **Opening Routines** and **Transition Tips** turn to pages 178–181 and visit DLMExpressOnline.com for more ideas.

📖 Read **"Inside Out"**/**"Por dentro y por fuera"** from the *Teacher's Treasure Book*, page 106, for your morning Read Aloud.

Language Time

  large group / 15 minutes

👥 **Social and Emotional Development** Ask children why it is important to listen carefully, follow directions, and to be careful of others around them during group activities.

Oral Language and Vocabulary

✓ **Can children describe and repeat a series of movements or exercises?**

First, Second, Third Review and practice sequential words and actions with children.

● Tell children to watch closely as you show them three movements. For example: touch your head, touch your waist, touch your knees. Ask: **What did I do first? second? third? ¿Qué hice primero? ¿Segundo? ¿Y tercero?** Have children show you the three movements in order.

● Repeat several times using different movements or exercises. Increase the complexity, such as: 2 steps, 2 claps, 4 hops.

● Then tell children what to do instead of showing them. For example: **First hop. Second clap. Third hop.** *Primero, brinquen. Segundo, den una palmada. Tercero, brinquen.* Ask: **What did you do first, second, third?** *¿Qué hicieron primero, segundo y tercero?* Repeat several times. You might also expand the activity into a game of *Simon Says*.

ELL Use the Sequence Card set "Building a Snowman" to help children understand sequential words *first, second, third, fourth*. Describe the steps involved in building the snowman. Say the sequential words as you work with children to put the pictures in order. Then have children repeat what you say and do.

Phonological Awareness

✓ **Can children blend two-phoneme words?**

Blending Phonemes Display the Dog Puppets. Tell children they are going to play a game of "Echo," repeating sounds after the dogs and then blending the sounds to say a word. For example: the first dog says /m/...children echo /m/...the second dog says /ē/...children echo /ē/...the dogs ask: **What's the word?** *¿Cuál es la palabra?* Children reply **me!** Use two-phoneme words such as *me, you, us, we, bee, knee, two, toe*. Then have children take turns playing the role of the dogs.

Center Time

▶ **Center Rotation** Center Time includes teacher-guided activities and independent activities. Refer to the **Learning Centers** on pages 100–101 for independent activity ideas.

 small group 60–90 minutes

Creativity Center | Center Tip

 Observe children as they use their finger puppets to role-play exercising.

Materials paper finger puppet outlines (with cut-out finger holes for the legs), cardstock, colored pencils

Finger Puppet Stories Copy finger-puppet outlines onto cardstock, and cut out the holes for children.

- Have children color and cut out their puppets. Model how to insert two fingers into the holes of the puppet to make "legs."

- Have children use their finger puppets to tell creative stories about exercising and demonstrate different exercises. Ask: **What exercises do you know?** *¿Qué ejercicios conocen?*

Center Tip

If...children have difficulty recalling exercises,

then...suggest that they think of their own experiences on the playground, or remind them of this week's literature stories.

Construction Center | Center Tip

 Observe children as they work together to assemble the floor game.

Materials butcher paper, yardstick, large circles in four colors (red, blue, yellow, green), four-section spinners, markers, glue

Flexibility Game Have each group of four children assemble and play their own floor game.

- Help each group glue four rows of six circles on the butcher paper, using the same color for all circles in each row. Also make two spinners, one labeled *right hand, left hand, right foot, left foot;* the other colored red, blue, yellow, green.

- The game leader spins the two spinners and tells the players which hand or foot to place on a specific color. Players cannot choose the same circle or move a hand or foot off the circle until the leader spins that body part again. Players continue to put their hands or feet on circles as directed, moving around the other players without falling over. The winner is the last player upright.

Center Tip

If...children have difficulty with stretching or bending, **then...**have them be the group leader, spinning the spinners and directing the players. Monitor groups as they play, reminding them of appropriate behavior and teamwork as needed.

✓ Learning Goals

Language and Communication
- Child uses newly learned vocabulary daily in multiple contexts.

Science
- Child identifies and participates in exercises and activities to enhance physical fitness.

Fine Arts
- Child expresses ideas, emotions, and moods through individual and collaborative dramatic play.

Physical Development
- Child coordinates body movements in a variety of locomotive activities (such as walking, jumping, running, hopping, skipping, climbing).

Differentiated Instruction

🖐 Extra Support
Creative Play
If...children have difficulty thinking of a creative story to tell with their puppet, **then...** have children work with a partner or in trios to share their story. Suggest that they use their puppets to tell their own version of a favorite storybook. Remind them to include movement and/or exercises.

⭐ Enrichment
Creative Play
Challenge children to make a background set for their finger puppet story, drawing pictures for the backdrops of their finger-puppet show.

Accommodations for 3's
Construction Center
If...children have difficulty remembering right from left, **then...**put an *R* sticker on their right hand and right foot. You might also remind them that the word *hand* begins with /h/, just like *hi* (a hand waves "hi").

Circle Time

Literacy Time

 large group — 15 minutes

📖 Read Aloud

 Can children recall story events and relate them to real life?

Build Background Tell children that you will be reading a story about a man climbing a mountain. Explain that a mountain is a huge hill.

● Ask: ***How do you think the man will feel as he climbs the mountain? Why do you think so?*** *¿Cómo creen que se sentirá el hombre mientras sube la montaña?*

Listen for Enjoyment Read aloud "The Llama's Warning"/"La advertencia de la llama," *Teacher's Treasure Book* page 337. Tell children to listen carefully to what happens to the man each day as he climbs up the mountain.

● Ask: ***Why is the man climbing the mountain?*** *¿Por qué el hombre sube la montaña?*

● After each paragraph, ask: ***Does the man want to keep climbing the mountain? Why or why not? Who helps him keep going?*** *¿Quiere el hombre seguir subiendo la montaña? ¿Por qué? ¿Quién lo ayuda a seguir?* Ask: ***If you were climbing the mountain, would you keep going? Why or why not?*** *Si ustedes estuvieran en la montaña, ¿habrían seguido subiendo?*

Respond to the Story Ask children to describe each day of the climb. Ask: ***How does the man feel at the beginning of the climb? How does he feel at the end? Why?*** *¿Cómo se siente el hombre al principio? ¿Cómo se siente al final? ¿Por qué?*

TIP Use the sequential words in the story to check for understanding and have children predict what happens next. For example: ***What happened on the first day? What do you think will happen on the second day?*** *¿Qué sucede el primer día? ¿Qué creen que sucederá el segundo día?*

ELL Help children distinguish between homophones *see* and *sea* from the folktale. Show the word *sea* on a picture of the sea as you say the name. Tell children: ***The sea has water.*** For the word *see*, show two copies of the letter *e* drawn to look like a pair of eyes. Hold up your hands to your eyes like a pair of binoculars. Point to yourself, your eyes, and then a child as you say: ***I see you.***

Learn About Letters and Sounds

 Can children identify and match initial letters and letter sounds?

Folktale Letters Have children match letter cards to flannel board cutouts (*Teacher's Treasure Book* pages 439–440) to show the initial consonant.

● Give each child a set of Alphabet/Letter Tiles. Show the Llama character. Say the name slowly. Ask: ***What is the first letter of the name Llama.../l/, Llama? What letter stands for /l/? Show me that tile.*** *¿Con qué letra empieza la palabra llama? Muéstrenme esa letra.* Confirm the correct answer: Llama begins with *Ll* for /l/, so *Ll* is the first letter of Llama. Repeat for the rest of the flannel board cutouts. Give children their own paper cutouts. Have them write the initial letter on the front.

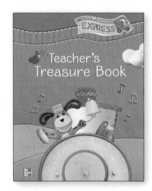

Teacher's Treasure Book, page 337

✓ Learning Goals

Emergent Literacy: Reading

• Child names most upper- and lowercase letters of the alphabet.

• Child identifies the letter that stands for a given sound.

• Child describes, relates to, and uses details and information from books read aloud.

• Child asks and answers questions about books read aloud (such as, "Who?" "What?" "Where?").

Vocabulary

climb	subir	exercise	ejercicio
mountain	montaña	quit	dejar
sea	mar	strong	fuerte
water	agua		

Differentiated Instruction

 Extra Support

Letter and Word Knowledge

If...children have difficulty identifying initial consonants for the cutouts, **then...**limit their choices to three letters. Display each letter, say the sound, and have children repeat after you. Then compare each letter sound to the first sound of the name. For example, say: ***This is letter P for /p/. Is /p/ the first sound in the word*** llama? *Esta letra es la P, y suena /p/. ¿Ése es el segundo sonido de la palabra* llama?

 Enrichment

Letter and Word Knowledge

Have children write the full name on the back of their cutouts. Display each name next to the flannel board pieces for children to copy.

 Special Needs

Speech/Language Delays

Use the flannel board pieces for the story and ask the child to put them in sequential order. Ask him or her to tell the story in his or her own words.

Online Math Activity

Children can complete Number Compare 2 and Number Snapshots 5 during computer time or Center Time.

Math Time

Observe and Investigate

☑ **Can children quickly add amounts?**

Snapshots (Adding) Secretly put three counters in one of your hands and two counters in the other. Tell children to watch carefully.

- Show your closed hands, and then open them for two seconds, closing them immediately.

- Ask children how many counters they saw in each hand, and then how many they saw altogether. Open both hands, and count counters with children to check.

- Repeat several times, adding with amounts up to ten.

⋆⋆⋆ Social and Emotional Development

Making Good Choices

☑ **Do children show a desire to work together?**

Working Together Display the Dog Puppets and a set of blocks. Tell children that the puppets are arguing about who gets to use the blocks. Have children give you suggestions as you model a dialogue between the puppets that ends with them agreeing to use the blocks together.

- Ask: *What problem did the puppets have? How did they solve their problem?*
  ¿Qué problema tuvieron los títeres? ¿Cómo lo resolvieron?

- Ask children why teamwork is important. Help them recognize that teamwork is a good way to finish a job faster, and it can be a lot of fun too. Remind children to work together when cleaning up after themselves at the centers.

- Play the song "We'll Take Good Care"/*"Las cuidaremos"* from the Making Good Choices Audio CD. Ask children how teamwork helps them take care of materials in the classroom.

ELL Some children may have difficulties following the conversation between the Dog Puppets. While role playing, act out the dogs' actions, such as arguing and happily taking turns stacking the blocks. Say simple phrases as you perform each action, such as: *We share. We take turns.*

For additional suggestions on how to meet the needs of children at the Beginning, Intermediate, Advanced, and Advanced-High levels of English proficiency, see pages 184–187.

☑ **Learning Goals**

Social and Emotional Development
- Child initiates interactions with others in work and play situations.

Mathematics
- Child uses concrete objects or makes a verbal word problem to add up to 5 objects.

Vocabulary

altogether	en total	count	contar
counters	fichas	help	ayudar
how many	cuánto	share	compartir
take turns	turnarse		

Differentiated Instruction

 Extra Support

Observe and Investigate

If...children have difficulty comparing amounts quickly, **then...**show the counters for a longer period of time.

 Enrichment

Observe and Investigate

For a greater challenge, increase the number of counters in one hand and then the other. You might also switch the manipulatives to cubes, to distinguish between quantity and size.

Learning Goals

Language and Communication
- Child follows two- and three-step oral directions.

Mathematics
- Child uses concrete objects or makes a verbal word problem to add up to 5 objects.
- Child uses concrete objects or makes a verbal word problem to subtract up to 5 objects from a set.

Vocabulary

altogether	en total	fingers	dedos
how many	cuántos	number	número
show	mostrar	thumbs	pulgares

Differentiated Instruction

 Extra Support

Math Time

If...children have difficulty making numbers with their fingers, **then...**show them one way, and ask: *How many fingers do I show on each hand? How many altogether? ¿Cuántos dedos muestro en cada mano? ¿Cuántos son en total?* Then ask: *How can I show the same number another way? ¿Como puedo mostrar el mismo número pero de otra manera?*

⭐ **Enrichment**

Math Time

Challenge children to use their fingers to show combinations for numbers greater than 5. You might also challenge partners to work together to show combinations for numbers greater than 10.

Math Time

 large group 20 minutes

Language and Communication Skills After you model making numbers using your fingers, provide 2-step directions for children to follow. For example, say: *Show me 2 fingers with one hand, and 1 finger with the other. How many altogether?* *Muéstrenme 2 dedos con una mano y 1 dedo con la otra. ¿Cuántos son en total?*

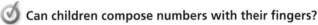 Can children explain how to compose numbers?

Talk About Making Numbers Explain to children that the same number can be made different ways.

- Show 4 fingers on your left hand together with 1 index finger from your right hand. Say: *4 and 1 make 5. 4 y 1 hacen 5.* Then show 3 fingers on the left hand and 2 fingers on the right. Say: *3 and 2 make 5 too. 3 y 2 también hacen 5.* Ask: *If I show 2 fingers on my first hand, how many do I show on my second hand to make 5 again? Si muestro 2 dedos en la primera mano, ¿cuántos muestro en la segunda para llagar a 5 otra vez?* (3)

- Then say: *Are there any other ways to make 5? Tell me how. ¿Hay otras maneras para llegar al 5? Díganme cómo.* Let children tell you how to show 5 in other ways (1 and 4; 0 and 5).

Can children compose numbers with their fingers?

Finger Games Tell children they will be making numbers with their fingers. This activity is an extension of the activity done on Day 3. Remind children to listen carefully and to keep their hands to themselves.

- Tell children to show 4 with their fingers. Discuss the different responses: Ask: *How many did you show on one hand? How many did you show on the other? How many fingers are showing altogether? ¿Cuántos dedos mostraron en una mano? ¿Cuántos mostraron en la otra? ¿Cuántos dedos hay en total?*

- Ask them to show another way to make 4, using both hands if they have not yet, and repeat the questions.

- Repeat, always asking children to describe their actions. Alternate the following: do not allow thumbs in responses; challenge children by asking them to show 3, 5, or 7 using the same number on each hand, discuss why it cannot be done (odd numbers), and then model equal numbers per hand using 4, 6, 8, and 10; and, show 4 on one hand by asking how many fingers up (4) and how many down (1), and repeat with 0, 1, 2, 3, and 5.

ELL Focus on the concept "altogether" as you work with children to compose numbers using fingers. Have children mirror your actions and repeat your words. Use combinations of 5. First show 4 fingers on your left hand as you say *four*, and then bring your right index finger next to the others to show 5 as you say questioningly: *altogether? 5.* Follow the same procedure for combination of 3 and 2 ...*three*...(add on 2 from right hand)...*altogether? 5*, and then again for combination 2 and 3, and then 4 and 1.

Center Time

> **Center Rotation** Center Time includes teacher-guided activities and independent activities. Refer to the **Learning Centers** on pages 100–101 for independent activity ideas.

small group **30 minutes**

Math and Science Center

✓ **Check that children are counting and adding numbers correctly.**

Materials masking tape, numeral cards 0–3, beanbags, counters

Number Toss Children add numbers as they play "beanbag toss."

- Use masking tape to make a large four-square grid on the floor for each group of children. Tape a numeral card in each square. Children take turns tossing two beanbags onto the grid. They add the numbers, and then choose an exercise and do that many repetitions. The rest of the group counts the number of repetitions, and then they confirm the total by using counters.

- For example: the beanbags land on 2 and 1, the chosen exercise is jumping jacks, so the player does 3 jumping jacks.

- Players keep the counters they earn each round. The first player to get more than 12 counters wins.

Center Tip

If... children have difficulty adding mentally,

then... have them add with counters before they exercise.

Encourage teammates to help each other add.

Learning Goals

Language and Communication
- Child communicates relevant information for the situation (for example, introduces herself; requests assistance).

Mathematics
- Child uses concrete objects or makes a verbal word problem to add up to 5 objects.

Science
- Child identifies and participates in exercises and activities to enhance physical fitness.

Writing

Recap the day. Have children tell about climbing, hiking, or camping outdoors. Ask: *How did you get some exercise?* *¿Cómo hacen ustedes ejercicio?* Record their answers in a list. Read them back as you track the print, and emphasize the correspondence between speech and print.

Purposeful Play

✓ **Observe children appropriately handling classroom materials.**

Children choose an open center for free playtime. Encourage cooperation skills by suggesting they work together to create another math game.

Let's Say Good-Bye

large group **15 minutes**

 Read Aloud Revisit "Inside Out"/"Por dentro y por fuera" for your afternoon Read Aloud. Remind children to listen for words that tell how to keep their body healthy and strong.

 Home Connection Refer to the Home Connections activities listed in the Resources and Materials chart on page 97. Remind children to tell families why it is important to exercise. Sing the "Good-Bye Song"/"Hora de ir a casa" as children prepare to leave.

Let's Start the Day

Focus Question

Why is exercise important?
¿Por qué es importante hacer ejercicio?

▶ **Opening Routines and Transition Tips**
For **Opening Routines** and **Transition Tips** turn to pages 178–181 and visit DLMExpressOnline.com for more ideas.

Read **"My Body Talks"/**"Mi cuerpo habla" from the *Teacher's Treasure Book*, page 183, for your morning Read Aloud.

✓ Learning Goals

Language and Communication
• Child follows two- and three-step oral directions.

Emergent Literacy: Reading
• Child blends two phonemes to form a word.

Science
• Child identifies and participates in exercises and activities to enhance physical fitness.

Physical Development
• Child coordinates body movements in a variety of locomotive activities (such as walking, jumping, running, hopping, skipping, climbing).

Vocabulary

climb	subir	exercise	ejercicio
hop	brincar	jump	saltar
run	saltar	swing	balancearse

Differentiated Instruction

 Extra Support

Phonological Awareness
If...children have difficulty blending phonemes to find the correct picture, **then...**give them a visual clue, such as touching each knee as you say /n/-/ē/, or pointing your toe as you say /t/-/ō/.

⭐ **Enrichment**

Phonological Awareness
Challenge children to find pairs of pictures with names that begin or end with the same sound (for example, *bee/boy, two/toe,* and *knee/bee*). Ask: **What letter sound is the same? Is the sound at the beginning or end of the word?** *¿Qué letra y qué sonido es el mismo? ¿Está ese sonido al principio o al final de la palabra?*

Language Time

large group   15 minutes

Social and Emotional Development Tell children to stay within their own space and to be respectful of each other when doing activities together.

Oral Language and Vocabulary

✓ **Can children relate what they've learned about exercise?**

Listen and Play Revisit the *Rhymes and Chants Flip Chart*, p 35. Ask: **How are the children exercising? Why is it important to exercise?** *¿Qué hacen los niños? ¿Por qué es importante hacer ejercicio?*

• Then guide children through a series of fun movements, such as the following. Afterward, have children talk about what they did.

> Stretch your body. Lift your hands high.
>
> Now bend down. Try to touch your toes.
>
> Stand up and hop. Hop like a rabbit.
>
> Now walk like a monkey.
>
> Swing your arms. Bend your knees.
>
> Now pretend to climb a mountain.
>
> Climb up, up, up to the top. Now rest!

Phonological Awareness

✓ **Can children blend two-phoneme words?**

Blending Phonemes Give children a set of picture cards for these words: *knee, toe, bee, boy, two, eight*. Have children display the cards in front of them.

• Tell children to listen carefully as you say a word slowly. For example: */n/ /ē/*. Ask: **What's the word?** *¿Cuál es la palabra?* Children reply: **knee**. Tell children to find that picture card and show it to you. Then tell them to march in place, with knees up high, until you say stop.

• Continue with the rest of the cards. Include an exercise for each word. For example: *touch your toes; move like a bee; hop to a boy; do two sit-ups; do eight jumping jacks.*

ELL Display a pair of picture cards for two-phoneme words (*knee, toe, bee, boy, two, eight, egg, pie, ice*). Blend and say each word as you point to the picture, and have children repeat after you.

Rhymes and Chants Flip Chart, page 35

Center Time

▶ **Center Rotation** Center Time includes teacher-guided activities and independent activities. Refer to the **Learning Centers** on pages 100–101 for independent activity ideas.

 small group 60–90 minutes

Writer's Center

| Center Tip |

✓ Track the use of descriptive words as children tell about healthy habits.

Materials paper doll outlines, fill-in writing boxes, pencils, white construction paper, glue, crayons

A Healthy Happy Me

● Help children label the parts of the body on their paper doll outline. Have them label the location of the heart.

● Display the following sentence for children to copy into their writing box: *I take care of my body.*

● Have children glue their paper doll onto construction paper, and glue their writing box below it for a pedestal. Tell them to color details and draw pictures of healthy habits/activities around their body to complete their portrait. Ask: **What are some ways you keep your body healthy and strong?** *¿Cómo se mantienen sanos y fuertes?*

Center Tip

If...children have difficulty drawing pictures of healthy habits, **then...**provide a supply of health and fitness magazine pictures, stickers, and clip art for them to glue onto their paper.

Creativity Center

Center Tip

✓ Observe children as they demonstrate and explore animal actions and creative movements.

Materials variety of instrumental music, action songs

Music and Movement Play instrumental music and encourage children to move to the beat. Refer to the exercises they've learned this week.

● Prompt children to imitate the movements that animals make. For example, say: **Stretch like a cat...fly like a bird...hop like a frog... yawn like a lion...slide like a snail...wiggle like a worm.** *Estírense como un gato... vuelen como un pájaro... salten como una rana... rujan como un león...deslícense como una serpiente... menéense como un gusano.*

● Have children demonstrate other animal movements for classmates to do. Ask: **What part of your body are you moving?** *¿Qué partes del cuerpo están moviendo?*

Center Tip

If...children have difficulty thinking of other animal movements, **then...** play instructional action songs for children to follow along. Ask: **What do they tell you to do in the song?** *¿Qué dijo la canción que tienen que hacer?*

Learning Goals

Language and Communication
• Child names and describes actual or pictured people, places, things, actions, attributes, and events.

Emergent Literacy: Writing
• Child uses scribbles, shapes, pictures, symbols, and letters to represent language.

Science
• Child identifies and participates in exercises and activities to enhance physical fitness.

Fine Arts
• Child expresses thoughts, feelings, and energy through music and creative movement.

Physical Development
• Child coordinates body movements in a variety of locomotive activities (such as walking, jumping, running, hopping, skipping, climbing).

Differentiated Instruction

✋ Extra Support
Writer's Center
If...children have difficulty recalling the names of the body parts, **then...**provide a list of words with pictures for them to choose from, and read them aloud with children.

⭐ Enrichment
Writer's Center
Challenge children to label other parts of the body that move during exercise. Discuss and show examples of the movable parts. For example, ask: **What parts of your body allow you to wave your hand? What part do you use to move your head?** *¿Qué partes del cuerpo les permiten saludar con la mano? ¿Qué parte usan para mover la cabeza?* List the words for children to copy onto their paper.

Accommodations for 3's
Writer's Center
If...children have difficulty writing the labels, **then...**give them lightly written stick-on labels to trace and put onto their picture. Include picture symbols on the stickers to help children label the correct parts.

Focus Question
Why is exercise important?
¿Por qué es importante hacer ejercicio?

Learning Goals

Emergent Literacy: Reading
- Child names most upper- and lowercase letters of the alphabet.
- Child identifies the letter that stands for a given sound.
- Child produces the most common sound for a given letter.
- Child describes, relates to, and uses details and information from books read aloud.

Science
- Child identifies and participates in exercises and activities to enhance physical fitness.

Physical Development
- Child coordinates body movements in a variety of locomotive activities (such as walking, jumping, running, hopping, skipping, climbing).

Vocabulary

arm	brazo	bend	doblar
demonstrate	demostrar	knee	rodilla
leg	pierna	stretch	estirarse

Differentiated Instruction

 Extra Support

Learn About Letters and Sounds
If...children have difficulty recalling the names and sounds of many letters at one time, **then...** use only three or four letters repeatedly in the trail. You might also set up different trails for children to advance to as they complete a level.

 Enrichment

Learn About Letters and Sounds
Instead of saying the letter sound, have children say words that begin with each letter they step on while walking the trail.

 # Circle Time

Literacy Time

 large group 15 minutes

📖 Read Aloud

☑ **Can children describe, compare, and relate to information in the book?**

Build Background Tell children that you will be rereading a book about exercise.

- Ask: *What did we learn about exercise? ¿Qué apredimos sobre hacer ejercicio?*

Listen for Understanding Display the cover of *Rise and Exercise!*, and read the title aloud.

- Reread the story, stopping to have children describe and compare the exercises that the people in the book are doing.

- Ask: *What exercises do they do? What games do they play? What parts of their body do they move? ¿Qué ejercicios hacen los niños? ¿A qué juegos juegan? ¿Qué partes del cuerpo mueven?*

Respond and Connect Have children connect their new learning to their daily lives. Ask: *What exercises can you do? ¿Qué ejercicios pueden hacer?* Invite children to demonstrate an exercise for classmates to do. You might also play music while they exercise.

TIP Before children demonstrate and perform the exercises, remind them of appropriate behavior and safety rules.

ELL Role-play to help children understand the difference between *exercise, exercises, exercising*. Demonstrate an exercise as you say: *First exercise*. Show another one as you say: *Second exercise*. Do both exercises as you say: *Two exercises*. Repeat with children, and as you exercise together, say: *We are exercising!*

Learn About Letters and Sounds

☑ **Can children identify letters and sounds?**

Review and Practice Letters Make a trail of laminated letter cards around the play area, putting two or three of the same letters in a row.

- Use words from the book to review the name and sound of each letter. For example, say: *Repeat after me.../f/ -un, fun...fun begins with /f/. What letter makes the /f/ sound? Point to that letter. Repitan después de mí... /f/ -un, fun... fun comienza con /f/. ¿Qué letra tiene el sonido /f/?* Confirm the answer. Have children use their finger to write the letter in the air.

- Then have children walk along the letter trail. First have them say the name of the letter as they step on each card. Then have them go again, this time saying each letter sound.

- Suggest different ways for them to move along the trail, such as hopping, marching, walking with bended knees, or walking on tiptoes.

Rise and Exercise!
A ejercitarse, ¡uno, dos, tres!

Online Math Activity

Children can complete Number Compare 2 and Number Snapshots during computer time or Center Time.

Math Time

 large group 15 minutes

Observe and Investigate

✓ **Can children add and subtract amounts?**

Monsters and Raisins Tell children they are going to pretend to be monsters that eat raisins. Give each child a paper plate.

● Ask: *How many raisins do you have on your plate right now?* *¿Cuántas pasas tienen ahora en el plato?* (0) Then distribute some raisins, telling children to put a specific number of raisins on their plate. For example: *Put 3 raisins on your plate for the monster.* *Pongan 3 pasas en el plato para el monstruo.*

● Take turns having all children add or subtract raisins. Demonstrate first. For example: *The monster is hungry. He wants 2 more. Put two more raisins on your plate.* Ask: *How many are on your plate now?* *El monstruo tiene hambre. Quiere 2 más. Pongan 2 pasas más en el plato. ¿Cuántas pasas hay ahora?*

● For subtraction, have the "monsters" eat the raisins. For example: *The monster just ate 1 raisin. Yum!* *El monstruo se comió 1.* (Children eat 1 raisin.) *How many raisins are still left on your plate?* *¿Cuántas pasas hay ahora en el plato?*

● Have children create their own word problems for the group to act out.

ELL Focus on the concepts of "more" and "fewer" For example, after adding a raisin to the plate, say: *Now I have <u>more</u>.* After eating a raisin, say: *Now I have <u>fewer</u>.* Have children repeat these frames as they add and subtract raisins on their own plate.

⚝ Social and Emotional Development

 large group 15 minutes

Making Good Choices

✓ **Do children show a desire to work together?**

Working Together Display *Making Good Choices Flip Chart* page 35.

● Point to the flip chart illustration. Ask: *What did we learn about working together?* *¿Qué aprendimos sobre trabajar en equipo?*

● Place a mixed pile of red, blue, and green cubes and the three jars they belong in on the table. Say: *Let's work together to sort these cubes and put them away. We can work together to get the job done faster. Let's help each other and take turns putting the cubes into their jars.* *Vamos a trabajar juntos para ordenar y guardar estos cubos. Podemos trabajar juntos para hacerlo más rápido. Ayudémonos y trabajemos por turnos para poner los cubos en los tachos.* Encourage children to compare the amounts as they sort the colors.

Making Good Choices Flip Chart, page 35

Focus Question
Why is exercise important?
¿Por qué es importante hacer ejercicio?

Social and Emotional Development
• Child initiates play scenarios with peers that share a common plan and goal.

Language and Communication
• Child uses oral language for a variety of purposes.

Emergent Literacy: Reading
• Child describes, relates to, and uses details and information from books read aloud.

Fine Arts
• Child expresses ideas, emotions, and moods through individual and collaborative dramatic play.

Vocabulary

fox	zorro	frog	rana
llama	llama	man	hombre
monkey	mono	parrot	loro
turtle	tortuga		

Differentiated Instruction

 Extra Support

Explore and Express
If…children have difficulty remembering story details or sequence of events, **then**…give each group of children a set of labeled folktale cutouts to help them recall information.

 Enrichment

Explore and Express
Suggest that children create "cue cards" for the performers, holding up cards that show words or pictures of important vocabulary words and details from the story, such as sequence words (first, second, third), names of animals, and details about how the man feels climbing up the mountain.

Dramatic Play Time

  large group   20 minutes

Personal Safety Skills Remind children to be careful and respectful of others around them. Tell children they may not climb up (or on top of) anything for their performance. They should stay on flat ground.

Oral Language and Academic Vocabulary

☑ **Can children summarize the events and describe the characters?**

Recalling Story Details Have children recall details about the folktale "The Llama's Warning." Help children summarize the sequence of events and describe the animals involved in the man's climb to the top of the mountain.

• Ask: *Why is the man climbing the mountain? Who does he meet along the way? What does each animal say to help the man continue his climb?* *¿Por qué sube el hombre la montaña? ¿Con quiénes se encuentra en el camino? ¿Qué dice cada animal para animar al hombre a continuar hasta la cima?*

• Have children practice the movement and behavior of each character. For example, say: *Show me how a llama moves…a parrot moves…a monkey moves…a turtle moves…a frog moves…a fox moves…how a tired man climbing up a mountain moves.* *Muéstrenme cómo se mueve una llama… un loro… un mono… una tortuga… una rana… un zorro… un hombre cansado que sube una montaña.*

Explore and Express

☑ **Can children dramatize the story of "The Llama's Warning"?**

Dramatizing the Folktale Tell children that they will act out the story of "The Llama's Warning." Explain that they will be using very few props, so they must use their voice and actions to help show how each character feels.

• Have children get into small groups. Tell them that some children will need to play the role of more than one animal. Display labeled cutouts of the seven characters for reference: *man, llama, parrot, monkey, turtle, frog,* and *fox.*

• Have each group decide together how they will perform the story. Encourage them to show good teamwork. Remind them to only pretend to carry a heavy bag and to only pretend to climb.

• Have groups take turns performing their story as the rest of the children watch.

TIP Rotate from group to group to check and monitor progress as children plan. Encourage children to help each other recall story details and practice role-playing. As children perform the play, provide prompts and clues as needed to help them remember the story plot and sequence.

ELL Display labeled cutouts of the folktale characters and the setting of the story. Point to each picture, say the name, and have children repeat after you. You might also make picture-card necklaces of the characters for children to wear during their performance.

Center Time

▶ **Center Rotation** Center Time includes teacher-guided activities and independent activities. Refer to the **Learning Centers** on pages 100–101 for independent activity ideas.

 small group 30 minutes

Construction Center

✓ **Track children's use of body-part names and action words.**

Materials parts of a paper doll copied onto cardstock, hole puncher, brad fasteners, crayons or colored pencils, optional decorative supplies (yarn for hair, clothing patterns, wiggly eyes, glitter markers)

Paper Dolls in Motion Have children assemble moveable paper dolls. Provide parts to assemble at the joints (elbows, wrists, knees, ankles).

● Point to and name your joints. Have children do the same. Explain that joints allow us to bend and move our body. Say: *Your elbow is where your arm bends. Your knee is where your leg bends.* *El codo me permite doblar el brazo. La rodilla me permite doblar la pierna.*

● Have children color and cut out the parts of their paper doll. Help them punch holes and assemble the parts at the joints.

● Invite children to share their paper doll. Ask: *How does your doll move? How do you move? ¿Cómo se mueve el muñeco? ¿Cómo se mueven ustedes?* Have them use their doll for storytelling.

Center Tip

If...children have difficulty identifying parts of the body that move, **then...**refer to *Math and Science Flip Chart* page 65. Use self-stick notes on the chart to label different parts. Ask: *Where are your arms? Where are your legs? What part of your legs help you bend them? ¿Dónde están sus brazos? ¿Y sus piernas? ¿Qué parte de las piernas los ayuda a doblarlas?*

Learning Goals

Social and Emotional Development
● Child is aware of self in terms of abilities, characteristics and preferences, and respects personal boundaries.

Language and Communication
● Child names and describes actual or pictured people, places, things, actions, attributes, and events.

Science
● Child identifies and participates in exercises and activities to enhance physical fitness.

Writing

Recap the day and week. Say: *Tell me one thing you learned about exercise this week. Cuéntenme una cosa que hayan aprendido esta semana sobre hacer ejercicio.* Record their answers on chart paper. Share the pen with children as you write. Have children write their names beside their entries.

Purposeful Play

✓ **Observe children sharing classroom materials and working cooperatively.**

Children choose an open center for free playtime. Encourage cooperation skills by suggesting they use their paper dolls to tell a story about exercising.

Let's Say Good-Bye

 large group 15 minutes

 Read Aloud Revisit "My Body Talks"/"Mi cuerpo habla" for your afternoon Read Aloud. Remind children to act out the movements as you read.

 Home Connection Refer to the Home Connections activities listed in the Resources and Materials chart on page 97. Remind children to tell families what they learned this week about exercising. Sing the "Good-Bye Song"/"Hora de ir a casa" as children prepare to leave.

Focus Question

How can I stay healthy?
¿Cómo puedo mantenerme saludable?

This week children will learn about healthy habits. They will make growth charts, describe how much they have grown this year, discuss people's needs and how they are met, play exercise games, and read about healthy food and exercise and relate them to growth.

Unit 8
Healthy Foods/Healthy Body
Week 4

 Learning Goals

Social and Emotional Development	1	2	3	4	5
Child is aware of self in terms of abilities, characteristics and preferences, and respects personal boundaries.	✓	✓	✓	✓	✓

Language and Communication	1	2	3	4	5
Child demonstrates an understanding of oral language by responding appropriately.			✓	✓	✓
Child follows basic rules for conversations (taking turns, staying on topic, listening actively).				✓	
Child names and describes actual or pictured people, places, things, actions, attributes, and events.	✓		✓	✓	✓
Child exhibits an understanding of instructional terms used in the classroom.		✓		✓	✓
Child understands or knows the meaning of many thousands of words, many more than he or she uses.				✓	
Child uses newly learned vocabulary daily in multiple contexts.	✓		✓	✓	
Child understands and uses sentences having two or more phrases or concepts.			✓		

Emergent Literacy: Reading	1	2	3	4	5
Child enjoys and chooses reading-related activities.				✓	✓
Child explores books and other texts to answer questions.	✓				
Child blends two phonemes to form a word.	✓	✓	✓	✓	✓
Child names most upper- and lowercase letters of the alphabet.	✓	✓	✓	✓	✓
Child identifies the letter that stands for a given sound.	✓	✓	✓	✓	✓
Child produces the most common sound for a given letter.	✓	✓			
Child retells or reenacts poems and stories in sequence.	✓			✓	
Child asks and answers questions about books read aloud (such as, "Who?" "What?" "Where?").	✓	✓			✓

Emergent Literacy: Writing	1	2	3	4	5
Child uses scribbles, shapes, pictures, symbols, and letters to represent language.			✓		✓
Child writes own name or a reasonable approximation of it.			✓		
Child experiments with and uses some writing conventions when writing or dictating.					✓

Mathematics	1	2	3	4	5
Child counts 1–10 concrete objects correctly.			✓		
Child recognizes and names numerals 0 through 9.	✓				
Child divides sets from 2 to 10 objects into equal sets, using informal techniques.		✓		✓	
Child creates two-dimensional shapes; recreates two-dimensional shapes from memory.				✓	✓
Child measures the length and height of people or objects using standard or non-standard tools.	✓				

Science	1	2	3	4	5
Child understands and describes life cycles of plants and animals.	✓				
Child practices personal hygiene skills independently (for example, washes hands, blows nose, covers mouth, brushes teeth).	✓		✓		✓
Child recognizes and selects healthy foods.	✓	✓	✓		✓
Child identifies and participates in exercises and activities to enhance physical fitness.	✓				✓

Social Studies	1	2	3	4	5
Child understands basic human needs for food, clothing, shelter.			✓		
Child identifies common areas and features of home, school, and community.					✓

Fine Arts	1	2	3	4	5
Child expresses emotions or ideas through art.			✓		

Physical Development	1	2	3	4	5
Child coordinates body movements in a variety of locomotive activities (such as walking, jumping, running, hopping, skipping, climbing).					✓
Child engages in a sequence of movements to perform a task.					✓

Materials and Resources

	DAY 1	DAY 2	DAY 3	DAY 4	DAY 5
Program Materials	• Teacher's Treasure Book • Oral Language Development Card 79 • Rhymes and Chants Flip Chart • *Jamal's Busy Day* Big Book • ABC Big Book • Numeral Cards 0–5 • Building Blocks Math Activities • Making Good Choices Flip Chart • Math and Science Flip Chart • Home Connections Resource Guide	• Teacher's Treasure Book • Dog Puppets • ABC Picture Cards • *Jamal's Busy Day* Big Book • ABC Big Book • Two-Color Counters • Making Good Choices Flip Chart • Math and Science Flip Chart	• Teacher's Treasure Book • Oral Language Development Card 80 • Rhymes and Chants Flip Chart • Concept Big Book 4: *Staying Healthy* • ABC Big Book • Pizza Game 2 board • Two-Color Counters • Making Good Choices Flip Chart • Dog Puppets	• Teacher's Treasure Book • Dog Puppets • Flannel Board Patterns for "Monkey and the Fruit Tree" • ABC Big Book • Pattern Blocks • Pattern Block Puzzles 7-10 • Math and Science Flip Chart • Two-Color Counters • Home Connections Resource Guide	• Teacher's Treasure Book • Rhymes and Chants Flip Chart • *Jamal's Busy Day* Big Book • ABC Picture Cards • Making Good Choices Flip Chart
Other Materials	• books showing doctors • growth chart begun in Unit 2 • student photos • drawing paper • crayons	• pictures of objects whose names have two phonemes (see p. 146) • drawing paper • crayons and other art supplies • buttons • construction paper squares • glue	• clay • drawing paper and crayons • books about food and clothing from different cultures • blocks • empty food cartons or boxes • pictures of food and clothing • plastic fruit and vegetables	• index cards • flannel patterns • props for retelling "Monkey and the Fruit Tree" • drawing paper • crayons	• books about children playing outdoors • paper • crayons • paper squares • empty boxes • blocks • art materials
Home Connection	Encourage children to tell their families about how to stay healthy. Send home Weekly Family Letter, Home Connections Resource Guide, pp. 71–72.	Encourage children to tell their families about ways to stay healthy.	Encourage children to tell their families about why people need food and clothing to live.	Encourage children to tell their families about the monkey and the fruit tree. Send home Story Book 24, Home Connections Resource Guide, pp. 173–176.	Encourage children to tell their families what they learned this week about staying healthy.

Assessment

As you observe children throughout the week, you may fill out an Anecdotal Observational Record Form to document an individual's progress toward a goal or signs indicating the need for developmental or medical evaluation. You may also choose to select work for each child's portfolio. The Anecdotal Observational Record Form and Weekly Assessment rubrics are available in the assessment section on DLMExpressOnline.com.

More Literature Suggestions

- **You Are Healthy** by Todd Snow
- **A Good Heart** by Linda Rieger
- **The Healthy Body Book** by Ellen Sabin
- **Dinosaurs Alive and Well!: A Guide to Good Health** by Marc Brown and Laurie Krasney Brown
- **Equal Shmequal** by Virginia L. Kroll
- **Pachanga deliciosa** por Pat Mora
- **La casa adormecida** por Audrey Wood
- **Froggy se viste** por Jonathan London
- **¡A comer!** por Ana Zamorano
- **Mi día** por Sindy McKay

Daily Planner

	DAY 1	**DAY 2**
Let's Start the Day **Language Time** `large group`	**Opening Routines** p. 140 **Morning Read Aloud** p. 140 **Oral Language and Vocabulary** p. 140 Visiting the Doctor **Phonological Awareness** p. 140 Recognize Real Words	**Opening Routines** p. 146 **Morning Read Aloud** p. 146 **Oral Language and Vocabulary** p. 146 Finish the Sentence **Phonological Awareness** p. 146 Recognize Letter Sounds
Center Time `small group`	**Focus On:** **Pretend and Learn Center** p. 141 **Library and Listening Center** p. 141	**Focus On:** **ABC Center** p. 147 **Creativity Center** p. 147
Circle Time **Literacy Time** `large group`	**Read Aloud** *Jamal's Busy Day/* *El intenso día de Jamal* p. 142 **Learn About Letters and Sounds:** Review Letters p. 142	**Read Aloud** *Jamal's Busy Day/* *El intenso día de Jamal* p. 148 **Learn About Letters and Sounds:** I'm Thinking of a Letter p. 148
Math Time `large group`	**Compare Game** p. 143	**Fair-Sharing** p. 149
Social and Emotional Development `large group`	**Being Respectful** p. 143	**Being Respectful** p. 149
Content Connection `large group`	**Science:** **Oral Language and Academic Vocabulary** p. 144 Applying Knowledge about Healthy Habits **Observe and Investigate** p. 144 Making a Growth Chart	**Math:** p. 150 Talk About Shares p. 150 Model Equal Shares
Center Time `small group`	**Focus On:** **Math and Science Center** p. 145 **Purposeful Play** p. 145	**Focus On:** **Math and Science Center** p. 151 **Purposeful Play** p. 151
Let's Say Good-Bye `large group`	**Read Aloud** p. 145 **Writing** p. 145 **Home Connection** p. 145	**Read Aloud** p. 151 **Writing** p. 151 **Home Connection** p. 151

Building **B**locks

Focus Question
How can I stay healthy?
¿Cómo puedo mantenerme saludable?

DAY 3

Opening Routines p. 152
Morning Read Aloud p. 152
Oral Language and Vocabulary
p. 152 Visiting the Dentist
Phonological Awareness
p. 152 Recognize Letter Sounds

Focus On:
Creativity Center p. 153
Writer's Center p. 153

Read Aloud
Staying Healthy/
Mantente sano p. 154
Learn About Letters and Sounds:
My Letter p. 154

Pizza Game 2 p. 155

Being Helpful p. 155

Social Studies:
Oral Language and Academic Vocabulary
p. 156 Talking About People's Needs
Understand and Participate
p. 156 Looking at Food and Clothing Books

Focus On:
Construction Center p. 157
Purposeful Play p. 157

Read Aloud p. 157
Writing p. 157
Home Connection p. 157

DAY 4

Opening Routines p. 158
Morning Read Aloud p. 158
Oral Language and Vocabulary
p. 158 Make-Believe Stories
Phonological Awareness
p. 158 Blend Letter Sounds

Focus On:
ABC Center p. 159
Pretend and Learn Center p. 159

Read Aloud
"The Monkey and the
Fruit Tree"/"El mono y el
árbol frutal" p. 160
**Learn About Letters and
Sounds:** Review the Letters
p. 160

Discuss Pattern Block Puzzles p. 161

Being Helpful p. 161

Math:
p. 162 Talk About Equal Groups
p. 162 Play I Spy

Focus On:
Math and Science Center p. 163
Purposeful Play p. 163

Read Aloud p. 163
Writing p. 163
Home Connection p. 163

DAY 5

Opening Routines p. 164
Morning Read Aloud p. 164
Oral Language and Vocabulary
p. 164 Playing Outside
Phonological Awareness
p. 164 Recognize Phonemes

Focus On:
Library and Listening Center p. 165
Writer's Center p. 165

Read Aloud
Jamal's Busy Day/El intenso día de Jamal
p. 166
Learn About Letters and Sounds:
Review Letters p. 166

Folding Shapes p. 167

Being Helpful p. 167

Outdoor Play:
Oral Language and Academic Vocabulary
p. 168 Be Healthy
Move and Learn p. 168 Let's Run and Jump

Focus On:
Construction Center p. 169
Purposeful Play p. 169

Read Aloud p. 169
Writing p. 169
Home Connection p. 169

Week 4

Learning Centers

Staying Healthy

Math and Science Center

Observing Growth
Children use photographs and drawings to compare their growth from when they were babies to now. See p. 145.

Making Groups
Children group paper squares so they represent equal amounts. See p. 151.

Equal Blocks
Children add or subtract blocks to make groups of blocks equal. See p. 163.

Fair Share
Partners divide healthy play food items equally so each child gets an equal portion.

ABC Center

Find the Letter
Children locate their assigned letter among letter cards randomly placed. They say the letter sound and the picture name with same initial letter sound. See p. 147.

ABC Order
Children sort sets of alphabet cards into two groups— those that show the letters in alphabetical order and those that do not. Children identify the letter that is not in alphabetical order. See p. 159.

Letter Hide and Seek
Children write the alphabet on paper and then walk around the classroom in pairs locating each letter in environmental print. They mark off each letter as they find it and search until they find every letter.

Creativity Center

Food Pictures
Children draw, paint, and describe a healthy snack. See p. 147.

Making Foods
Children form clay sculptures of favorite foods and describe why they like these foods. See p. 153.

Slow Motion
Children think of an action such as jumping jacks or stretches. They make several pictures to show a body making the movements in sequence.

Sandman
Children discuss whether the Sandman is real or make-believe. They draw pictures of what a sandman would look like and how he would help children sleep.

Library and Listening Center

Browsing Books
Children look at books about doctors and describe how doctors help people. See p. 141.

Browsing Books on Outdoor Play
Children look through books about children playing outside, identify a favorite picture, and describe what the children pictured are doing and how it helps them stay healthy. They draw a picture of themselves doing the activity. See p. 165.

Healthy Eating
Children browse through books about food and draw a picture showing a favorite fruit and vegetable.

Construction Center

Build a Store
Children use blocks to build a clothing or grocery store. They describe the store and explain what they sell in it. See p. 157.

Build a Playground
Partners use blocks and art materials to make a model playground. They describe the playground equipment they made. See p. 169.

Washing Up
Children use blocks and art materials to build a sink and to mimic the tools they use to stay clean. They pretend a bristle block is a brush or a block is a bar of soap.

Writer's Center

Sound Pictures
Children blend two-phoneme words, and illustrate and write them. See p. 153.

Our Play Book
Children draw pictures of activities they do outdoors, describe the pictures, and label them. The pictures are fastened together to make a class book. See p. 165.

Healthy Signs
Children trace their hands to make hand washing signs. They discuss when people should wash their hands and where the signs should be posted.

Pretend and Learn Center

Act It Out
Children act out the rhyme "Outdoor Play." See p. 141.

Retell and Act Out Stories
Children act out or use a flannel board to retell "The Monkey and the Fruit Tree." See p. 159.

Healthy Call
Child pairs use a pretend phone to call relatives or friends and tell them something they can do to stay healthy.

Healthy Debate
Children discuss Goldilocks's health habits. She eats healthy food and naps. Children recommend exercises for Goldilocks.

DAY 1

Focus Question

How can I stay healthy?
¿Cómo puedo mantenerme saludable?

Learning Goals

Language and Communication
• Child uses newly learned vocabulary daily in multiple contexts.

Emergent Literacy: Reading
• Child blends two phonemes to form a word.

Vocabulary

check-up	chequeo	doctor	doctora
healthy	sano	office	consultorio
sick	enfermo	stethoscope	estetoscopio

Differentiated Instruction

Extra Support

Phonological Awareness
If...children have difficulty recognizing and blending two phonemes into real words, **then...** show a picture of a bee. Have children say the initial sound, /b/. Then have them say the final sound, /ē/. Say: *Put the sounds together to make the word. Unamos los sonidos para formar la palabra.*

Enrichment

Phonological Awareness
On the *Rhymes and Chants Flip Chart*, point to the word *go*. Challenge children to say the two phonemes and blend them into the word.

Special Needs

Speech/Language Delays
Designate a "rhyme-time". Go around the room, and point to an object such as "chair." Then, ask, "What rhymes with chair?" If you don't get a response, give a hint. "I know a big animal that growls that rhymes with chair. Right, bear rhymes with chair."

Let's Start the Day

▶ Opening Routines and Transition Tips

For **Opening Routines** and **Transition Tips** turn to pages 178–181 and visit DLMExpressOnline.com for more ideas.

 Read **"Summer at the Beach"/***"Verano en la playa"* from the *Teacher's Treasure Book,* page 221, for your morning Read Aloud.

Language Time

Social and Emotional Remind children to stay in their seats without kicking their feet or leaning on other children who are near them.

Oral Language and Vocabulary

✓ **Can children show understanding by responding appropriately?**

Visiting the Doctor Talk about going to the doctor. Ask: *Have you ever gone to the doctor? Why did you go? ¿Alguna vez han visitado al doctor? ¿Por qué fueron?*

● Display *Oral Language Development Card 79*. Identify the people (doctor, girl) and where they are (the doctor's office). Then follow the suggestions on the back of the card.

Oral Language Development Card 79

Phonological Awareness

✓ **Can children blend two phonemes to make a real word?**

Recognize Real Words Display *Rhymes and Chants Flip Chart*, page 36. Point to the boy's knee in the picture of the boy riding a horse. Have the children say the initial sound, /n/. Then have them say the final sound, /ē/. Have children blend the two phonemes to make the word. Repeat by pointing to the bow in the hair of the girl eating a snack and having children blend sounds to make *bow*.

ELL Use the *Rhymes and Chants Flip Chart* to revisit *bee, knee,* and *bow.* Say the two phonemes in each word and have children blend them.

Rhymes and Chants Flip Chart, page 36

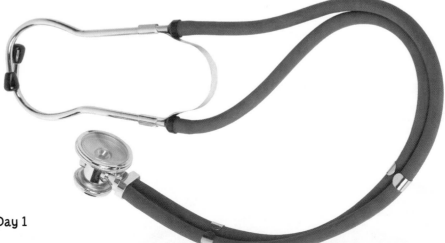

Center Time

▶ **Center Rotation** Center Time includes teacher-guided activities and independent activities. Refer to the **Learning Centers** on pages 138–139 for independent activity ideas.

 small group 60–90 minutes

Pretend and Learn Center

Center Tip

☑ **Look for examples of children staying in their designated spaces, and point them out as examples of being respectful to others.**

Act It Out Explain to children that they will act out the rhyme "Outdoor Play." Refer to the Rhymes and Chants Chart, page 36, and recite "Outdoor Play" with the children.

- Recite the first verse, and assign a small group to act it out, pretending to go outside.

- Continue by having three or four children act out the actions for verse 2 as you recite aloud; then continue with verse 3.

If...children have difficulty moving around the room without disrupting others or materials, **then...**provide a specific space for children to act out the rhyme.

Library and Listening Center

Center Tip

☑ **Track understanding of the characters in a book.**

Materials books showing doctors (real and make-believe)

Browsing Books Have children browse through books that show real doctors or animals as doctors.

- Have children choose their favorite picture of a doctor, identify who is in the picture, tell where they are, and describe what is happening.

- Ask: *How is the doctor helping?* ¿Cómo ayuda el doctor?

- Have children choose and draw their favorite character.

If...children have difficulty identifying the characters in a book, **then...**point to clues in the pictures.

 Learning Goal

Language and Communication
- Child uses newly learned vocabulary daily in multiple contexts.

Emergent Literacy: Reading
- Child explores books and other texts to answer questions.

- Child retells or reenacts poems and stories in sequence.

Differentiated Instruction

 Extra Support

Library and Listening Center
If...children have difficulty understanding a book showing an animal as a doctor, **then...**remind them about make-believe stories. Explain that the animal doctor in the story is acting like a real doctor.

★ Enrichment

Library and Listening Center
Choose a word made up of two phonemes. Challenge children to say each sound and blend them to make a real word.

Accommodations for 3's

Pretend and Learn Center
If...children have difficulty working in small groups, **then...**have children, one at a time, act out each verse, or specific sentences.

Focus Question

How can I stay healthy?
¿Cómo puedo mantenerme saludable?

Learning Goals

Emergent Literacy: Reading
• Child names most upper- and lowercase letters of the alphabet.
• Child identifies the letter that stands for a given sound.
• Child produces the most common sound for a given letter.
• Child asks and answers questions about books read aloud (such as, "Who?" "What?" "Where?").

Vocabulary

brush	cepillar	day	día
healthy	saludable	numbers	números
wash	lavarse	work	trabajo

Differentiated Instruction

 Extra Support

Learn About Letters and Sounds
If...children have difficulty writing a letter such as *Zz*, **then...**write the letter on the board and have children trace over the letter with colored chalk.

 Enrichment

Learn About Letters and Sounds
Challenge children to choose words from *Jamal's Busy Day* and then use the Alphabet/Letter Tiles to spell those words. Read the words children make.

Literacy Time

 large group — 15 minutes

Read Aloud

 Can children begin to recognize story elements and structure?

Build Background Tell children that you will be reading a book about a boy named Jamal and his busy day.

● Ask: **Why might Jamal be so busy?** *¿Por qué creen que Jamal está tan ocupado?*

Listen for Enjoyment Display the Big Book *Jamal's Busy Day,* and read the title. Conduct a picture walk.

● Browse through the pages. Describe what is happening on each page.

● Ask: **How does Jamal start his busy day? What does he do with his family to get ready for his day?** *¿Cómo comienza Jamal su día? ¿Qué hace con su familia para prepararse para su día?*

Respond to the Story Have children name some of the things that Jamal does during the day. Ask: **Who is this story about? Where does most of the story take place? What does Jamal do first in school?** *¿Acerca de quién trata este cuento? ¿Dónde sucede la mayor parte del cuento? ¿Qué es lo que Jamal hace primero en la escuela?*

TIP Be sure children use picture details to understand that Jamal is in school. Point out the desks, the other children, and the teacher. Ask: **What in the picture lets you know that Jamal is studying math?** *¿Qué parte del dibujo les indica que Jamal está estudiando matemáticas?*

ELL As you browse *Jamal's Busy Day,* stop at a picture. Encourage children to point and name things they know in the illustration. Then reread the text.

For additional suggestions on how to meet the needs of children at the Beginning, Intermediate, Advanced, and Advanced-High levels of English proficiency, see pages 184–187.

Learn About Letters and Sounds

 Can children identify all the letters of the alphabet?

Review Letters Sing the "ABC Song" with children. Then page through the *ABC Big Book,* stopping randomly, and have children identify the pictures. Point to the initial letter of a word and have children say its name and sound. Model how to write the upper case and lower case letter using the *ABC Picture Cards.* Have children trace the upper case letter with their fingers.

● While one child is tracing, the other children can be writing the letter in the air or on the floor using their finger. Have them say the letter sound each time they write the letter.

● Repeat for the lower case letter.

Jamal's Busy Day
El intenso día de Jamal

ABC Big Book

Math Time

Observe and Investigate

 Can children compare objects in groups?

Compare Game For each pair of children, use two or more sets of Numeral Cards (0–5), found on *Teacher's Treasure Book* page 510.

- Mix the cards, and deal them equally, facing down, to each player. Players simultaneously flip their top cards to compare which is greater. The player with more says "I have more!" and takes the opponent's card. If cards are equal, each player flips another card to break the tie.

- The game ends when all the cards have been played, and the winner is the player with more cards. Or, play the game without a winner by not allowing players to collect cards.

ELL After setting up two equal groups of eggs from *Building Blocks,* have children describe what they see by repeating this sentence frame *These groups are [equal].*

Online Math Activity

Introduce Egg-stremely Equal in which children divide sets of eggs into equal groups. Each child should complete the activity this week.

Social and Emotional Development

Making Good Choices

 Do children respect each other's personal space?

Being Respectful Invite children to give examples of how to respect each other's space in a classroom. Display the *Making Good Choices Flip Chart,* page 36. Point to the girl near the boy who is working on the puzzle.

- Ask: *Do you think the boy wants the girl to help him? How could the girl be sitting if she wanted to help the boy work on the puzzle?* *¿Creen que el niño quiere que la niña lo ayude? ¿Cómo debería sentarse la niña si quisiera ayudar al niño con el rompecabezas?*

- Then discuss the children drinking juice. Ask: *How are they sitting? What do you think might happen?* *¿Cómo están sentados? ¿Qué creen que podría pasar?*

Making Good Choices Flip Chart, page 36

Learning Goal

Social and Emotional Development
- Child is aware of self in terms of abilities, characteristics and preferences, and respects personal boundaries.

Mathematics
- Child recognizes and names numerals 0 through 9.

Vocabulary

equal	igual a	fewer	menor
greater	mayor	less	menos
more	más		

Differentiated Instruction

✋ Extra Support

Observe and Investigate
If...children struggle identifying which is more, **then...**have them count out counters first, place them on the card to show the number, and then compare the counters.

⭐ Enrichment

Observe and Investigate
Have children use Numeral Cards 0–10 and repeat the Compare Game.

Accommodations for 3's

Observe and Investigate
If...children have difficulty identifying numerals, **then...**use Counting Cards or Dot Cards instead of Numeral Cards.

Focus Question
How can I stay healthy?
¿Cómo puedo mantenerme saludable?

Differentiated Instruction

 Extra Support

Oral Language and Academic Vocabulary
If... children have difficulty identifying what is happening in each picture, **then...** suggest specific things for them to look at: **Look at the two children playing with the ball. Why is that a good way to stay healthy?** *Observen a los dos niños jugando con la pelota. ¿Por qué jugar a la pelota es una buena forma de mantenerse saludable?*

 Enrichment

Oral Language and Academic Vocabulary
Challenge children to think of other things they can do to stay healthy. Have them draw pictures and then paste their pictures on a chart.

Science Time

 large group 20 minutes

Health Skills Model good cleanliness routines by washing your hands before and after you eat.

Oral Language and Academic Vocabulary

✓ **Can children apply their knowledge about healthy habits and the needs of pets?**

Applying Knowledge about Healthy Habits Point to each photograph on the *Math and Science Flip Chart*, page 67. Ask: **What is happening in this picture?** *¿Qué sucede en esta imagen?*

• For each habit, ask children to explain why it helps us stay healthy. Ask children to expand on photos by describing other things they do to stop germs and keep their teeth healthy, other foods they eat that are nutritious, and other exercises they can do to keep their bodies strong.

• Remind children that they have learned a lot about pets and how people take care of them. Ask children to think about ways that people help their pets stay healthy. Examples include taking pets to the doctor (veterinarian), feeding them food that is healthy for animals, giving them enough water, and helping them get exercise.

Math and Science Flip Chart, page 67

Observe and Investigate

✓ **Can children use words to describe ways they are growing and staying healthy?**

Making a Growth Chart Show children the growth chart begun in Unit 2. Say: **Let's see how much you've grown this year.** *Vamos a ver cuánto han crecido este año.*

• Measure children and point out that they are taller.

• Explain that eating healthy snacks and exercising affects how we grow. Use chart paper to show children's favorite snacks and exercises. Label the chart **We Like to Be Healthy!** ¡Nos gusta estar saludables! Draw rows, one for each child in your class. Then make two columns: **My Favorite Snack, My Favorite Exercise** Mi comida favorita, Mi ejercicio favorito.

• Record each child's name, his or her favorite healthy snack, and favorite form of exercise.

ELL Have children respond yes/no to your questions about favorite exercises and favorite snacks. For example: **Is a banana a healthy snack? Is running good exercise? Is watching TV good exercise?**

Center Time

▶ **Center Rotation** Center Time includes teacher-guided activities and independent activities. Refer to the **Learning Centers** on pages 138–139 for independent activity ideas.

  small group 30 minutes

Math and Science Center

 **Center Tip**

☑ **Encourage children to describe how they have changed since they were younger.**

Materials growth chart from Science Time, children's personal photos, drawing paper, crayons

Observing Growth Invite children to bring in a baby photo.

- Invite volunteers to describe how they looked when they were babies.

- Have children paste their baby photos on half of a large sheet of drawing paper. On the other half, have children draw self-portraits.

- Have children discuss how they have changed since infancy and how they have grown over the past year.

- Remind children how important it is to exercise and eat healthy foods so they can continue to grow and be strong.

Center Tip

If...children need help drawing their self-portraits, **then...** provide mirrors and have children just draw their faces.

Purposeful Play

☑ **Observe children respecting each other's personal space.**

Children choose an open center for free playtime. Encourage children to give each other enough space at a table to draw pictures.

Let's Say Good-Bye

  large group 15 minutes

 Read Aloud Revisit "Summer at the Beach"/ *"Verano en la playa"* for your afternoon Read Aloud. Ask children to listen for words that begin with /s/ and /w/.

 Home Connection Refer to the Home Connections activities listed in the Resources and Materials chart on page 135. Remind children to tell families about how to stay healthy. Sing the "Good-Bye Song"/*"Hora de ir a casa"* as children prepare to leave.

✓ **Learning Goal**

Mathematics
- Child measures the length and height of people or objects using standard or non-standard tools.

Science
- Child understands and describes life cycles of plants and animals.
- Child recognizes and selects healthy foods.
- Child identifies and participates in exercises and activities to enhance physical fitness.

Writing

Recap the day. Have children name some of the things they can do to stay healthy. Ask: *What did you learn about how to stay healthy?* ¿Qué aprendieron sobre mantenerse saludables? Record their answers. Read them back as you track the print, and emphasize the correspondence between speech and print.

DAY 2

Focus Question
How can I stay healthy?
¿Cómo puedo mantenerme saludable?

Let's Start the Day

▶ **Opening Routines and Transition Tips**
For **Opening Routines** and **Transition Tips** turn to pages 178–181 and visit **DLMExpressOnline.com** for more ideas.

📖 Read **"Pancho and the Sky"/**"Pancho y Cielo" from the *Teacher's Treasure Book*, page 306, for your morning Read Aloud.

 Learning Goals

Social and Emotional Development
• Child is aware of self in terms of abilities, characteristics and preferences, and respects personal boundaries.

Language and Communication
• Child understands and uses sentences having two or more phrases or concepts.

Emergent Literacy: Reading
• Child blends two phonemes to form a word.

Vocabulary

brush	cepillarse	busy	ocupado
dinner	cena	healthy	saludable
wash	lavarse	work	trabajar

 **Differentiated Instruction**

 **Extra Support**
Oral Language and Vocabulary
If...children have difficulty completing the sentence, **then...**offer clues through questions about specific habits, such as: *Do you brush your teeth every day? Do you comb your hair? Do you eat vegetables? ¿Se cepillan los dientes todos los días? ¿Se peinan el cabello? ¿Comen vegetales?*

⭐ **Enrichment**
Oral Language and Vocabulary
Children can expand their vocabularies during the discussion. Ask them to state two or more sentences to add to the sentence frame that they just completed.

Language Time

large group — 15 minutes

👪 **Social and Emotional Development** Ask children why it is important to respect each other's space.

Oral Language and Vocabulary

✓ **Can children answer questions using complete sentences?**
Finish the Sentence Talk about ways to stay healthy. Ask: *What should you eat to stay healthy? What exercise can you do to stay healthy? ¿Qué deben comer para mantenerse saludables? ¿Qué ejercicios deben hacer para mantenerse saludables?*

● Tell children that they will play a sentence game by repeating a sentence and adding their own ending. Begin by saying: "I stay healthy because I ride my bike." Call on children, in turn to complete the sentence "I stay healthy because _____."

● Encourage children to use their imaginations. Accept all reasonable responses.

Phonological Awareness

✓ **Can children identify two phonemes in real words?**
Recognize Letter Sounds Display the Dog Puppets. Tell children that one puppet will hold up a picture. Children will say each sound in the pictured word and then blend the sounds. The second puppet will cheer if children are correct. Have the puppet hold up pictures, one at a time, of a bee, tie, and bow.

🔲 ELL Pair children. Give each pair picture cards of two-phoneme words, with the word written below the picture. Use words such as *toe, knee,* and *boy*. Have one child show the card to the other child. The other child says the two phonemes that make up the word and blends them. Then partners reverse roles.

Center Time

> **Center Rotation** Center Time includes teacher-guided activities and independent activities. Refer to the **Learning Centers** on pages 138–139 for independent activity ideas.

small group | 60–90 minutes

Refer to the **Learning Centers** on pages 138–139 for independent activity ideas.

ABC Center

 Keep track of the letter-sounds children know.

Materials *ABC Picture Cards*

Find the Letter Assign each child a letter.

- Place the *ABC Picture Cards* face up in random order on the table.

- Have children, in turn, find their assigned letter and first say the sound for the letter and then say the picture name.

- Encourage children to also trace the letter on their card with their finger before turning it face down.

- Repeat with the other letters until all the letters are found.

Center Tip

If…children have difficulty remembering the sound for their letter, **then…**have them say the picture name first.

Creativity Center

 Listen for words children use to describe their favorite healthy foods.

Materials drawing paper, crayons and other art supplies

Food Pictures Tell children that they will draw a picture of their favorite healthy snack.

- Distribute paper and art supplies. Have children draw a picture of their favorite healthy food (popcorn, apple, pear, etc.).

- Then have children color or paint their picture. Say: *Tell me about your picture. What is the name of the food? What color is it? How does it taste? Why do you like it? Describan sus dibujos. ¿Cómo se llama ese alimento? ¿De qué color es? ¿Qué sabor tiene? ¿Por qué les gusta?*

Center Tip

If…children have difficulty deciding on a healthy snack to draw, **then…**provide four pictures of fruits and vegetables from the *Photo Library CD-ROM* and have children choose one to draw.

Learning Goal

Emergent Literacy: Reading
- Child names most upper- and lowercase letters of the alphabet.

- Child produces the most common sound for a given letter.

Science
- Child recognizes and selects healthy foods.

Differentiated Instruction

 Extra Support

ABC Center

If…children have difficulty remembering the sound of a letter, **then…**have them write the letter in sand or on paper with shaving cream as they say the sound.

Enrichment

ABC Center

Challenge children to name two or three other words that begin with their assigned letter.

Accommodations for 3's

ABC Center

If…children have difficulty finding their assigned letter, **then…**arrange the letters in ABC order. Point to each letter and say its name. Then ask a child to find his or her assigned letter.

Special Needs

Behavioral Social/Emotional

This unit provides a great opportunity to encourage 'picky eaters' to try something new that they haven't tried before. Some children (especially those with autism) are very resistant to trying new foods.

Circle Time

Literacy Time

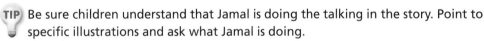

large group   15 minutes

📖 Read Aloud

✓ **Can children recall important story details about Jamal?**

Build Background Tell children that you will read about a boy named Jamal and all the things he does in one day.

● Ask: *Why is Jamal so busy? ¿Por qué Jamal y su familia se preparan para un día intenso?*

Listen for Understanding Display *Jamal's Busy Day,* and read the title. Discuss with children that print is what is read rather than the picture. Ask: *Where should I start reading? ¿Por dónde debo empezar a leer?* Point to the place.

● Read the first two pages. Have a volunteer point to the first word in the first sentence.

● Ask: *Where does this part of the story take place? ¿Dónde sucede esta parte del cuento?*

● Ask: *What does Jamal do after he comes home from school? ¿Qué hace Jamal después de regresar de la escuela?*

Respond to the Story Have children discuss why Jamal thinks going to school is a job. Ask: *How does Jamal work hard in school? What does Jamal do at the end of the story? What does Jamal do that helps him stay healthy? ¿Por qué Jamal dice que él también trabaja mucho? ¿Qué hace en la escuela? ¿Qué hace Jamal al final del cuento? ¿Qué hace Jamal para mantenerse saludable?*

TIP Be sure children understand that Jamal is doing the talking in the story. Point to specific illustrations and ask what Jamal is doing.

ELL As you read *Jamal's Busy Day*, explain the concept of work and job in the story. Point out that Jamal thinks school is like a job. Explain that because Jamal is so busy like his mother and father, he feels he goes to work, too.

For additional suggestions on how to meet the needs of children at the Beginning, Intermediate, Advanced, and Advanced-High levels of English proficiency, see pages 184–187.

Learn About Letters and Sounds

✓ **Can children identify the correct letter in a sequence?**

I'm Thinking of a Letter Sing the "ABC Song" with children as you page through the *ABC Big Book*.

● Tell children that they will play a game called, "I'm Thinking of a Letter." Say, *I'm thinking of a letter that comes right after F (or right before). Say the letter name. Then say the sound the letter stands for. Estoy pensando en una letra que viene justo después (o justo antes) de la F. Digan el nombre de la letra, y luego digan qué sonido tiene.* Repeat with other letters.

Jamal's Busy Day
El intenso día de Jamal

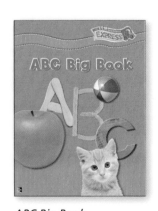

ABC Big Book

---

large group 15 minutes

Math Time

Observe and Investigate

Can children make fair shares?

Fair-Sharing Model how to divide 10 objects into two equal or "fair" groups.

- Use 10 objects such as counters. Select a child with whom to share. Say: ***I am going to share my counters with [child's name].*** *Voy a compartir mis fichas con [nombre del niño].*Give one counter to the child and one to yourself as you say: ***One for you, and one for me.*** *Una para ti y una para mí.* Then have the child continue dividing the counters equally by sharing and using your model.
- Then have pairs of children share six, eight, or ten counters using the appropriate language "one for me" and "one for you." When children finish, ask: ***Did you share your counters equally?*** *¿Compartieron sus fichas en partes iguales?*

Building Blocks

Online Math Activity

Children can complete Egg-stremely Equal during computer time or Center Time.

Learning Goal

Social and Emotional Development

• Child is aware of self in terms of abilities, characteristics and preferences, and respects personal boundaries.

Mathematics

• Child divides sets from 2 to 10 objects into equal sets, using informal techniques.

Vocabulary

counters	fichas
divide	dividir
equal	igual
fair share	en partes iguales
group	grupo

large group 15 minutes

Social and Emotional Development

Making Good Choices

Do children respect each other's personal space?

Being Respectful Revisit *Making Good Choices Flip Chart*, page 36, "How Do I Act in Class?"

- Display a Dog Puppet. Say: ***Tell the puppet what this girl is doing while the boy tries to work on a puzzle. Explain how she could be helpful.*** *Díganle al títere lo que hace esta niña mientras el niño arma el rompecabezas. Expliquen qué podría hacer para ayudar.*
- Provide each child a turn to tell the puppet about a child on the chart. Remind children not to bother other children who are working in a center.

ELL Provide sentence frames to help during the conversation with the dog puppet. Use these and others: ***The girl is* ______. *She is* ______.** Model the use of each frame. Have children repeat, then apply using their own words. Encourage more advanced children to form more complex sentences.

Making Good Choices Flip Chart, page 36

Differentiated Instruction

Extra Support

Observe and Investigate

If...children struggle sharing counters equally, **then...**have them line up their counters one below the other and compare the two groups. Children should determine if there is an equal number of items without counting by comparing the two groups.

Enrichment

Observe and Investigate

Have children share more than 10 objects equally with a friend. Encourage them to experiment with different strategies for making sure the groups are equal.

Focus Question
How can I stay healthy?
¿Cómo puedo mantenerme saludable?

Language and Communication
• Child exhibits an understanding of instructional terms used in the classroom.

Mathematics
• Child divides sets from 2 to 10 objects into equal sets, using informal techniques.

Vocabulary

divide	dividir	equal	igual
fair	justo	objects	objetos
share	compartir		

Differentiated Instruction

 Extra Support

Math Time

If...children have difficulty identifying equal groups on the chart, **then...**point to each group and tell them to look at the trees, apples, flowers, etc. Ask how they can tell each group has the same number of objects.

 Enrichment

Math Time

Challenge children to share a set of hidden counters covered with a piece of paper. A child takes the objects one at a time and shares them with a classmate.

Math Time

Language and Communication Skills Use instructional terms while discussing fair shares and groups. Model as needed.

☑ **Can children make fair shares?**

Talk About Shares Provide each child in the class a certain even number of buttons.

● Ask each child to divide their buttons into two fair shares.

● Ask: *How did you divide the buttons? What did you say as you made the groups? How do you know the groups are fair?* *¿Cómo dividieron los botones? ¿Qué dijeron mientras los dividían en grupos? ¿Cómo saben que los dividieron de una manera justa?*

● After children made fair shares, invite volunteers to show their fair shares. Then put the buttons together, and have them use the appropriate language to divide the set, saying "one for you, one for me"/"uno para ti y uno para mí."

☑ **Can children identify and model equal shares?**

Model Equal Shares Have children identify and model with counters equal shares.

● Display *Math and Science Flip Chart* page 68, "A Nature Scene." Discuss the scene. Point out that there are equal groups shown such as two groups of 2 trees, one rabbit on each side, and two groups of 3 flowers.

● Ask: *What are on two of the trees?* (apples) *How can we show that these are fair shares or equal groups?* *¿Qué hay en los árboles? (manzanas) ¿Cómo podemos mostrar que son partes iguales?* Have children use counters to show two equal groups with 4 counters each to represent the apples.

● Continue with other items shown on the chart.

ELL Children should go to the chart and point out the equal groups of objects/animals. Then work with them to model making equal shares. Use the appropriate language as you model, and have children repeat after you to explain what you are doing.

Math and Science Flip Chart, page 68

Center Time

▶ **Center Rotation** Center Time includes teacher-guided activities and independent activities. Refer to the **Learning Centers** on pages 138–139 for independent activity ideas.

   small group 30 minutes

Learning Goal

Social and Emotional Development
• Child is aware of self in terms of abilities, characteristics and preferences, and respects personal boundaries.

Language and Communication
• Child exhibits an understanding of instructional terms used in the classroom.

Mathematics
• Child divides sets from 2 to 10 objects into equal sets, using informal techniques.

Math and Science Center

| | Center Tip |

✓ **Observe children as they use paper items to make equal groups.**

Materials drawing paper, precut small construction-paper squares, glue

Making Groups Prepare construction-paper squares, all the same size but different colors. Say: ***Let's use these shapes to make fair shares.***
Vamos a usar estas figuras para formar partes iguales.

- Give each child a sheet of drawing paper folded in half and 6, 8 or 10 paper squares.

- Have children use the squares to make two fair shares. They glue an equal number of squares on each side of the paper.

- Children show their work when completed.

Center Tip

If...children need help dividing the paper squares equally, **then...**have them work with a friend and divide the squares by saying "one for you" and "one for me." Each child glues his or her squares on one side of the paper.

Writing

Recap the day. Say: ***Tell me one thing you learned about healthy habits***. *Díganme una cosa hayan aprendido acerca de los hábitos saludables.* Record their answers on chart paper. Share the pen with children as you write. Children can write their name beside their entry.

Purposeful Play

✓ **Observe children's awareness of their own body in a space**

Children choose an open center for free playtime. Encourage children to sit near each other and draw pictures of equal groups of items.

Let's Say Good-Bye

  large group 15 minutes

 Read Aloud Revisit "Pancho and the Sky"/"*Pancho y Cielo*" for your afternoon Read Aloud. Ask children to listen for words that begin with /p/ and /k/.

 Home Connection Refer to the Home Connections activities listed in the Resources and Materials chart on page 135. Remind children to tell families about ways to stay healthy. Sing the "Good-Bye Song"/"*Hora de ir a casa*" as children prepare to leave.

GLUE

DAY 3

Let's Start the Day

Focus Question

How can I stay healthy?
¿Cómo puedo mantenerme saludable?

▶ **Opening Routines and Transition Tips**
For **Opening Routines** and **Transition Tips** turn to pages 178–181 and visit **DLMExpressOnline.com** for more ideas.

 Read **"Weather"/**"El tiempo" from the T*eacher's Treasure Book*, page 234, for your morning Read Aloud.

✓ Learning Goals

Language and Communication
• Child uses newly learned vocabulary daily in multiple contexts.

Emergent Literacy: Reading
• Child blends two phonemes to form a word.

Vocabulary

chair	sillón	cleaning	limpieza
dentist	dentista	office	consultorio
teeth	dientes	tools	instrumentos

 **Differentiated Instruction**

Extra Support

Phonological Awareness

If...children have difficulty recognizing and blending two phonemes into real words, **then...** point to the child's knee on the Rhymes and Chants Flip Chart. Say: *Say the first sound in the word.* (/n/) *Say the next sound in the word.* (/ē/) *Put the sounds together to form the word.* (knee) *Digan el primer sonido de la palabra.* (/n/) *Digan el siguiente sonido.* (/ē/) *Ahora, unan los sonidos para formar la palabra* (knee).

⭐ Enrichment

Phonological Awareness

Act out the following words, one at a time: run, sit, hop. Challenge children to say the sounds at the beginning, middle, and end of the word and blend them.

Language Time

 large group **15 minutes**

👤👤👤 **Social and Emotional Development** Remind children to stay in their seats without kicking their feet or leaning on other children who are near them.

Oral Language and Vocabulary

✓ **Can children respond to questions in complete sentences?**

Visiting the Dentist Ask children how many of them have been to the dentist. Ask: **What does a dentist do?** *¿Qué hace un dentista?*

● Display *Oral Language Development Card 80*. Point out the girl in the dentist's chair. Ask: **What is happening in this picture?** *¿Qué está pasando en esta imagen?* Then follow the suggestions on the back of the card.

Phonological Awareness

✓ **Can children identify two letter sounds in words?**

Recognize Letter Sounds Revisit *Rhymes and Chants Flip Chart,* page 36. Remind children that they can put sounds together to make a word. Point to the following in the illustration, one at a time: eat, bow, knee, up (the girl in the swing is up). Have children say the two sounds in each word and then blend them. To extend oral language, have children then use each word in their own sentence.

ELL Use the *Rhymes and Chants Flip Chart* to revisit the words *go* and *we*. Have children use actions and gestures to illustrate each word, as they say each phoneme in the word and blend them.

For additional suggestions on how to meet the needs of children at the Beginning, Intermediate, Advanced, and Advanced-High levels of English proficiency, see pages 184–187.

Oral Language Development Card 80

Rhymes and Chants Flip Chart, page 36

Center Time

▶ **Center Rotation** Center Time includes teacher-guided activities and independent activities. Refer to the **Learning Centers** on pages 138–139 for independent activity ideas.

 small group  60–90 minutes

Creativity Center

| Center Tip |

☑ **Track children's ability to make and describe their favorite food.**

Materials play clay

Making Foods Tell children that they will make their favorite food out of play clay.

● Give each child a ball of clay. Ask: **What food will you make?** *¿Qué comida prepararán?*

● Prompt children to describe their food and tell why they like it.

Center Tip

If...children have difficulty remembering how to make a certain food,

then...provide food books or food pictures as a reference.

Writer's Center

| Center Tip |

☑ **Track children's ability to identify letters and sounds of words.**

Materials drawing paper, crayons

Sound Pictures Tell children that they will draw pictures of words.

● Help children fold a sheet of paper into thirds.

● Say a two-phoneme word, such as *bee,* phoneme by phoneme (/b/ /ē/).

● Have children blend the word and draw a picture. Ask children to label the picture with the lower case letter that starts the word.

● Repeat with the words *key* and *pie*.

Center Tip

If...children have difficulty drawing the objects,

then...display photos from the *ABC Big Book* and have children copy the picture. Cover the letters on each picture and have children write the letters.

Learning Goal

Emergent Literacy: Reading
● Child blends two phonemes to form a word.

Emergent Literacy: Writiing
● Child uses scribbles, shapes, pictures, symbols, and letters to represent language.

Fine Arts
● Child expresses emotions or ideas through art.

Differentiated Instruction

 Extra Support

Creativity Center

If...children have difficulty using the play clay,

then...model how to roll the clay with their hands to soften it before making an object.

Enrichment

Creativity Center

Challenge children to work in pairs or small groups and make a healthy meal out of clay. Have them explain what they made.

Accommodations for 3's

Writer's Center

If...children have difficulty writing letters,

then...lightly write the letters for children to trace and then copy.

Focus Question
How can I stay healthy?
¿Cómo puedo mantenerme saludable?

Circle Time

Learning Goals

Language and Communication
• Child demonstrates an understanding of oral language by responding appropriately.

Emergent Literacy: Reading
• Child identifies the letter that stands for a given sound.

Emergent Literacy: Writing
• Child writes own name or a reasonable approximation of it.

Science
• Child practices personal hygiene skills independently (for example, washes hands, blows nose, covers mouth, brushes teeth).

Vocabulary

exercise	ejercicios	food	comida
grow	crecer	habits	hábitos
healthy	saludable	strong	fuerte

Differentiated Instruction

 Extra Support
Read Aloud
If...children have difficulty answering questions, **then...**point to the picture that gives the answer. Describe what is happening in the picture and then have children answer the question.

Enrichment
Read Aloud
Challenge children to think of other ways to exercise that are not shown in the Read Aloud. Have them make up a sentence using this sentence frame "I get exercise when I _____." "Hago ejercicio cuando _____."

Literacy Time

 large group · 15 minutes

Read Aloud

✓ **Can children use picture details to understand the text?**

Build Background Tell children that you will be reading about ways to stay healthy.

Listen for Understanding Display *Concept Big Book 4: Staying Healthy,* page 18, and read the title. Read pages 26–28. Point to photographs as you read aloud.

● Ask: *How do the photographs help you understand what I'm reading? ¿Cómo les ayudan las fotos a entender lo que estoy leyendo?*

Respond to the Story Have children name some of the healthy habits that were shown. *Why do you think washing up is a healthy habit? What else is a healthy habit? What makes you grow strong? Do you think you have grown taller since the beginning of the year? ¿Por qué creen que lavarse es un hábito saludable? ¿Qué otra cosa es un hábito saludable? ¿Qué los ayuda a crecer fuertes? ¿Creen que han crecido desde que comenzó el año?*

TIP Help children use the picture details by describing what is going on in each picture.

ELL As you read the book, explain the word *habit* to children. Explain that a habit is something you do every day or very often, such as brushing your teeth, washing your hands, or combing your hair. Help children understand that healthy habits are important for good health.

Learn About Letters and Sounds

✓ **Can children identify the first letter in their name?**

My Letter Sing the "ABC Song" with children as you page through the *ABC Big Book.* Then call on children, in turn, to find the letter that begins their first name.

● Have them trace their letter with their finger and say its sound.

● Encourage children to add a sticky note with their first name to the appropriate letter page.

Staying Healthy
Mantente sano

ABC Big Book

Building Blocks

Online Math Activity

Children can complete Egg-stremely Equal during computer time or Center Time.

Math Time

Observe and Investigate

✓ **Can children demonstrate one to one correspondence?**

Pizza Game 2 Demonstrate this game by playing it with children. Each player needs a Pizza Game 2 sheet (*Teacher's Treasure Book,* page 503) and flat, round counters. Choose a target number, such as 5.

- Player One rolls a number cube, and puts that many counters ("toppings") on the sheet's plate, for example, 6. Once Player Two agrees that Player One chose the correct number of counters, Player One moves the counters to one or more of the sheet's pizzas, trying to get 5 on each. If a 6 was rolled, Player One could put 5 on one pizza and start another with 1.

- Players take turns, and the winner is the first player to get the target number of counters on each pizza. Repeat if time permits with a different target number.

ELL During the counting activity, focus on the concept of "how many." As you count and add a counter, ask: *How many counters do I have now?* Have the child point to each counter and count aloud.

✗✗✗ Social and Emotional Development

Making Good Choices

✓ **Are children respectful of other children's space?**

Being Helpful Display *Making Good Choices Flip Chart* page 36, "How Do I Act in Class?" Review with children the way the children are respecting or not respecting each other's space, themselves, others, and their environment.

- With both Dog Puppets, role play other situations to model how children show respect. For example, explain that the puppets will show how to sit at the lunch table.

- After the role play, ask: *Did the puppet stay in one seat? Did the first puppet kick the other puppet? Did the first puppet lean on the second puppet while the second puppet was eating? ¿Se quedó el títere en su asiento? ¿Dio patadas al otro títere? ¿Se reclinó sobre el otro títere mientras comía?*

Making Good Choices Flip Chart, page 36

Learning Goals

Language and Communication
• Child names and describes actual or pictured people, places, things, actions, attributes, and events.
• Child understands or knows the meaning of many thousands of words, many more than he or she uses.

Science
• Child recognizes and selects healthy foods.

Social Studies
• Child understands basic human needs for food, clothing, shelter.

Vocabulary

clothing	ropa	food	alimentos
needs	necesidades	people	personas
shelter	refugio	water	agua

Differentiated Instruction

 Extra Support
Understand and Participate
If...children have difficulty identifying kinds of food, **then...**display pictures of healthy foods from the Photo Library. Ask: *What is the name of this food? What color is it? How does it taste? Do you like it? ¿Cómo se llama este alimento? ¿De qué color es? ¿Qué sabor tiene? ¿Les gusta?*

 Enrichment
Understand and Participate
Challenge children to play a game using pictures of clothing from the *Photo Library CD-ROM.*

Social Studies Time

Health Skills During the discussion, invite children to talk about what they learned this week about eating healthy snacks and other foods.

Oral Language and Academic Vocabulary

✔ **Can children identify their needs?**

Talking About People's Needs Remind children that they read about Jamal at home, getting dressed, eating breakfast, and then going to school. Explain that all people need food, clothing and shelter.

● Ask: *Do you remember what the word shelter means? ¿Recuerdan lo que significa la palabra refugio?* (a safe place to live)

● Ask: *Do you need food to live? A home? Clothing? Why? ¿Necesitan alimento para vivir? ¿Un hogar? ¿Ropa? ¿Por qué?*

● Point out that people all over the world need food, a place to live, and clothing.

Understand and Participate

✔ **Can children understand why food and clothing are important to people?**

Looking at Food and Clothing Books Display books showing foods from different cultures and books about clothing. Make sure some of the photos contain people.

● Page through the books with children, pointing out the types of clothing people wear, and the foods people eat.

● Discuss with children why some people are wearing warm clothing; others, lightweight clothing. Help children understand that people dress according to the weather/climate. Ask: *What kind of clothing are you wearing today? ¿Qué tipo de ropa llevan hoy?*

● Continue the discussion by pointing out that people also need food. Remind children that they learned food gives them energy. Then ask: *What kinds of food do you like to eat? Which kinds of healthy foods do you eat as snacks? ¿Qué tipos de alimentos les gusta comer? ¿Qué tipos de alimentos saludables comen en la merienda?*

● Make a class chart of Favorite Foods. Invite each child to draw his or her favorite food on the chart. (There can be duplication.) Label children's pictures with the food name.

ELL Use the *Photo Library CD-ROM* pictures to teach children words associated with homes, food, and clothing. Have children look at the pictures and repeat the names of the items seen. Encourage children to use one of the words in a sentence.

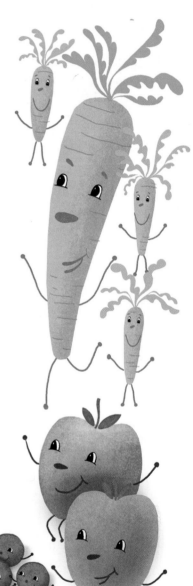

Center Time

▶ **Center Rotation** Center Time includes teacher-guided activities and independent activities. Refer to the **Learning Centers** on pages 138–139 for independent activity ideas.

   small group 30 minutes

Construction Center

	Center Tip
✓ **Monitor children as they make and describe a store.**	**If...**children need help sharing the blocks and materials, **then...**assign each child a part to build.

Materials blocks, empty food cartons or boxes, pictures of food or clothing, plastic vegetables and fruit

Build a Store Tell children that they will use blocks to build a grocery store or a clothing store. Invite children to use their imaginations; for example, they could make a fruit and vegetable store.

- Have children work in small groups. Ask: *What kind of store will you build?* *¿Qué tipo de tienda construirán?*

- Have children describe their finished store. Encourage them to explain their decisions.

Purposeful Play

✓ **Observe children as they work in pairs or small groups.**

Children choose an open center for free playtime. Encourage children to pretend they are shopping at the store. Remind children to respect each other's space and allow enough room for all children to play.

Let's Say Good-Bye

  large group 15 minutes

 Read Aloud Revisit "Weather"/"El tiempo" for your afternoon Read Aloud. Ask children to listen for the kinds of weather the children in the story see.

 Home Connection Refer to the Home Connections activities listed in the Resources and Materials chart on page 135. Remind children to tell families about why people need food and clothing to live. Sing the "Good-Bye Song"/"Hora de ir a casa" as children prepare to leave.

✓ Learning Goal

Language and Communication
- Child names and describes actual or pictured people, places, things, actions, attributes, and events.

Social Studies
- Child understands basic human needs for food, clothing, shelter.

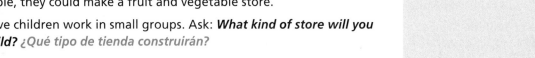

Writing

Recap the day. Have children name articles of clothing that they wear. Ask: *What did you learn about why people need clothing?* *¿Qué aprendieron sobre la razón por la que las personas necesitan ropa?* Ask them to draw a picture showing an article of clothing and label it.

Focus Question

How can I stay healthy?
¿Cómo puedo mantenerme saludable?

Social and Emotional Development
• Child is aware of self in terms of abilities, characteristics and preferences, and respects personal boundaries.

Language and Communication
• Child demonstrates an understanding of oral language by responding appropriately.

• Child follows basic rules for conversations (taking turns, staying on topic, listening actively).

Emergent Literacy: Reading
• Child blends two phonemes to form a word.

Vocabulary

animals	animales	fruit	fruta
greedy	glotón	politely	amablemente
problem	problema	treat	delicia

Differentiated Instruction

Extra Support

Oral Language and Vocabulary
If...children have difficulty distinguishing real animals from make-believe, **then...**show pictures of animals from fiction and nonfiction books. Ask: *Do animals in real-life wear clothes like people do? Do real animals look like this? ¿Usan ropa los animales en la vida real? ¿Son así los animales reales?*

Enrichment

Oral Language and Vocabulary
Have children work in small groups and look at fiction books about animals. Invite them to talk about what they see and what is happening in the pictures.

Let's Start the Day

> **Opening Routines and Transition Tips**
> For **Opening Routines** and **Transition Tips** turn to pages 178–181 and visit DLMExpressOnline.com for more ideas.
>
> Read **"Stop, Look, and Listen"**/*"Para, mira y escucha bien"* from the *Teacher's Treasure Book,* page 77, for your morning Read Aloud.

Language Time

large group · 15 minutes

Social and Emotional Development Ask: *Why do you think it's important to give classmates enough space as they work and play?*

Oral Language and Vocabulary

✓ **Can children distinguish real from make-believe?**

Make-Believe Stories Remind children that they have read many stories that were make-believe. Ask: *How did the animals act in those stories? ¿Cómo actuaban los animales en estos cuentos?* Children should realize that they acted and talked like people do. Point out that only make-believe animals talk or dress like people do.

● Discuss what the animals in some of those stories say and do. Ask questions using Who, What, Where, and How.

● Ask: *If a monkey could talk like a person, what do you think it would say to you? What would a rabbit say? What would a squirrel say? Si un mono pudiera hablar como una persona, ¿qué creen que les diría? ¿Qué diría un conejo? ¿Qué diría una ardilla?*

Phonological Awareness

✓ **Can children blend two phonemes to make a word?**

Blend Letter Sounds Play "What's My Word?" Display the Dog Puppets. Hold one puppet and give the other to a child. Ask, "What's my word?" Then say a two-phoneme word to your puppet, phoneme by phoneme, e.g. /d/ /ā/. Have the child say the word to his or her puppet. (*day*) Ask the class: *Is that my word? ¿Es ésa mi palabra?* Provide corrective feedback, as needed. Then have the child pass the puppet and repeat with other two-phoneme words, such as *so, my, it, eat, me, up,* and *go.*

 Pair ELL learners with more proficient English-speaking peers to carry out the role-playing with the dog puppets.

For additional suggestions on how to meet the needs of children at the Beginning, Intermediate, Advanced, and Advanced-High levels of English proficiency, see pages 184–187.

Center Time

▶ **Center Rotation** Center Time includes teacher-guided activities and independent activities. Refer to the **Learning Centers** on pages 138–139 for independent activity ideas.

 small group 60–90 minutes

ABC Center

☑ **Track children's ability to recognize ABC order.**

Materials index cards

ABC Order Write letters of the alphabet on index cards.

- On each card write four letters of the alphabet.

- On several cards write letters in proper alphabetical order. On the other cards include one letter that is not in alphabetical order. For example: C D E F, K L N M, p q r s, W X Y P.

- Have children sort the cards in two piles: One pile for the letters that are in the correct order; the other pile for the letters that are not in the correct order. Have children identify the letter that is not in the correct order. Ask: **What letter does not belong in that space?** *¿Qué letra no está en el lugar correcto?*

Center Tip

If...children have difficulty remembering letter sequence, **then...** have them refer to the *ABC Big Book*.

Pretend and Learn Center

☑ **Track how well children can retell stories read aloud to them.**

Materials flannel patterns, props

Retell and Act Out Stories Have children act out a story that they have heard.

- Explain to children that they will retell a new story after you read it aloud today

- Display the flannel board patterns for "The Monkey and the Fruit Tree." Have children use the patterns as they retell or act out the story.

- Encourage children to use other props available in the classroom to retell the story.

Center Tip

If...children have difficulty retelling the story, **then...** ask questions and provide clues about story details, such as: **How did Monkey remember the name of the tallest, most beautiful tree?** *¿Cómo recordó el mono el nombre del árbol más alto y bello?*

✓ Learning Goal

Language and Communication
- Child uses newly learned vocabulary daily in multiple contexts.

Emergent Literacy: Reading
- Child enjoys and chooses reading-related activities.

- Child retells or reenacts poems and stories in sequence.

Differentiated Instruction

✋ Extra Support

Pretend and Learn Center

If...children have difficulty retelling "Monkey and the Fruit Tree" in the correct sequence, **then...**prompt children as to which pattern should be used first, next, etc.

⭐ Enrichment

ABC Center

Challenge children to take turns, and say the alphabet in order. The first child will name the first letter of the alphabet, the second child will name the second letter, and so on. Children continue until all letters are named.

Accommodations for 3's

Pretend and Learn Center

If...children have difficulty retelling the story, **then...**ask what kind of animal was in the story and what the animal did.

Focus Question
How can I stay healthy?
¿Cómo puedo mantenerme saludable?

Circle Time

Literacy Time

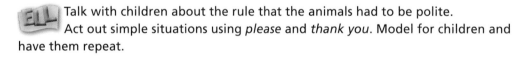
Read Aloud

 Can children answer questions about information read aloud?

Build Background Tell children that you will be reading a make-believe story about animals that live in a beautiful garden.

- Ask: **What kinds of animals would you usually find in a garden?** *¿Qué tipos de animales suelen encontrar en un jardín?* (Accept all reasonable responses.)

Listen for Enjoyment Read aloud "The Monkey and the Fruit Tree"/"*El mono y el árbol frutal*" on *Teacher's Treasure Book* page 339. Act out the story using flannel board patterns (pages 438–439).

- Tell children to listen to what the rabbit, monkey, and squirrel say and do.

- Ask: **What do all the animals eat? How did the animals get the fruit from the trees?** *¿Qué comían los animales? ¿Cómo obtenían los animales la fruta de los árboles?*

Respond to the Story Have children tell how Monkey remembered the name of the tallest tree. Ask: **Why do you think Monkey said his stomach hurt at the end of the story?** *¿Por qué creen que al mono le dolía el estómago al final?*

TIP Use a different voice for each animal.

 Talk with children about the rule that the animals had to be polite. Act out simple situations using *please* and *thank you*. Model for children and have them repeat.

Learn About Letters and Sounds

 Can children identify sounds of letters?

Review the Letters Sing the "ABC Song" with children as you page through the *ABC Big Book*.

- Place animal photos on a table or on an easel ledge.

- Name an animal and have a volunteer find that photo. Have the initial letter and sound identified.

- Have all children write the upper case letter in the air as they say the letter name and sound.

- Repeat for the lower case letter.

- Continue with other photos.

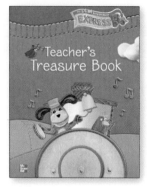
Teacher's Treasure Book page 339

ABC Big Book

Online Math Activity

Children can complete Egg-stremely Equal during computer time or Center Time.

Math Time

Observe and Investigate

 Can children make their own puzzles using shapes?

Discuss Pattern Block Puzzles Display Pattern Block Puzzles 7–10 (*Teacher's Treasure Book* pages 516–517) and discuss them with children.

- Discuss each puzzle. Make a big deal when new puzzles are introduced, as it motivates children.

- Encourage students to experiment with turning and flipping Pattern Blocks to make them fit into the puzzle outlines.

- For reinforcement, suggest children make their own unique puzzles using actual Pattern Blocks, and then trace what they created to "see" the puzzle.

- Ask: *How did you figure out which shapes to use in the puzzles?* *¿Cómo descubrieron las figuras que debían usar para el rompecabezas?*

𝑥𝑥𝑥 Social and Emotional Development

Making Good Choices

 Do children observe physical boundaries?

Being Helpful Display the Dog Puppets and set out drawing paper and crayons. Tell children that one puppet is drawing. Show the puppet drawing. Then while the first dog puppet is drawing, have the second dog puppet lean on the first dog puppet saying, "Move over and give me room to draw."

- Ask: *What would you say to the second puppet if you were the first puppet? What are some other things the second puppet could have done?* *¿Qué le dirían al segundo títere si fueran el primer títere? ¿Qué otras cosas podría haber hecho el segundo títere?*

- Play the song "You're Playing Too Rough"/"*Juegas muy fuerte*" from the Making Good Choices Audio CD. Ask children what the song says about why playing rough is not a good choice.

 Some children may have difficulties following the conversation between the dog puppets. Remind children that you are pretending with the puppets. While role playing, stop and ask: *What did he say?*

✓ **Learning Goal**

Social and Emotional Development
• Child is aware of self in terms of abilities, characteristics and preferences, and respects personal boundaries.

Mathematics
• Child creates two-dimensional shapes; recreates two-dimensional shapes from memory.

Vocabulary

corners	vértices	parts	partes
puzzle	rompecabezas	shape	figura
sides	lados	trace	trazar

Differentiated Instruction

Extra Support
Observe and Investigate
If...children have difficulty making their own puzzles, **then**...draw lines within puzzles to guide children.

Enrichment
Observe and Investigate
Challenge children by having them solve one puzzle as many ways as they can or by allowing pairs to take turns completing a puzzle.

Accommodations for 3's
Observe and Investigate
If...children struggle with Pattern Block Puzzles, **then**...have them explore making their own puzzle with actual Pattern Blocks.

Learning Goals

Social and Emotional Development
• Child is aware of self in terms of abilities, characteristics and preferences, and respects personal boundaries.

Language and Communication
• Child exhibits an understanding of instructional terms used in the classroom.

Mathematics
• Child divides sets from 2 to 10 objects into equal sets, using informal techniques.

Vocabulary

divide objects	dividir objetos
equal	igual
equal parts	partes iguales
share	compartir

Differentiated Instruction

 Extra Support

Math Time

If...children have difficulty identifying equal groups, **then...**use counters to show the groups. Place the counters in each group in a row, one below the other. Have children compare the groups.

 Enrichment

Math Time

Challenge children to divide a container or bag of popcorn into equal parts by dividing the popcorn into smaller containers. Then have all children enjoy the popcorn as a healthy snack.

Math Time

large group · 20 minutes

Language and Communication Skills After you model making two equal groups of counters, ask children to tell what you did using the appropriate math language.

✓ **Can children draw equal groups?**

Talk About Equal Groups Draw two large circles on the board.

• Call on two children to come to the chalkboard. Ask them to draw two equal groups of dots inside the circle using colored chalk.

• Ask the class how they should go about making two equal groups. Children may say one child draws one dot, and the other child draws one dot to show a fair share. Make sure children respect each other's personal space while drawing the dots.

• Ask: *Are these two equal groups? ¿Son iguales estos dos grupos?*

• Then have children work in pairs and make their own equal groups by drawing dots on paper.

✓ **Can children identify equal groups?**

Play I Spy Display *Math and Science Flip Chart*, page 68, "A Nature Scene." Discuss the scene again.

• Point to the trees with apples. Ask: *I spy two groups of apples. Are there equal groups of apples on each tree? Veo, veo... dos grupos de manzanas. ¿Tienen la misma cantidad de manzanas los dos árboles?* (Yes, there are four apples on each tree.) Invite a child to point to the trees.

• Say: *I see two bunnies. Can anyone find another group of bunnies? Are the groups equal? Veo, veo... dos conejos. ¿Alguien ve otro grupo de conejos? ¿Son iguales los grupos?*

• Continue with other items shown on the chart.

ELL Focus on the concept *equal group*. Display 10 crayons and two sheets of paper. Make two equal groups by placing one crayon at a time on each paper using appropriate math language. Have children repeat your actions and language.

Math and Science Flip Chart, page 68

Center Time

Center Rotation Center Time includes teacher-guided activities and independent activities. Refer to the **Learning Centers** on pages 138–139 for independent activity ideas.

small group — 30 minutes

Math and Science Center

  Track children's ability to identify and make equal groups.

Materials Two-color Counters

Equal Blocks Tell children that they will continue to make equal groups.

- Show two groups of counters. One group should have more than the other. Ask: *Are these two groups equal? How do you know? ¿Son iguales estos dos grupos? ¿Cómo lo saben?* Have a volunteer make the groups equal.

- Then give each pair of children a certain number of counters. Have them make equal groups.

Center Tip

If...children need help deciding if your two groups are equal, **then...**place the objects from each group side by side.

Purposeful Play

Observe children appropriately handling classroom materials.

Children choose an open center for free playtime. Encourage respect of each other's space by having a group of children work together at a table making equal groups of items or drawing pictures of equal groups.

Learning Goal

Social and Emotional Development
- Child is aware of self in terms of abilities, characteristics and preferences, and respects personal boundaries.

Language and Communication
- Child names and describes actual or pictured people, places, things, actions, attributes, and events.

Mathematics
- Child divides sets from 2 to 10 objects into equal sets, using informal techniques.

Writing

Recap the day. Have children tell about a make-believe animal they have read about. Ask: *How do you know it's a make-believe animal? What did it do that shows you it is not a real animal? ¿Cómo saben que es un animal de fantasía? ¿Cómo se dan cuenta de que no es un animal real?* Record their answers in a list. Read answers back as you track the print, and emphasize the correspondence between speech and print.

Let's Say Good-Bye

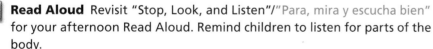

large group — 15 minutes

 Read Aloud Revisit "Stop, Look, and Listen"/"Para, mira y escucha bien" for your afternoon Read Aloud. Remind children to listen for parts of the body.

Home Connection Refer to the Home Connections activities listed in the Resources and Materials chart on page 135. Remind children to tell families about the monkey and the fruit tree. Sing the "Good-Bye Song"/"Hora de ir a casa" as children prepare to leave.

DAY 5

Focus Question

How can I stay healthy?
¿Cómo puedo mantenerme saludable?

 Learning Goals

Social and Emotional Development
• Child is aware of self in terms of abilities, characteristics and preferences, and respects personal boundaries.

Language and Communication
• Child demonstrates an understanding of oral language by responding appropriately.

Emergent Literacy: Reading
• Child blends two phonemes to form a word.

Vocabulary

friends	amigos
seesaw	subibaja
snack	merienda
springs	vueltas
teacher	maestro(a)
trampoline	cama elástica

Differentiated Instruction

 Extra Support

Oral Language and Vocabulary
If...children have difficulty answering the questions, **then...**use picture clues and read the sentence from the rhyme that answers the question. Then have children respond to the question.

⭐ **Enrichment**

Oral Language and Vocabulary
Encourage children to work in pairs. Have pairs choose two sentences from the rhyme to learn and sing to the class.

Let's Start the Day

▶ **Opening Routines and Transition Tips**
For **Opening Routines** and **Transition Tips** turn to pages 178–181 and visit DLMExpressOnline.com for more ideas.

📖 Read **"The Three Little Kittens"/***"Los tres gatitos"* from the *Teacher's Treasure Book,* page 118, for your morning Read Aloud.

Language Time

  large group / 15 minutes

🧍 **Social and Emotional Development** Ask children why it is important to sit in their chairs without kicking their feet.

Oral Language and Vocabulary

✓ **Can children respond to questions appropriately?**

Playing Outside Talk about what children have learned this week about staying healthy. Ask: *What do you know about staying healthy? ¿Qué saben sobre cómo mantenerse sanos?*

● Display *Rhymes and Chants Flip Chart* page 36. Sing "Outdoor Play" with children. Ask: *Where do the children go to play? How do the children get exercise? What do the children eat? Why is taking a nap a good way to stay healthy? ¿Adónde van a jugar los niños? ¿Cómo hacen ejercicio? ¿Qué comen? ¿Por qué creen que dormir la siesta es un buen modo de mantenerse saludable?*

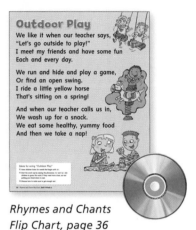

Rhymes and Chants Flip Chart, page 36

Phonological Awareness

✓ **Can children identify at least two phonemes in words?**

Recognize Phonemes Using the *Rhymes and Chants Flip Chart*, sing "Outdoor Play" once more with children. Remind children that every letter has at least one sound.

● Point to the bow in the picture. Have children say the initial sound, /b/. Then have them say the final sound, /ō/. Have children blend the two phonemes to make the word. Repeat with the picture of the shoe.

ELL Show a picture card of a bee. Point to the picture. Model blending the two phonemes that make up the word, /b/ /ē/, *bee*. Have children repeat. Continue with a card showing a key and a card showing a pie.

Center Time

▶ **Center Rotation** Center Time includes teacher-guided activities and independent activities. Refer to the **Learning Centers** on pages 138–139 for independent activity ideas.

 small group 60–90 minutes

Library and Listening Center

	Center Tip
☑ **Encourage children to talk about various ways to exercise to stay healthy.** **Materials** books showing children playing outdoors **Browsing Books on Outdoor Play** Have children browse through books that show children playing outdoors. • Have children choose their favorite picture and describe what is happening. • Ask: **What is the child playing? Is this a good way to stay healthy? Why?** *¿A qué está jugando el niño? ¿Es una buena manera de mantenerse saludable? ¿Por qué?* • Then have children draw a picture of themselves doing some form of outdoor exercise. • Encourage children to explain their choices.	**If...**children have difficulty thinking of something to draw, **then...**have them choose a picture from one of the books and draw themselves doing that exercise.

Writer's Center

	Center Tip
☑ **Track the use of action words as children tell about their pictures.** **Materials** drawing paper, crayons **Our Play Book** Have children write a book about what they like to do outside, such as play games, exercise, or go on a picnic. • Have children draw a picture of one thing they do outside. Have them write their first name at the top of the page. • Ask: **What word can you use to tell about your picture?** *¿Qué palabra podrían usar para describir su dibujo?* Encourage children to write the word or phrase that tells about their picture such as *skip, jump,* or *run.* You can write the word on a card and children can copy it onto their papers. • Fasten the pages together to make a class Play Book.	**If...**children have difficulty thinking of what they like to do, **then...**generate a list of activities with the children. Then have them choose one to illustrate.

✓ **Learning Goal**

Language and Communication
• Child names and describes actual or pictured people, places, things, actions, attributes, and events.

Emergent Literacy: Reading
• Child enjoys and chooses reading-related activities.

Emergent Literacy: Writiing
• Child uses scribbles, shapes, pictures, symbols, and letters to represent language.

• Child experiments with and uses some writing conventions when writing or dictating.

Science
• Child identifies and participates in exercises and activities to enhance physical fitness.

Differentiated Instruction

 Extra Support
Writer's Center
If...children have difficulty copying your words or writing their own, **then...**write the word or phrase they dictate.

 Enrichment
Writer's Center
Challenge children to make up a sentence about their picture. Encourage children to write or dictate their sentences.

Accommodations for 3's
Library and Listening Center
If...children have difficulty describing a picture, **then...**describe what is happening in each picture and ask children to choose their favorite picture.

Focus Question
How can I stay healthy?
¿Cómo puedo mantenerme saludable?

Circle Time

Literacy Time

 large group   15 minutes

📖 Read Aloud

✓ **Can children describe and use pictures to construct meaning?**

Build Background Tell children that you will be rereading the story about Jamal.

● Ask: *What did we learn about Jamal?* *¿Qué aprendimos sobre Jamal?*

Listen for Understanding Display *Jamal's Busy Day*, and read the title.

● Reread *Jamal's Busy Day*. Stop and have children talk about how Jamal stays healthy.

● Ask: *What does Jamal do to relax? What game does he play with his dad? How does that help him stay healthy?* *¿Qué hace Jamal para descansar? ¿A qué juega con su papá? ¿Cómo lo ayuda esto a mantenerse sano?*

Respond and Connect Have children connect their new learning to their daily lives. Ask: *Do you have breakfast in the morning like Jamal does? What do you do after school? Do you play outside? Do you like to play games inside?* *¿Desayunan por la mañana como Jamal? ¿Qué hacen después de terminar las clases? ¿Juegan afuera? ¿Les gusta jugar adentro?*

 TIP Be sure children can use picture details to tell more about what Jamal does during his busy day.

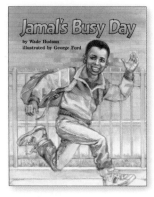

Jamal's Busy Day
El intenso día de Jamal

Learn About Letters and Sounds

✓ **Can children identify letters and sounds?**

Review Letters Play a matching game with children.

● Give each child an *ABC Picture Card*.

● Say a word. Have the child who is holding the letter that begins that word stand up. The child says the beginning sound as he or she shows the letter card to the rest of the class.

● Repeat with other letters. If time permits, have children exchange letters with classmates and play again.

ELL Provide words that include sounds common to both languages students are learning to speak.

For additional suggestions on how to meet the needs of children at the Beginning, Intermediate, Advanced, and Advanced-High levels of English proficiency, see pages 184–187.

ABC Picture Cards

large group 15 minutes

Building Blocks

Online Math Activity

Children can complete Egg-stremely Equal during computer time or Center Time.

Math Time

Observe and Investigate

Can children identify equal parts of a whole?

Folding Shapes Cut out large paper squares. Hold up a square and say: ***This is a whole square.*** *Este es un cuadrado entero.* Then ask children to watch carefully as you fold each square.

- Fold one square in half to show equal parts. Fold the other square into two different-sized parts. Hold up both squares.
- Ask: ***Which shows equal parts? What can you say about the equal parts?*** *¿Cuál tiene partes iguales? ¿Qué pueden decir sobre esas partes iguales?* (They are the same size.) ***If you fold a shape into two parts, will the parts always be equal?*** *Si doblan una figura en dos, ¿serán siempre iguales las partes?* (No, it depends on how the paper is folded.)
- Distribute paper squares to children and have them practice folding the square into equal parts.

ELL Continue to focus on the concept of equal parts. Hold up a straw. Say: ***I want to cut this straw into 2 pieces the same size.*** Show children how you fold the straw in 2 equal parts and then cut it. Say: ***These two parts are the same size. They are equal parts.*** Have children repeat the phrase "equal parts."

large group 15 minutes

Making Good Choices Flip Chart, page 36

Social and Emotional Development

Making Good Choices

Do children show a desire to be respectful of each other's space?

Being Helpful Display *Making Good Choices Flip Chart* page 36, "How Do I Act in Class?"

- Point to the flip chart illustrations. Ask: ***What did we learn about how to use our bodies in class? Do we kick our feet? Do we lean on our friend? Do we bother other children when they are working?*** *¿Qué aprendimos sobre cómo debemos usar nuestro cuerpo en clase? ¿Debemos dar patadas? ¿Debemos reclinarnos sobre nuestros amigos? ¿Debemos molestar a otros niños cuando están trabajando?*
- Have children discuss other ways to be respectful.

Learning Goal

Social and Emotional Development
- Child is aware of self in terms of abilities, characteristics and preferences, and respects personal boundaries.

Language and Communication
- Child exhibits an understanding of instructional terms used in the classroom.

Mathematics
- Child creates two-dimensional shapes; recreates two-dimensional shapes from memory.

Vocabulary

blocks	bloques	pattern	patrón
shape	figura	whole	entero
equal parts	partes iguales		

Differentiated Instruction

Extra Support

Observe and Investigate

If...children have difficulty identifying equal parts of a whole, **then...**fold a square and cut it apart to show that the parts match (are equal).

Enrichment

Observe and Investigate

Challenge children to fold a paper plate in half then draw a line down the fold to show equal parts. Have them color each part a different color.

Accommodations for 3's

Observe and Investigate

If...children struggle identifying equal parts of a whole, **then...**place a strip of paper on the table. Say: ***This is one whole.*** *Esto es una tira entera.* Fold the strip into 2 equal parts and fold another strip into 2 unequal parts. Model how to identify the strip with 2 equal parts.

Focus Question
How can I stay healthy?
¿Cómo puedo mantenerme saludable?

large group   20 minutes

Outdoor Play

Personal Safety Skills Model how to properly use any indoor or outdoor equipment.

Oral Language and Academic Vocabulary

Can children show understanding of healthy habits?

Be Healthy Remind children that they learned about ways to stay healthy.

- Ask: *What can you eat to stay healthy? What exercise can you do to stay healthy?* *¿Qué pueden comer para mantenerse saludables? ¿Qué ejercicios pueden hacer para mantenerse saludables?*

- Ask: *Why is resting or sleeping a good way to stay healthy too?* *¿Por qué descansar y dormir también los ayuda a mantenerse saludables?*

- Have children discuss other healthy habits regarding personal hygiene.

Move and Learn

Can children show mastery of gross motor skills?

Let's Run and Jump Tell children that they will move their bodies in different ways to get exercise. Provide a large open space in the room, in the gym or outdoors. Explain to children that they will move their bodies any way they want and then stop. Model walking and swinging arms. Then have children move as you say: *We are moving, moving, moving our bodies. Now stop.* *Movemos, movemos, movemos nuestro cuerpo. Ahora, nos detenemos.*

- Then have children run or jump. Model how to run in place, beginning slowly and then running faster. Then have children run in place, or run to a specific spot and stop on your signal. Have children rest after each activity.

- You may continue today or another time by having children jump as high as they can, jump and turn around, or jump as far as they can.

- Continue with other movements such as hopping or taking giant steps.

TIP Modify activities according to the needs of individual children.

ELL Display the Unit 8 Oral Language Development Card photos to discuss other healthy habits with children. Use the vocabulary for each photo as you help describe what is happening. Have children repeat the vocabulary words.

Learning Goals

Social and Emotional Development
- Child is aware of self in terms of abilities, characteristics and preferences, and respects personal boundaries.

Science
- Child practices personal hygiene skills independently (for example, washes hands, blows nose, covers mouth, brushes teeth).
- Child recognizes and selects healthy foods.
- Child identifies and participates in exercises and activities to enhance physical fitness.

Physical Development
- Child coordinates body movements in a variety of locomotive activities (such as walking, jumping, running, hopping, skipping, climbing).
- Child engages in a sequence of movements to perform a task.

Vocabulary

healthy	saludable	move	moverse
outdoor	afuera	play	jugar

Differentiated Instruction

 Extra Support

Move and Learn

If...children have difficulty hopping on one foot, **then...**let them just jump. Provide positive feedback as they move.

 Enrichment

Move and Learn

Make a straight line with masking tape on the floor or a chalk line outside on the playground. Have children walk on the line, then walk on tiptoes on the line.

 Special Needs

Delayed Motor Development

Adapt the Outdoor Play activity by giving the child an alternative to running and jumping such as beating a drum, ringing a bell, or moving her/his wrist (attach jingle bells to her/his wrist with an elastic band).

Center Time

▶ **Center Rotation** Center Time includes teacher-guided activities and independent activities. Refer to the **Learning Centers** on pages 138–139 for independent activity ideas.

 small group 30 minutes

Learning Goal

Social and Emotional Development
• Child is aware of self in terms of abilities, characteristics and preferences, and respects personal boundaries.

Language and Communication
• Child names and describes actual or pictured people, places, things, actions, attributes, and events.

Social Studies
• Child identifies common areas and features of home, school, and community.

Construction Center

Center Tip

If...children need more space to build, **then...**arrange classroom furniture in a manner that allows children to have their own space.

✓ **Monitor children as they make equipment for a playground.**

Materials empty boxes, blocks, other art materials

Build a Playground Tell children that they will use blocks, empty boxes and other art materials to build a pretend playground.

● Have children work with a partner. Ask: *What kind of things would you like to see in your outdoor playground? Would you like a seesaw? Would you like a swing set? Would you like a slide?* *¿Qué les gustaría tener en su patio? ¿Un subibaja? ¿Columpios? ¿Un tobogán?*

● Have pairs make one piece of equipment using any available materials.

● Have children describe what they made. Then point out how all the "equipment" makes a wonderful big playground.

Writing

Recap the day and week. Say: *Tell me one thing you learned about how to stay healthy.* *Díganme una cosa que hayan aprendido sobre cómo mantenerse sanos.* Record their answers on chart paper. Share the pen with children as you write. Have each child write his/her name beside the entry.

Purposeful Play

✓ **Observe children's awareness of personal boundaries.**

Children choose an open center for free playtime. Encourage children to sit together and draw a picture of a playground.

Let's Say Good-Bye

 large group  15 minutes

 Read Aloud Revisit "The Three Little Kittens"/"*Los tres gatitos*" for your afternoon Read Aloud. Remind children to listen for sounds that real cats make.

 Home Connection Refer to the Home Connections activities listed in the Resources and Materials chart on page 135. Remind children to tell families what they learned this week about staying healthy. Sing the "Good-Bye Song"/"*Hora de ir a casa*" as children prepare to leave.

In general, the purpose of assessing young children in the early childhood classroom is to collect information necessary to make important decisions about their developmental and educational needs. Because assessment is crucial to making informed teaching decisions, it is necessarily a vital component of **DLM Early Childhood Express.** The guidelines and forms found online allow the teacher to implement assessment necessary in the pre-kindergarten classroom.

Effective assessment is an ongoing process that always enhances opportunities for optimal growth, development, and learning. The process of determining individual developmental and educational needs tailors early childhood education practices and provides a template for setting individual and program goals.

Pre-kindergarten assessment should be authentic; that is, it should be a natural, environmental extension of the classroom. Assessments should be incorporated into classroom activities whenever possible, not completed as separate, pull-out activities in which the teacher evaluates the student one-on-one. Whenever possible, assessment should evaluate children's real knowledge in the process of completing real activities. For example, observing children as they equally distribute snacks would be a better assessment of their ability to make groups than observing an exercise in which children group counters would be.

It is also important to note that assessments should be administered over time, as environmental influences can greatly impact single outcomes. If a pre-kindergarten child is tired or ill, for example, the child may not demonstrate knowledge of a skill that has actually been mastered. It is also important to consider the length of assessment for children of this age, as attention spans are still developing and can vary greatly based on environmental influences. Most assessments should be completed within half an hour.

If possible, use multiple types of assessment for the same content area when working with pre-kindergarten children. Some children may be able to demonstrate mastery kinesthetically if they are not able to use expressive language well; others may not process auditory instruction adequately, but will be able to complete an assessment after observing someone model the task. It is vital that the assessment process should never make the child anxious or scared.

Informal Assessment

INFORMAL assessments rely heavily on observational and work-sampling techniques that continually focus on child performance, processes, and product over selected periods of time and in a variety of contexts.

ANECDOTAL assessments are written descriptions that provide a short, objective account of an event or an incident. Only the facts are reported—where, what, when, and how. Anecdotal records are especially helpful when trying to understand a child's behavior or use of skills. These recordings can be used to share the progress of individual children and to develop and individualize curriculum.

The Anecdotal Observational Record Form can be used at any time to document an individual child's progress toward a goal or signs indicating the need for developmental or medical evaluation. Observations can reflect the focused skills for the week, but are not limited to those skills. You may pair the form with video or audio recordings of the child to complete an anecdotal record.

Anecdotal Observational Record Form

CHECKLISTS are lists of skills or behaviors arranged into disciplines or developmental domains and are used to determine how a child exhibits the behaviors or skills listed. Teachers can quickly and easily observe groups of children and check the behaviors or skills each child is demonstrating at the moment.

Weekly Assessments measure progress toward specific guidelines that are addressed in the weekly curriculum. The Performance Assessment Checklist measures progress toward the guidelines of the entire curriculum. It is intended to be used three times per year.

Weekly Assessment

Performance Assessment Checklist

When using either type of checklist, it is important to remember that the skills and behaviors on the list are only guidelines. Each child is unique and has his or her own developmental timetable. It is also important to remember that the checklist only documents the presence or absence of a specific skill or behavior during the time of observation. It does not necessarily mean the skill is consistently present or lacking, though consistency may be noted when the skill has been observed over time.

PORTFOLIO assessments are collections of thoughtfully selected work samples, or artifacts, and accompanying reflections indicative of the child's learning experiences, efforts, and progress toward and/or attainment of established curriculum goals. They are an authentic, performance-based method to allow teachers to analyze progress over time. As children choose work samples for their portfolios, they become involved in their own learning and assessment and begin to develop the concept of evaluating their own work.

Although early childhood activities tend to focus on processes as opposed to products, there are numerous opportunities to collect samples of children's work. Items to collect include drawings, tracings, cuttings, attempts to print their names, and paintings. You may also include informal assessments of a child's ability to recognize letters, shapes, numbers, and rhyming words.

Formal Assessment

FORMAL assessments involve the use of standardized tests. They are administered in a prescribed manner and may require completion within a specified amount of time. Standardized tests result in scores that are usually compared to the scores of a normative group. These tests generally fall into the following categories: achievement tests, readiness tests, developmental screening tests, intelligence tests, and diagnostic tests.

Assessing Children with Special Needs

Children with special needs may require a more thorough initial assessment, more frequent on-going assessments, and continuous adaptation of activities. Assessment is essentially the first task for the teacher or caregiver in developing the individualized instruction program required for children with disabilities.

Assessing Children Who Are English Language Learners

Whenever possible, assessments should be given in both the child's first language and in English.

Celebrate the Unit

Essential Question

Why is healthy food and exercise good for me?

Health Fair

Organize a Health Fair in the Classroom

- Before the event, set up stations where children can perform simple exercises, such as a Jumping Station for jumping jacks, a Running Station for running in place, and a Stretching Station for bending and stretching up high.

- Organize the classroom into four areas, focusing each area on one of the weekly themes for the unit: Being Healthy, Healthy Foods, Healthy Fun, and Staying Healthy. In each area, display the appropriate focus question and have children display examples of their completed work, such as:

  healthy habits posters

  fruit and vegetable stands

  streamers in vegetable colors

  moveable paper dolls

  writing pieces, drawings, and other creative work

- Have partners walk from area to area and take turns describing their work to each other. Encourage them to tell each other what they learned about staying healthy.

- After viewing their work, have partners take turns at the exercise stations. Provide a simple timer that children can use to time each other for one or two minutes at each station.

- Provide nutritional snacks for children to enjoy after their exercise, such as low-fat yogurt with toppings (seeds or dried fruit), cut vegetables, low-sugar juice and water. Check for food allergies before serving snacks.

Evaluate and Inform

- Review the informal observation notes you recorded for each child during the four weeks of the unit. Identify areas in which individual children will need additional support.

- Send a summary of your observation notes home with children. Encourage parents to respond to the summary with questions or comments.

- Review dated samples of children's work in their portfolios. Copy some of these samples to send home to families along with the observation summary.

- Send home the Unit 8 My Library Book, *Healthy Kids*, for children to read with their families.

Celebrar la unidad

Pregunta esencial
¿Por qué me conviene consumir alimentos saludables y hacer ejercicio?

Feria de la Salud

Organice en el salón una Feria de la Salud

- Antes del evento, coloque estaciones donde los niños puedan realizar ejercicios sencillos, como una Estación de brincos para saltar estirando las extremidades; una Estación de Carreras para correr sin avanzar; y una Estación de estiramiento para inclinarse y estirarse hacia arriba y abajo.

- Organice a la clase en cuatro áreas, asignándole a cada área uno de los temas semanales de la unidad: Estar sano, Alimentos saludables, Diversiones saludables y Mantenerse sanos. En cada área, presente la pregunta de enfoque correspondiente y pídales a los niños que exhiban ejemplos de sus trabajos completados, como:

   afiches de hábitos saludables

   puestos de frutas y verduras

   serpentinas con colores de verduras

   muñecas movibles de papel

   piezas de escritura, dibujos y otros trabajos creativos

- Organice a los niños para que vayan en parejas de un área a otra y se turnen para describir mutuamente su trabajo. Anime a los compañeros de cada pareja para que platiquen entre ellos lo que aprendieron sobre cómo mantenerse sanos.

- Después de revisar su trabajo, pídales a los compañeros de cada pareja que se turnen en las estaciones de ejercicio. Deles un cronómetro sencillo que puedan usar para medir uno o dos minutos de ejercicio individual en cada estación.

- Deles a los niños bocadillos nutritivos para que los disfruten después de sus ejercicios, como yogurt bajo en grasa con ingredientes extra (semillas o frutas secas), verduras cortadas, jugos bajos en azúcar y agua. Antes de servir los bocadillos, verifique que no haya alergias a ciertos alimentos entre la clase.

Evaluar e informar

- ✓ Revise las observaciones informales que anotó para cada niño durante las cuatro semanas de la unidad. Identifique las áreas en las que cada niño podría requerir un apoyo adicional.

- ✓ Deles a los padres de los niños el resumen respectivo de sus observaciones. Insístales que respondan a este informe con preguntas o comentarios.

- ✓ Revise las muestras fechadas que hay en el portafolios de trabajo de cada niño. Haga copias de algunas de estas muestras para que las vean sus padres junto con el resumen de observaciones.

- ✓ Deles a los niños el librito de la Unidad 8, *Niños sanos,* para leer con sus familias.

Appendix

About the Authors

NELL K. DUKE, ED.D., is Professor of Teacher Education and Educational Psychology and Co-Director of the Literacy Achievement Research Center at Michigan State University. Nell Duke's expertise lies in early literacy development, particularly among children living in poverty, and integrating literacy into content instruction. She is the recipient of a number of awards for her research and is co-author of several books including *Literacy and the Youngest Learner: Best Practices for Educators of Children from Birth to 5* and *Beyond Bedtime Stories: A Parent's Guide to Promoting Reading, Writing, and Other Literacy Skills From Birth to 5.*

DOUG CLEMENTS is SUNY Distinguished Professor of Education at the University of Buffalo, SUNY. Previously a preschool and kindergarten teacher, Clements currently researchs the learning and teaching of early mathematics and computer applications. He has published over 100 research studies, 8 books, 50 chapters, and 250 additional publications, including co-authoring the reports of President Bush's National Mathematics Advisory Panel and the National Research Council's book on early mathematics. He has directed twenty projects funded by the National Science Foundation and Department of Education's Institute of Education Sciences.

JULIE SARAMA Associate Professor at the University at Buffalo (SUNY), has taught high school mathematics and computer science, gifted and talented classes, and early childhood mathematics. She directs several projects funded by the National Science Foundation and the Institute of Education Sciences. Author of over 50 refereed articles, 4 books, 30 chapters, 20 computer programs, and more than 70 additional publications, she helped develop the Building Blocks and Investigations curricula and the award-winning Turtle Math. Her latest book is *Early Childhood Mathematics Education Research: Learning Trajectories for Young Children.*

WILLIAM TEALE is Professor of Education at the University of Illinois at Chicago. Author of over one hundred publications on early literacy learning, the intersection of technology and literacy education, and children's literature, he helped pioneer research in emergent literacy. Dr. Teale has worked in the area of early childhood education with schools, libraries, and other organizations across the country and internationally. He has also directed three U.S. Department of Education-funded Early Reading First projects that involve developing model preschool literacy curricula for four-year-old children from urban, low-income settings in Chicago.

Contributing Authors

Kimberly Brenneman, PhD, is an Assistant Research Professor of Psychology at Rutgers University. She is also affiliated with the Rutgers Center for Cognitive Science (RuCCS) and the National Institute for Early Education Research (NIEER). Brenneman is co-author of *Preschool Pathways to Science (PrePS): Facilitating Scientific Ways of Thinking, Talking, Doing, and Understanding* and is an educational advisor for PBS's *Sid the Science Kid* television show and website. Research interests include the development of scientific reasoning and methods to improve instructional practices that support science and mathematics learning in preschool.

Peggy Cerna is an independent Early Childhood Consultant. She was a bilingual teacher for 15 years and then served as principal of the Rosita Valley Literacy Academy, a Pre-Kindergarten through Grade 1 school in Eagle Pass, Texas. Cerna then opened Lucy Read Pre-Kindergarten Demonstration School in Austin, Texas, which had 600 Pre-Kindergarten students. During her principalship at Lucy Read, Cerna built a strong parental community with the collaboration of the University of Texas, AmeriCorps, and Austin Community College. Her passion for early literacy drove her to create book clubs where parents were taught how to read books to their children.

Dan Cieloha is an educator with more than 30 years' experience in creating, implementing, and evaluating experientially based learning materials, experiences, and environments for young children. He believes that all learners must be actively and equitably involved in constructing, evaluating, and sharing what they learn. He has spearheaded the creation and field-testing of a variety of learning materials including *You & Me: Building Social Skills in Young Children*. He is also president of the Partnership for Interactive Learning, a leading nonprofit organization dedicated to the development of children's social and thinking skills.

Paula A. Jones, M.Ed., is an Early Childhood Consultant at the state and national levels. As a former Early Childhood Director for the Lubbock Independent School District, she served as the Head Start Director and co-founded three of their four Early Childhood campuses which also became a model design and Best Practices Program for the Texas Education Agency. She was a contributing author for the first Texas Prekindergarten Guidelines, served as president for the Texas Association of Administrators and Supervisors of Programs for Young Children, and is a 2010 United Way Champions for Children Award winner.

Bobbie Sparks is a retired educator who has taught biology and middle school science as well as being the K-12 district science consultant for a suburban district. At Harris County Department of Education she served as the K-12 science consultant in Professional Development. During her career as K-12 science consultant, Sparks worked with teachers at all grade levels to revamp curriculum to meet the Texas science standards. She served on Texas state committees to develop the TEKS standards as well as committees to develop items for tests for teacher certification in science.

Rita Abrams is a composer, lyricist, educator, and author whose music has won two Emmy Awards, multiple ASCAP Awards, and a variety of others including Parents' Choice, American Education Foundation, and Associated Press. As a teacher she sang her international hit, "Mill Valley," with the Strawberry Point School Third Grade Class. Since then, Abrams has continued to blend her classical music background, special education graduate work, and early childhood teaching experience into a prolific recording career including myriad children's albums, videos and film scores. She also creates musical theatre for both children and adults.

Opening Routines

Below are a few suggested routines to use for beginning your day with your class. You can rotate through them, or use one for a while before trying a new approach. You may wish to develop your own routines by mixing and matching ideas from the suggestions given.

1. Days of the Week

Ask children what day of the week it is. When they respond, tell them that you are going to write a sentence that tells everyone what day of the week it is. Print "Today is Monday." on the board. If you have a helper chart, have children assist you in finding the name of the day's helper. Print: "Today's helper is Miguel." Ask the helper to come forward and find the Letter Tiles or ABC Picture Cards that spell his or her name.

As the year progresses, you might want to have the helper find the letters that spell the day of the week. Eventually some children may be able to copy the entire sentence with Letter Tiles or ABC Picture Cards.

Mm moon | **Ii** iguana icicle | **Gg** giraffe girl | **Uu** umbrella unicycle | **Ee** egg eagle | **Ll** leaf

2. Calendar Search

Print "Today is _____." on the board. Ask children to help you fill in the blank. Print the day of the week in the blank. Invite children to look at the calendar to determine today's date. Write the date under the sentence that tells what day of the week it is. Invite children to clap out the syllables of both the sentence and the date.

Review the days of the week and the months of the year using the "Days of the Week Song"/"Canción de los dias de la semana" and the "Months of the year"/ "Los meses del año."

Ask children what day of the week it was yesterday. When they respond, ask them what day it is today. Place a seasonal sticker on today's date. Have children follow your lead and recite "Yesterday was Monday, September 12. Today is Tuesday, September 13. Tomorrow will be Wednesday, September 14."

3. Feelings

Make happy- and sad-faced puppets for each child by cutting yellow circles from construction paper and drawing happy and sad faces on them. Laminate the faces, and glue them to tongue depressors. Cover two large coffee cans. On one can glue a happy face, and write the sentence "I feel happy today." Glue the sad face to the second can, and write the sentence "I feel sad today."

Give each child a happy- and a sad-faced puppet. Encourage children to tell how they feel today and to hold up the appropriate puppet. Encourage children to come forward and place their puppets in the can that represents their feelings. Later in the year you can add puppets to represent other emotions.

You can vary this activity by using a graph titled "How I Feel Today"/"Como me siento hoy." Have children place their puppets in the appropriate column on the graph instead of in the cans.

4. Pledge of Allegiance/ Moment of Silence

Have children locate the United States flag. Recite the Pledge of Allegiance to the U.S. flag. Then allow a minute for a moment of silence.

Discuss these activities with children, allowing them to volunteer reasons the Pledge of Allegiance is said and other places they have seen the Pledge recited.

5. Coming to Circle

Talk with children about being part of a class family. Tell children that as part of a class family they will work together, learn together, respect each other, help each other, and play together. Explain that families have rules so that jobs get done and everyone stays safe. Let children know they will learn rules for their classroom. One of those rules is how they will come together for circle. Sing "This is the Way We Come to Circle" (to the tune of "This is the Way We Wash Our Clothes").

This is the way we come to circle.
Come to circle, come to circle.
This is the way we come to circle,
So early in the morning.

This is the way we sit right down,
Sit right down, sit right down.
This is the way we sit right down,
So early in the morning.

This is the way we fold our hands,
Fold our hands, fold our hands.
This is the way we fold our hands,
So early in the morning.

Transition Tips

Sing songs or chants such as those listed below while transitioning between activities:

1. I Am Now in Pre-K

To the tune of "I'm a Little Teapot"

I am now in Pre-K,
I can learn.
I can listen. I can take a turn.
When the teacher says so,
I can play.
Choose a center and together we'll play.

2. Did You Clean Up?

To the tune of "Are You Sleeping, Are You Sleeping, Brother John?"

Did you clean up?
Did you clean up?
Please make sure.
Please make sure.
Everything is picked up.
Everything is picked up.
Please. Thank you!
Please. Thank you!

Chant: Red, Yellow, Green
Red, yellow, green
Stop, change, go
Red, yellow, green
Stop, change, go
Green says yes.
And red says no.
Yellow says everybody wait in a row.
Red, yellow, green
Stop, change, go
Red, yellow, green
Stop, change, go

3. The Five Senses Song

To the tune of "If You're Happy and You Know It"

I can see with my eyes every day (clap clap)
I can see with my eyes every day (clap clap)
I can see with my eyes
I can see with my eyes
I can see with my eyes every day (clap clap)
(Repeat with smell with my nose, hear with my ears, feel with my hands, and taste with my mouth.)

4. Eat More Vegetables

To the tune of "Row, Row, Row Your Boat"

Eat, eat, eat more,
Eat more vegetables.
Carrots, carrots, carrots, carrots
Eat more vegetables.
(Repeat with broccoli, lettuce, celery, and spinach.)

5. Circle Time

To the tune of "Here We Go 'Round the Mulberry Bush"

This is the way we come to circle
Come to circle, come to circle.
This is the way we come to circle
So early in the morning.

This is the way we sit right down,
Sit right down, sit right down.
This is the way we sit right down,
So early in the morning.

Play a short game such as one of the following to focus children's attention:

Name That Fruit!

Say: *It's red on the outside and white on the inside. It rhymes with chapel!*

Children answer, "Apple!" and then repeat twice, "Apple/Chapel."

Repeat with other fruits, such as cherry and banana.

I Spy

Use a flashlight to focus on different letters and words in the classroom. Have children identify them.

Monkey See Monkey Do

Choose one child to be the monkey leader. He or she will act out a motion such as twist, jump, clap, or raise hand, and the rest of the monkeys say the word and copy the motion.

Let's Play Pairs

Distribute one *ABC Picture Card* to each child. Draw letters from an additional set of cards. The child who has the matching letter identifies it and goes to the center of his or her choice.

That's My Friend!

Take children's name cards with their pictures from the wall and distribute making sure no one gets his or her own name. When you call a child's name, she or he has to say something positive about the child on the card and end with "That's my friend!"

Name Game

Say: *If your name begins with ____, you may choose a center.* Have the child say his or her name as he or she gets up. Repeat the child's name, emphasizing the beginning sound.

Center Management

Learning Centers provide children with additional opportunities to practice or extend each lesson's skills and concepts either individually or in small groups. The activities and materials that are explored in the centers not only promote oral language but also help develop children's social skills as they work together. The use of these Learning Centers encourages children to explore their surroundings and make their own choices.

Teacher's Role

The Learning Centers allow time for you to:

- Observe children's exploration of the centers.

- Assess children's understanding of the skills and concepts being taught.

- Provide additional support and encouragement to children who might be having difficulty with specific concepts or skills. If a child is having difficulty, model the correct approach.

Classroom Setup

The materials and activities in the centers should support what children are learning. Multiple experiences are necessary for children's comprehension. The centers should also engage them in learning by providing hands-on experiences. Every time children visit a center and practice skills or extend concepts being taught in the lessons, they are likely to broaden their understanding or discover something new.

In order to support children's learning, the materials and activities in the Learning Centers should change every week. It is important that all the children have a chance to explore every center throughout each week. Be sure they rotate to different centers and do not focus on only one activity. You might also consider adding new materials to the centers as the week progresses. This will encourage children to expand on their past work. Modify or add activities or materials based on your classroom needs.

It is crucial that children know what is expected of them in each center. To help children understand the expectation at each center, display an "I can" statement with an illustration or photograph of a student completing the activity. Discuss these expectations with children in advance, and reinforce them as needed. These discussions might include reviewing your typical classroom rules and talking about the limited number of children allowed in each center. Remind them that they may work individually or in small groups.

Library and Listening Center

Children should feel free throughout the day to explore books and other printed materials. Create a comfortable reading area in the room, and fill it with as many children's books as possible. Include a number of informational books that tell why things happen and books of rhymes, poems, and songs, as well as storybooks and simple alphabet books.

Before beginning each unit in the program, bring in books about the specific concepts or themes in a unit. Encourage children to bring in books they have enjoyed and would like to share with classmates. Even though they may not be actually reading, have children visit the area often. Here they can practice their book handling, apply their growing knowledge of print awareness, and look at pictures and talk about them. Have them read the books to you or to classmates.

Big Book literature selections from the program have been recorded and are available as part of the *Listening Library Audio CDs*. After each literature reading, encourage children to listen to the recordings. Provide CD players that work both with and without earphones. This way, individual children may listen to selections without disturbing the rest of the class. You will also be able to play the recordings for the whole class, if you choose. Encourage children to record their own stories and then share these stories with their classmates.

As you set up the Learning Centers, here are a few ideas you might want to implement in your classroom.

- Create a separate Workshop Center sign-up chart for children to use when choosing a center to explore.

- Provide an area for children who want to be alone to read or to simply reflect on the day's activities.

- Separate loud areas and quiet areas.

- Hang posters or art at eye level for the children.

- Place on shelves materials, such as books or art supplies, that are easily accessible to the children.

English Language Learners

Teaching the English Language Learner

Stages of English-Language Proficiency

An effective learning environment is an important goal of all educators. In a supportive environment, all English learners have the opportunity to participate and to learn. The materials in this guide are designed to support children while they are acquiring English, allowing them to develop English-language reading skills and the fluency they need to achieve in the core content areas as well.

This guide provides direction in supporting children in four stages of English proficiency: Beginning, Intermediate, Advanced, and Advanced-High. While children at a beginning level by definition know little English and will probably have difficulty comprehending English, by the time they progress to the intermediate or early advanced levels of English acquisition, their skills in understanding more complex language structures will have increased. These stages can be described in general terms as follows:

BEGINNING AND INTERMEDIATE Children identified at these levels of English-language proficiency demonstrate dramatic growth. During these stages, children progress from having no receptive or productive English to possessing a basic command of English. They are learning to comprehend and produce one- or two-word responses to questions, are moving to phrases and simple sentences using concrete and immediate topics, and are learning to interact in a limited fashion with text that has been taught. They progress to responding with increasing ease to more varied communication tasks using learned material, comprehending a sequence of information on familiar topics, producing basic statements and asking questions on familiar subjects, and interacting with a variety of print. Some basic errors are found in their use of English syntax and grammar.

ADVANCED Children who have reached the Advanced level of English-language proficiency have good comprehension of overall meaning and are beginning to demonstrate increased comprehension of specific details and concepts. They are learning to respond in expanded sentences, are interacting more independently with a variety of text, and in using newly acquired English vocabulary to communicate ideas orally and in writing. They demonstrate fewer errors in English grammar and syntax than at the beginning and early intermediate levels.

ADVANCED-HIGH Children who are identified at this level of English-language proficiency demonstrate consistent comprehension of meaning, including implied and nuanced meaning, and are learning the use of idiomatic and figurative language. They are increasingly able to respond using detail in compound and complex sentences and sustain conversation in English. They are able to use standard grammar with few errors and show an understanding of conventions of formal and informal usage.

It is important to provide an instructional scaffold for phonemic awareness, phonics, words structure, language structures, comprehension strategies and skills, and grammar, usage, and mechanics so that children can successfully learn to read while advancing along the continuum of English acquisition. For example, at the Beginning level, you might ask children for *yes* or *no* answers when answering questions about selection comprehension or grammar. Children at the Advanced-High level should be asked to provide answers in complete and expanded sentences. By the time children achieve an Advanced level, their knowledge of English will be more sophisticated because they are becoming more adept at comprehending English and using techniques such as making inferences or using persuasive language.

The following charts illustrate how to use sentence stems with children at each level of English-language proficiency:

Teaching Sentence Stems

- Write the sentence stems on the board, chart paper, or sentence strips. Choose stems that are appropriate for the four general levels of English proficiency.

- Model using the sentence stem(s) for the comprehension strategy or skill.

- Read each phrase as you insert the appropriate words to express an idea. Have children repeat the sentences after you. For Beginning and Intermediate children, use the stems within the questions you ask them.

Linguistic Pattern: *I predict that* _____.

Beginning	Intermediate	Advanced	Advanced-High
Simple questions about the text. Yes-or-no responses or responses that allow children to point to an object or picture.	Simple questions about the text which allow for one- or two-word responses or give children two options for a response to select from.	Questions that elicit a short response or a complete simple sentence using the linguistic pattern.	Have children make predictions on their own. Children should use the linguistic pattern and respond with a complete complex sentence.

Practicing Sentence Stems

- To give children multiple opportunities to generate the language they have just been taught, have them work in pairs or small groups and utilize cooperative learning participation strategies to facilitate this communicative practice.

- Pair children one level of proficiency above or below the other. For example, have Beginning children work with Intermediate level children.

- Use differentiated prompts to elicit the responses that incorporate the linguistic patterns and structures for the different proficiency levels. See the following sample of prompts and responses.

Beginning	Intermediate	Advanced	Advanced-High
Do you predict _____? *Yes/No*	Do you predict _____ or _____? *I predict* _____.	What do you predict _____? *I predict* _____.	Give a prediction about _____. *I predict* _____.

- Select some common cooperative learning participation strategies to teach to children. Once they have learned some language practice activities, they can move quickly into the various routines. See the examples on the next page.

English Language Learners

My Turn, Your Turn

Children work in pairs.

1. The teacher models a sentence and the whole group repeats, or echoes it.

2. One child generates an oral phrase, and the partner echoes it.

3. Partners switch and alternate roles so that each child has a chance to both generate and repeat phrases.

Talking Stick

Children work in small groups. This strategy allows every child to have an opportunity to speak several times and encourages more reflective or reticent participants to take a turn. Children can "pass" only one time.

1. The teacher charts sentence graphic organizers and linguistic patterns children will use in their responses.

2. The teacher models use of linguistic patterns from the lesson.

3. The teacher asks a question or gives a prompt, and then passes a stick, eraser, stuffed animal, or any other designated object to one child.

4. A child speaks, everyone listens, and then the child passes the object on to the person next to him or her.

5. The next child speaks, everyone listens, and the process continues until the teacher or facilitator gives a signal to return the object.

Think-Pair-Share

This strategy allows children time for processing ideas by building in sufficient wait time to process the question and frame an answer. It is an appropriate strategy to use during small- or large-group discussions or lessons, giving all children a chance to organize their thoughts and have a turn sharing their responses with a partner. It also allows for small group verbal interaction to practice language before sharing with the larger group.

1. After reading or listening to a section of text, the teacher presents a question or task. It is helpful to guide with a specific prompt, modeling the language to be used in the response.

2. Children think about their responses for a brief, designated amount of time.

3. Partners share and discuss their responses with each other.

4. An adaptation can be to have each child share his or her partner's response within a small group to promote active listening.

Teaching Vocabulary

Building the background knowledge and a context for children to learn new words is critical in helping children understand new vocabulary. Primary language can be a valuable tool for preteaching, concept development, and vocabulary. Cognates, or words similar in English counterparts, often provide an opportunity for bridging the primary language and English. Also, children who have background knowledge about a topic can more easily connect the new information they are learning with what they already know than children without a similar context from which to work. Therefore, giving children background information and encouraging them to make as many connections as possible with the new vocabulary word they encounter will help them better understand the selection they are about to read.

In addition to building background knowledge, visual displays such as pictures, graphs, charts, maps, models, or other strategies offer unambiguous access to new content. They provide a clear and parallel correspondence between the visual objects and the new vocabulary to be learned. Thus, because the correlation is clear, the negotiation of meaning is established. Additionally, this process must be constant and reciprocal between you and each child if the child is to succeed in effectively interacting with language.

Included in this guide is a routine for teaching vocabulary words. In addition to this routine, more detailed explanations of the ways to teach vocabulary are as follows:

REAL OBJECTS AND REALIA: Because of the immediate result visuals have on learning language, when explaining a word such as *car,* the best approach is simply to show a real car. As an alternative to the real object, you can show realia. Realia are toy versions of real things, such as plastic eggs to substitute for real eggs, or in this case, a toy car to signify a real car. A large, clear picture of an automobile can also work if it is absolutely recognizable.

If, however, the child has had no experience with the item in the picture, more explanation might be needed. For example, if the word you are explaining is a zoo animal such as an *ocelot,* and children are not familiar with this animal, one picture might be insufficient. They might confuse this animal with a cat or any one of the feline species. Seeing several clear pictures, then, of each individual type of common feline and comparing their similarities and differences might help clarify meaning in this particular instance. When children make a connection between their prior knowledge of the word *cat* with the new word *ocelot,* it validates their newly acquired knowledge, and thus they process learning more quickly.

PICTURES: Supplement story illustrations with visuals such as those found in the **Photo Library CD, ABC Picture Cards,** magazine pictures, and picture dictionaries. Videos, especially those that demonstrate an entire setting such as a farm or zoo, or videos where different animals are highlighted in the natural habitat, for instance, might be helpful. You might also wish to turn off the soundtrack to avoid a flood of language that children might not be able to understand. This way children can concentrate on the visual-word meaning correlation.

PANTOMIME: Language is learned through modeling within a communicative context. Pantomiming is one example of such a framework of communication. Some words, such as *run* and *jump,* are appropriate for pantomiming. Throughout this guide, you will find suggestions for pantomiming words like *sick* by coughing, sneezing, and holding your stomach. If children understand what you are trying to pantomime, they will more easily engage in the task of learning.

Letter Formation Guide

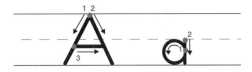 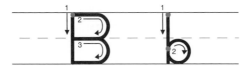 

A Starting point, slanting down left
Starting point, slanting down right
Starting point, across the middle: capital *A*

a Starting point, around left all the way
Starting point, straight down,
touching the circle: small *a*

B Starting point, straight down
Starting point, around right and in
at the middle, around right and in
at the bottom: capital *B*

b Starting point, straight down, back
up, around right all the way: small *b*

C Starting point, around left to
stopping place: capital *C*

c Starting point, around left to
stopping place: small *c*

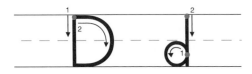 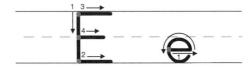 

D Starting point, straight down
Starting point, around right and in
at the bottom: capital *D*

d Starting point, around left all the way
Starting point, straight down, touching
the circle: small *d*

E Starting point, straight down
Starting point, straight out
Starting point, straight out
Starting point, straight out: capital *E*

e Starting point, straight out, up and
around to the left, curving down
and around to the right: small *e*

F Starting point, straight down
Starting point, straight out
Starting point, straight out: capital *F*

f Starting point, around left and straight down
Starting point, straight across: small *f*

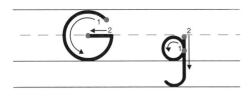 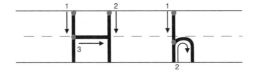 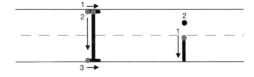

G Starting point, around left, curving up and
around
Straight in: capital *G*

g Starting point, around left all the way
Starting point, straight down, touching the
circle, around left to stopping place: small *g*

H Starting point, straight down
Starting point, straight down
Starting point, across the middle: capital *H*

h Starting point, straight down, back
up, around right, and straight down: small *h*

I Starting point, across
Starting point, straight down
Starting point, across: capital *I*

i Starting point, straight down
Dot exactly above: small *i*

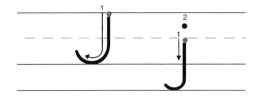

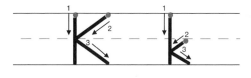

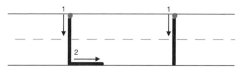

J Starting point, straight down, around left to stopping place: capital *J*

j Starting point, straight down, around left to stopping place
Dot exactly above: small *j*

K Starting point, straight down
Starting point, slanting down left, touching the line, slanting down right: capital *K*

k Starting point, straight down
Starting point, slanting down left, touching the line, slanting down right: small *k*

L Starting point, straight down, straight out: capital *L*

l Starting point, straight down: small *l*

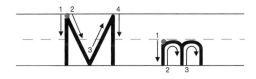

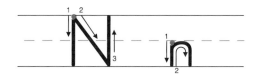

M Starting point, straight down
Starting point, slanting down right to the point, slanting back up to the right, straight down: capital *M*

m Starting point, straight down, back up, around right, straight down, back up, around right, straight down: small *m*

N Starting point, straight down
Starting point, slanting down right, straight back up: capital *N*

n Starting point, straight down, back up, around right, straight down: small *n*

O Starting point, around left all the way: capital *O*

o Starting point, around left all the way: small *o*

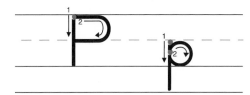

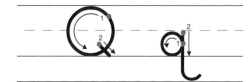

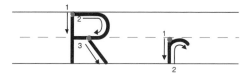

P Starting point, straight down
Starting point, around right and in at the middle: capital *P*

p Starting point, straight down
Starting point, around right all the way, touching the line: small *p*

Q Starting point, around left all the way
Starting point, slanting down right: capital *Q*

q Starting point, around left all the way
Starting point, straight down, touching the circle, curving up right to stopping place: small *q*

R Starting point, straight down
Starting point, around right and in at the middle, touching the line, slanting down right: capital *R*

r Starting point, straight down, back up, curving around right to stopping place: small *r*

Letter Formation Guide

S Starting point, around left, curving right and down around right, curving left and up: capital *S*

S Starting point, around left, curving right and down around right, curving left and up to stopping place: small *s*

T Starting point, straight across
Starting point, straight down: capital *T*

t Starting point, straight down
Starting point, across short: small *t*

U Starting point, straight down, curving around right and up, straight up: capital *U*

u Starting point, straight down, curving around right and up, straight up, straight back down: small *u*

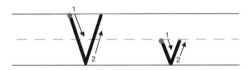

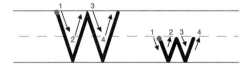

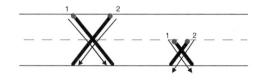

V Starting point, slanting down right, slanting up right: capital *V*

v Starting point, slanting down right, slanting up right: small *v*

W Starting point, slanting down right, slanting up right, slanting down right, slanting up right: capital *W*

W Starting point, slanting down right, slanting up right, slanting down right, slanting up right: small *w*

X Starting point, slanting down right
Starting point, slanting down left: capital *X*

X Starting point, slanting down right
Starting point, slanting down left: small *x*

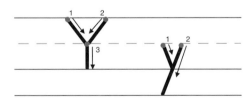

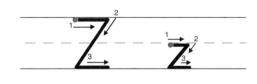

Y Starting point, slanting down right, stop
Starting point, slanting down left, stop
Starting point, straight down: capital *Y*

y Starting point, slanting down right
Starting point, slanting down left, connecting the lines: small *y*

Z Starting point, straight across, slanting down left, straight across: capital *Z*

z Starting point, straight across, slanting down left, straight across: small *z*

Number Formation Guide

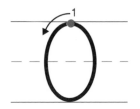

0 Starting point, curving left all the way around to starting point: *0*

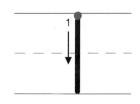

1 Starting point, straight down: *1*

2 Starting point, around right, slanting left and straight across right: *2*

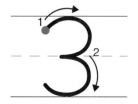

3 Starting point, around right, in at the middle, around right: *3*

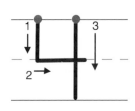

4 Starting point, straight down
Straight across right
Starting point, straight down, crossing line: *4*

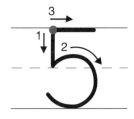

5 Starting point, straight down, curving around right and up
Starting point, straight across right: *5*

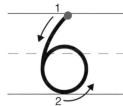

6 Starting point, slanting left, around the bottom curving up, around right and into the curve: *6*

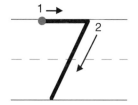

7 Starting point, straight across right, slanting down left: *7*

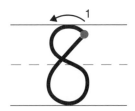

8 Starting point, curving left, curving down and around right, slanting up right to starting point: *8*

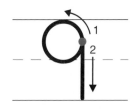

9 Starting point, curving around left all the way, straight down: *9*

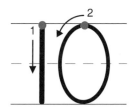

10 Starting point, straight down
Starting point, curving left all the way around to starting point: *10*

Vocabulary Development

Vocabulary development is a key part of **The DLM Early Childhood Express**. Children learn new words through exposure during reading and class discussion. They build language and vocabulary through activities using key words and phrases and by exploring selected vocabulary. After vocabulary words have been introduced, encourage children to use the words in sentences. Again, providing linguistic structures gives children a context for using new vocabulary and building oral language and gives you the opportunity to assess children's understanding of new words. For example, use sentence patterns such as the following:

- A _____ can _____.

- A _____ is a _____.
  (Use this for classification activities. *A tulip is a flower. A rabbit is an animal.*)

- The _____ is _____.
  (Use for describing. *The rabbit is soft.*)

Define words in ways children in your class can understand. When possible, show pictures of objects or actions to help clarify the meanings of words. Provide examples or comparisons to help reinforce the meanings of words and to connect new words to previously learned words. For example, say *The rabbit's FUR is soft like COTTON.* Connect words to categories. For example, say: *Pears are fruits. Are apples fruits? What else is a fruit?* Demonstrate the meaning of words when possible.

During reading, be sure children feel comfortable asking questions and sharing their reactions to what you are reading. Encourage children to share explanations, make predictions, compare and contrast ideas, sequence story events, and describe what you are reading. Encourage children's engagement by modeling reactions and responses while reading. For example, say *I like the part where _____ did _____.* or *This story is about _____.* Support children who are reluctant to speak by using linguistic structures that encourage them to talk about stories and use vocabulary words. You might use the following linguistic structures:

- This story is about _____.

- First _____.

- Next _____.

- Last _____. (Use this for retelling stories.)

- The _____ is the same as _____.

- The _____ is different from _____.

- We read about _____.

Model asking questions before, during, and after reading:

- I wonder what this story is going to be about.

- Who is _____?

- What is _____?

- What did _____ do?

- Why did _____ do _____?

- What happened first? Middle? Last?

Be sure to ask open-ended questions. Unlike questions that simply require a *yes* or *no* or one-word answer, open-ended questions encourage children to think about responses and use new vocabulary in sentences.

Throughout the day, create opportunities for children to talk to each other as they share daily experiences, discuss and explain what they are doing, and talk about what they are learning.

Vocabulary Words by Topic

Animals

alligator/caimán
ant/horminga
anteater/oso hormiguero
bat/murciélago
bear/oso
beaver/castor
bee/abeja
beetle/escarabajo
bobcat/lince
butterfly/mariposa
camel/camello
cat/gato
chicken/gallina/pollo
chipmunk/ardilla
cow/vaca
crab/cangrejo
deer/venado/ciervo
dog/perro
dolphin/delfin
donkey/burro
dragonfly/libélula
duck/pato
eagle/águila
elephant/elefante
flamingo/flamingo
fly/mosca
fox/zorro
frog/rana
giraffe/jirafa
goat/cabra
gorilla/gorila
grasshopper/saltamontes
hamster/hámster
hippopotamus/hipopótamo
horse/caballo
kangaroo/canguro
koala/coala

ladybug/catarina
leopard/leopardo
lion/león
llama/llama
lobster/langosta
monkey/mono
moose/alce
mosquito/mosquito
mouse/ratón
octopus/pulpo
opossum/zarigüeya
owl/búho
panda/oso panda
parakeet/periquito
peacock/pavo real
pelican/pelicano
penguin/pingüino
pig/cerdo
polar bear/oso polar
porcupine/puerco espín
rabbit/conejo
raccoon/mapache
rhinoceros/rinoceronte
robin/petirrojo
salamander/salamandra
sea horse/caballo de mar
shark/tiburón
sheep/oveja
skunk/mofeta/zorrillo
snake/serpiente
squirrel/ardilla
starfish/estrella de mar
swan/cisne
tiger/tigre
toad/sapo
turkey/pavo
turtle/tortuga
walrus/morsa

whale/ballena
zebra/cebra

Colors and Shapes

blue/azul
green/verde
red/rojo
yellow/amarillo
circle/círculo
diamond/diamante
oval/óvalo
rectangle/rectángulo
square/cuadrado
triangle/triángulo

Signs

deer crossing/cruce de venado
handicapped parking/
    estacionamiento para inválidos
railroad crossing/paso del tren
school crossing/cruce escolar
speed limit/limite de velocidad
stop sign/señal de alto
traffic light/semáforo
yield sign/señal de ceder el paso

Earth

beach/playa
blizzard/tormenta de nieve
cloud/nube
coral reef/arrecife de coral
desert/desierto
dry season/temporada seca
fall/otoño
fog/niebla
forest/bosque
geyser/géiser
glacier/glaciar

hail/granizo
hurricane/huracán
ice/hielo
island/isla
lake/lago
lightning/relámpago
mountain/montaña
ocean/océano
plain/llano
rain/lluvia
rain forest/selva tropical
rainy season/temporada de lluvias
rapids/rápidos
river/río
snow/nieve
spring/primavera
stream/arroyo
summer/verano
sun/sol
tornado/tornado
tundra/tundra
volcano/volcán
waterfall/cascada
wind/viento
winter/invierno

Human Body

ankle/tobillo
arm/brazo
body/cuerpo
ear/oreja
elbow/codo
eyes/ojos
feet/pies
fingers/dedos
hair/pelo
hands/manos

Vocabulary Words by Topic

head/cabeza
hearing/oído
heel/talón
hips/caderas
knee/rodilla
legs/piernas
mouth/boca
nose/nariz
sense/sentido
shoulders/hombros
sight/vista
smell/olfato
taste/gusto
teeth/dientes
toes/dedos de los pies
touch/ tacto

Plants

cactus/cactus
carrot/zanahoria
clover/trébol
cornstalk/planta de maíz
dandelion/diente de león
fern/helecho
grapevine/parra
grass/hierba
lettuce/lechuga
lilac bush/lila de monte
marigold/caléndula
moss/musgo
oak tree/árbol de roble
onion/cebolla
orange tree/naranjo
palm tree/palma
pine tree/pino
poison ivy/hiedra venenosa
rice/arroz
rose/rosa

seaweed/alga marina
sunflower/girasol
tomato/tomate
tulip/tulipán
water lily/nenúfar
wheat/trigo

Clothing

belt/cinturón
blouse/blusa
boots/botas
boy's swimsuit/traje de baño para
    niños
coat/abrigo
dress/vestido
earmuffs/orejeras
girl's swimsuit/traje de baño para
    niñas
gloves/guantes
hat/sombrero
jacket/chaqueta
jeans/pantalones vaqueros
mittens/manoplas
pajamas/pijama
pants/pantalones
raincoat/impermeable
robe/bata
scarf/bufanda
shirt/camisa
shoes/zapatos
shorts/pantalones cortos
skirt/falda
slippers/pantuflas
socks/calcetines
sweat suit/chandal
sweater/suéter
tie/corbata
vest/chaleco

Food

apples/manzanas
bacon/tocino
bagels/roscas de pan
bananas/plátanos
beans/frijoles
beef/carne
beets/betabel
blueberries/arándanos
bread/pan
broccoli/brécol
butter/mantequilla
cake/pastel
cantaloupe/cantalupo
carrots/zanahoria
cauliflower/coliflor
celery/apio
cereal/cereal
cheese/queso
cherries/cerezas
chicken/pollo
clams/almejas
cookies/galletas
corn/maíz
cottage cheese/requesón
crackers/galletas saladas
cream cheese/queso crema
cucumbers/pepinos
eggs/huevos
figs/higos
fish/pescado
grapefruit/toronja
grapes/uvas
green peppers/pimientos verdes
ham/jamón
ice-cream cone/cono de helado
jelly/gelatina
lemons/limones

lettuce/lechuga
limes/limas
macaroni/macarrones
milk/leche
mushrooms/champiñones
nuts/nueces
onions/cebollas
orange juice/jugo de naranja
oranges/naranjas
peaches/duraznos
peanut butter/crema de cacahuete
pears/peras
peas/guisantes
pie/tarta
pineapples/piñas
plums/ciruelas
pork chop/chuleta de puerco
potatoes/papas
radishes/rábanos
raisins/pasas
rice/arroz
rolls/panecillos
salad/ensalada
sausage/salchicha
shrimp/camarón
soup/sopa
spaghetti/espaguetis
squash/calabaza
strawberries/fresas
sweet potatoes/camotes
tomatoes/tomates
watermelon/sandía
yogurt/yogur

Recreation

archery/tiro el arco
badminton/bádminton
baseball/béisbol
basketball/baloncesto
biking/ciclismo
boating/paseo en bote
bowling/boliche
canoeing/piragüismo
climbing/montañismo
croquet/croquet
discus/disco
diving/buceo
fishing/pesca
football/fútbol
golf/golf
gymnastics/gimnasia
hiking/excursionismo
hockey/hockey
horseback riding/equitación
ice-skating/patinaje sobre hielo
in-line skating/patines en línea
lacrosse/lacrosse
pole-vaulting/salto con pértiga
running/atletismo
scuba diving/buceo
shot put/lanzamiento de peso
skiing/esquí
soccer/fútbol
surfing/surfing
swimming/natación
T-ball/T-ball
tennis/tenis
volleyball/voleibol
walking/caminar
waterskiing/esquí acuático
weight lifting/levantamiento

School

auditorium/auditorio
book/libro
cafeteria/cafetería
cafeteria table/mesa de cafetería
calculator/calculadora
chair/silla
chalk/tiza
chalkboard/pizarrón
chart paper/rotafolio
classroom/aula
computer/computadora
construction paper/papel para
   construir
crayons/crayones
desk/escritorio
easel/caballete
eraser/borrador
globe/globo
glue/pegamento
gym/gimnasio
hallway/vestíbulo
janitor's room/conserjería
learning center/centro de
   aprendizaje
library/biblioteca
markers/marcadores
music room/salón de música
notebook paper/papel de cuaderno
nurse's office/enfermería
paint/pintura
paintbrush/pincel
pen/pluma
pencil/lápiz
pencil sharpener/sacapuntas
playground/patio de recreo
principal's office/oficina del
   director

ruler/regla
science room/salón de ciencias
scissors/tijeras
stairs/escaleras
stapler/grapadora
supply room/almacén
tape/cinta adhesiva

Toys

ball/pelota
balloons/globos
bike/bicicleta
blocks/cubos
clay/arcilla
coloring book/libro para colorear
doll/muñeca
doll carriage/careola de muñecas
dollhouse/casa de muñecas
farm set/juego de la granja
game/juego
grocery cart/carro de compras
hats/sombreros
in-line skates/patines
instruments/instrumentos
jump rope/cuerda para saltar
kite/cometa
magnets/imanes
marbles/canicas
puppet/títere
puzzle/rompecabezas
scooter/motoneta
skateboard/patineta
slide/tobogán
stuffed animals/peluches
tape recorder/grabadora
top/trompo
toy cars/carro de juguete
toy trucks/camión de juguete

train set/juego de tren
tricycle/triciclo
wagon/vagón
yo-yo/yó-yó

Equipment

baggage cart/carro para equipaje
baseball/béisbol
bat/bate
mitt/manopla
basketball/pelota de baloncesto
basketball net/canasta
blueprints/planos
computer/computadora
drafting tools/borradores
bow/arco
arrow/flecha
bowling ball/pelota de boliche
bowling pin/bolos de boliche
bridle/freno
saddle/silla de montar
saddle pad/montura
broom/escoba
bulldozer/aplanadora
canoe/canoa
paddle/paleta
cash register/caja registradora
computer/computadora
crane/grúa
dishwasher/lavaplatos
drill/taladro
drum/tambor
drumsticks/palillos
dryer/secadora
dustpan/recogedor
figure skates/patinaje artístico

Vocabulary Words by Topic

football/balón
shoulder pads/hombreras
football helmet/casco
goggles/gafas
golf ball/pelota de golf
golf clubs/palo de golf
tee/tee
hammer/martillo
handcuffs/esposas
badge/placa
hat/gorra
hockey stick/palo de hockey
hockey puck/disco de hockey
ice skates/patines
hoe/azadón
hose/manguera
coat/chaqueta
hat/sombrero
sprinkler/rociador
iron/plancha
ironing board/tabla de planchar
lawn mower/cortacéspedes
mail pouch/bolsa de correo
mirror/espejo
probe/sonda
pick/pico
mop/estropajo
paintbrush/brocha de pintar
piano/piano
pliers/alicates
rake/rastrillo
roller skates/patines
saw/sierra
screwdriver/desarmador
scuba tank/tanque de buceo
mask/máscara
flippers/aletas
shovel/pala

sketch pad/cuaderno para dibujo
palette/paleta
skis/esquís
ski boots/botas para esquiar
poles/palos
soccer ball/balón de fútbol
shoes/zapatos de tenis
stepladder/escalera doble
stethoscope/estetoscopio
surfboard/tabla de surf
tennis ball/pelota de tenis
tennis racket/raqueta de tenis
tractor/tractor
vacuum cleaner/aspiradora
washer/lavadora
water skis/esquís acuáticos
rope/cuerda
life jacket/chaleco salvavidas
watering can/regadera
wheelbarrow/carretilla
wrench/llave inglesa

Home

basement/sótano
bathroom/baño
bathroom sink/lavabo
bathtub/bañera
bed/cama
bedroom/recámara/habitación
blanket/cobija/manta
chair/silla
circuit breaker/cortocircuito
dresser/cómoda
electrical outlet/enchufe
end table/mesa auxiliar
fireplace/chimenea
furnace/horno
kitchen/cocina

kitchen chair/silla de cocina
kitchen sink/fregadero
kitchen table/mesa de cocina
lamp/lámpara
light switch/interruptor de la luz
living room/sala
medicine cabinet/botiquín
nightstand/mesilla de noche
pillow/almohada
refrigerator/refrigerador
shower/ducha
smoke alarm/alarma de incendios
sofa/sofá
stove/estufa
thermostat/termostato
toilet/el baño
water heater/calentador de agua

Occupations

administrative assistant/asistente
   administrativo
air traffic controller/controlador
   aéreo
airline pilot/piloto
architect/arquitecto
artist/artista
astronaut/astronauta
athlete/atleta
author/autor
ballerina/bailarina
banker/banquero
bus driver/conductor de autobús
camera operator/operador de
   cámara
carpenter/carpintero
cashier/cajero
chef/jefe de cocina
computer technician/técnico en

   computación
cosmetologist/cosmetólogo
dancer/bailarín
dentist/dentista
doctor/doctor
electrician/electricista
engineer/ingeniero
farmer/granjero
firefighter/bombero
forest ranger/guardabosques
lawyer/abogado
manicurist/manicurista
musician/músico
nurse/enfermera
paramedic/paramédico
photographer/fotógrafo
police officer/policía
postal worker/empleado postal
real estate agent/corridor de
   bienes raíces
refuse collector/recolector de
   basura
reporter/reportero
school crossing guard/guarda
   escolar
server/mesero
ship captain/capitán de barco
singer/cantante
skater/patinador
teacher/maestro
truck driver/conductor de camión
veterinarian/veterinario
weaver/tejedora

Structures

adobe/casa de adobe
airplane hangar/hangar de avión
airport/aeropuerto
apartment building/edificio de
    departamentos/edificio de pisos
arena/arena
art museum/museo de arte
bakery/panadería
bank/banco
barn/granero
bridge/peunte
bus shelter/parada cubierta
city hall/ayuntamiento
clothing store/tienda de ropa
condominium/condominio
courthouse/tribunal
covered bridge/puente cubierto
dam/presa
dock/muelle
drawbridge/puente levadizo
duplex/dúplex
fire station/estación de bomberos
flower shop/floristeria
garage/garaje
gas station/gasolinera
gazebo/mirador
grain elevator/elevador de granos
grocery store/supermercado
hospital/hospital
house/casa
library/biblioteca
log cabin/cabaña de madera
marina/marina
monument/monumento
movie theater/cine
opera house/teatro de la ópera
palace/palacio

parking garage/estacionamiento
pizza shop/pizzaría
police station/estación de policía
power plant/central eléctrica
pyramid/pirámide
restaurant/restaurante
school/escuela
shelter house/albergue
shopping mall/centro comercial
skyscraper/rascacielos
stadium/estadio
swimming pool/alberca/piscina
tent/tienda
toy store/juguetería
train station/estación del tren
windmills/molino de viento

Transportation

airplane/avión
bicycle/bicicleta
bus/autobús
canoe/canoa
car/coche
four-wheel-drive vehicle/coche con
    doble tracción
helicopter/helicóptero
hot air balloon/globo de aire
    caliente
kayak/kayac
moped/ciclomotor
motor home/casa motora
motorboat/lancha motora
motorcycle/motocicleta
pickup truck/camioneta
rowboat/bote de remos
sailboat/velero
school bus/camión escolar

semitrailer truck/camión con semi-
    remolque
ship/barco
submarine/submarino
subway/metro
taxi/taxi
train/tren
van/furgoneta

Learning Trajectories for Math

Children follow natural developmental progressions in learning. Curriculum research has revealed sequences of activities that are effective in guiding children through these levels of thinking. These developmental paths are the basis for *Building Blocks* learning trajectories.

Learning Trajectories for Primary Grades Mathematics

Learning trajectories have three parts: a mathematical goal, a developmental path along which children develop to reach that goal, and a set of activities matched to each of the levels of thinking in that path that help children develop the next higher level of thinking. The ***Building Blocks*** learning trajectories give simple labels, descriptions, and examples of each level. Complete learning trajectories describe the goals of learning, the thinking and learning processes of children at various levels, and the learning activities in which they might engage. This document provides only the developmental levels.

The following provides the developmental levels from the first signs of development in different strands of mathematics through approximately age 8. Research shows that when teachers understand how children develop mathematics understanding, they are more effective in questioning, analyzing, and providing activities that further children's development than teachers who are unaware of the development process. Consequently, children have a much richer and more successful math experience in the primary grades.

Each of the following tables, such as "Counting," represents a main developmental progression that underlies the learning trajectory for that topic.

For some topics, there are "subtrajectories"—strands within the topic. In most cases, the names make this clear. For example, in Comparing and Ordering, some levels are "Composer" levels and others involve building a "Mental Number Line." Similarly, the related subtrajectories of "Composition" and "Decomposition" are easy to distinguish. Sometimes, for clarification, subtrajectories are indicated with a note in italics after the title. For example, Parts and Representing are subtrajectories within the Shape Trajectory.

Frequently Asked Questions (FAQ)

1. Why use learning trajectories? Learning trajectories allow teachers to build the mathematics of children—the thinking of children as it develops naturally. So, we know that all the goals and activities are within the developmental capacities of children. Finally, we know that the activities provide the mathematical building blocks for success.

2. When are children "at" a level? Children are at a certain level when most of their behaviors reflect the thinking—ideas and skills—of that level. Most levels are levels of thinking. However, some are merely "levels of attainment" and indicate a child has gained knowledge. For example, children must learn to name or write more numerals, but knowing more numerals does not require more complex thinking.

3. Can children work at more than one level at the same time? Yes, although most children work mainly at one level or in transition between two levels. Levels are not "absolute stages." They are "benchmarks" of complex growth that represent distinct ways of thinking.

4. Can children jump ahead? Yes, especially if there are separate subtopics. For example, we have combined many counting competencies into one "Counting" sequence with subtopics, such as verbal counting skills. Some children learn to count to 100 at age 6 after learning to count objects to 10 or more, some may learn that verbal skill earlier. The subtopic of verbal counting skills would still be followed.

5. How do these developmental levels support teaching and learning? The levels help teachers, as well as curriculum developers, assess, teach, and sequence activities. Through planned teaching and encouraging informal, incidental mathematics, teachers help children learn at an appropriate and deep level.

6. Should I plan to help children develop just the levels that correspond to my children's ages? No! The ages in the table are typical ages children develop these ideas. (These are rough guides only.) These are "starting levels" not goals. We have found that children who are provided high-quality mathematics experiences are capable of developing to levels one or more years beyond their peers.

Developmental Levels for Counting

The ability to count with confidence develops over the course of several years. Beginning in infancy, children show signs of understanding numbers. With instruction and number experience, most children can count fluently by age 8, with much progress in counting occurring in kindergarten and first grade. Most children follow a natural developmental progression in learning to count with recognizable stages or levels. This developmental path can be described as part of a learning trajectory.

Age Range	Level Name	Level	Description
1–2	Precounter	1	At the earliest level a child shows no verbal counting. The child may name some number words with no sequence.
1–2	Chanter	2	At this level, a child may sing-song or chant indistinguishable number words.
2	Reciter	3	At this level, the child may verbally count with separate words, but not necessarily in the correct order.
3	Reciter (10)	4	A child at this level may verbally count to 10 with some correspondence with objects. He or she may point to objects to count a few items, but then lose track.
3	Corresponder	5	At this level, a child may keep one-to-one correspondence between counting words and objects—at least for small groups of objects laid in a line. A corresponder may answer "how many" by recounting the objects.
4	Counter (Small Numbers)	6	At around 4 years of age, the child may begin to count meaningfully. He or she may accurately count objects in a line to 5 and answer the "how many" question with the last number counted. When objects are visible, and especially with small numbers, the child begins to understand cardinality (that numbers tell how many).
4	Producer (Small Numbers)	7	The next level after counting small numbers is to count out objects to 5. When asked to show four of something, for example, this child may give four objects.
4	Counter (10)	8	This child may count structured arrangements of objects to 10. He or she may be able to write or draw to represent 1–10. A child at this level may be able to tell the number just after or just before another number, but only by counting up from 1.
5	Counter and Producer— Counter to (10+)	9	Around 5 years of age, a child may begin to count out objects accurately to 10 and then beyond to 30. He or she has explicit understanding of cardinality (that numbers tell how many). The child may keep track of objects that have and have not been counted, even in different arrangements. He or she may write or draw to represent 1 to 10 and then 20 and 30, and may give the next number to 20 or 30. The child also begins to recognize errors in others' counting and is able to eliminate most errors in his or her own counting.

Age Range	Level Name	Level	Description
5	Counter Backward from 10	10	Another milestone at about age 5 is being able to count backward from 10 to 1, verbally, or when removing objects from a group.
6	Counter from N (N+1, N–1)	11	Around 6 years of age, the child may begin to count on, counting verbally and with objects from numbers other than 1. Another noticeable accomplishment is that a child may determine the number immediately before or after another number without having to start back at 1.
6	Skip Counting by 10s to 100	12	A child at this level may count by 10s to 100 or beyond with understanding.
6	Counter to 100	13	A child at this level may count by 1s to 100. He or she can make decade transitions (for example, from 29 to 30) starting at any number.
6	Counter On Using Patterns	14	At this level, a child may keep track of a few counting acts by using numerical patterns, such as tapping as he or she counts.
6	Skip Counter	15	At this level, the child can count by 5s and 2s with understanding.
6	Counter of Imagined Items	16	At this level, a child may count mental images of hidden objects to answer, for example, "how many" when 5 objects are visible and 3 are hidden.
6	Counter On Keeping Track	17	A child at this level may keep track of counting acts numerically, first with objects, then by counting counts. He or she counts up one to four more from a given number.
6	Counter of Quantitative Units	18	At this level, a child can count unusual units, such as "wholes" when shown combinations of wholes and parts. For example, when shown three whole plastic eggs and four halves, a child at this level will say there are five whole eggs.
6	Counter to 200	19	At this level, a child may count accurately to 200 and beyond, recognizing the patterns of ones, tens, and hundreds.
7	Number Conserver	20	A major milestone around age 7 is the ability to conserve number. A child who conserves number understands that a number is unchanged even if a group of objects is rearranged. For example, if there is a row of ten buttons, the child understands there are still ten without recounting, even if they are rearranged in a long row or a circle.
7	Counter Forward and Back	21	A child at this level may count in either direction and recognize that sequence of decades mirrors single-digit sequence.

Developmental Levels for Comparing and Ordering Numbers

Comparing and ordering sets is a critical skill for children as they determine whether one set is larger than another in order to make sure sets are equal and "fair." Prekindergartners can learn to use matching to compare collections or to create equivalent collections. Finding out how many more or fewer in one collection is more demanding than simply comparing two collections. The ability to compare and order sets with fluency develops over the course of several years. With instruction and number experience, most children develop foundational understanding of number relationships and place value at ages four and five. Most children follow a natural developmental progression in learning to compare and order numbers with recognizable stages or levels. This developmental path can be described as part of a learning trajectory.

Age Range	Level Name	Level	Description
2	Object Corresponder	1	At this early level, a child puts objects into one-to-one correspondence, but may not fully understand that this creates equal groups. For example, a child may know that each carton has a straw, but does not necessarily know there are the same numbers of straws and cartons.
2	Perceptual Comparer	2	At this level, a child can compare collections that are quite different in size (for example, one is at least twice the other) and know that one has more than the other. If the collections are similar, the child can compare very small collections.
3	First-Second Ordinal Counter	3	At this level the child can identify the "first" and often "second" object in a sequence.
3	Nonverbal Comparer of Similar Items	4	At this level, a child can identify that different organizations of the same number are equal and different from other sets (1–4 items). For example, a child can identify ••• and ••• as equal and different from •• or •••.
4	Nonverbal Comparer of Dissimilar Items	5	At this level, a child can match small, equal collections of dissimilar items, such as shells and dots, and show that they are the same number.
4	Matching Comparer	6	As children progress, they begin to compare groups of 1–6 by matching. For example, a child gives one toy bone to every dog and says there are the same number of dogs and bones.

Age Range	Level Name	Level	Description
4	Knows-to-Count Comparer	7	A significant step occurs when the child begins to count collections to compare. At the early levels, children are not always accurate when a larger collection's objects are smaller in size than the objects in the smaller collection. For example, a child at this level may accurately count two equal collections, but when asked, says the collection of larger blocks has more.
4	Counting Comparer (Same Size)	8	At this level, children make accurate comparisons via counting, but only when objects are about the same size and groups are small (about 1–5 items).
5	Counting Comparer (5)	9	As children develop their ability to compare sets, they compare accurately by counting, even when a larger collection's objects are smaller. A child at this level can figure out how many more or less.
5	Ordinal Counter	10	At this level, a child identifies and uses ordinal numbers from "first" to "tenth." For example, the child can identify who is "third in line."
6	Counting Comparer (10)	11	This level can be observed when the child compares sets by counting, even when a larger collection's objects are smaller, up to 10. A child at this level can accurately count two collections of 9 items each, and says they have the same number, even if one collection has larger blocks.
6	Mental Number Line to 10	12	As children move into this level, they begin to use mental images and knowledge of number relationships to determine relative size and position. For example, a child at this level can answer which number is closer to 6, 4 or 9 without counting physical objects.
6	Serial Orderer to 6+	13	At this level, the child orders lengths marked into units (1–6, then beyond). For example, given towers of cubes, this child can put them in order, 1 to 6.
7	Place Value Comparer	14	Further development is made when a child begins to compare numbers with place value understanding. For example, a child at this level can explain that "63 is more than 59 because six tens is more than five tens, even if there are more than three ones."
7	Mental Number Line to 100	15	Children demonstrate the next level when they can use mental images and knowledge of number relationships, including ones embedded in tens, to determine relative size and position. For example, when asked, "Which is closer to 45, 30 or 50?" a child at this level may say "45 is right next to 50, but 30 isn't."
8+	Mental Number Line to 1,000s	16	At about age 8, children may begin to use mental images of numbers up to 1,000 and knowledge of number relationships, including place value, to determine relative size and position. For example, when asked, "Which is closer to 3,500—2,000 or 7,000?" a child at this level may say "70 is double 35, but 20 is only fifteen from 35, so twenty hundreds, 2,000, is closer."

Developmental Levels for Recognizing Number and Subitizing (Instantly Recognizing)

The ability to recognize number values develops over the course of several years and is a foundational part of number sense. Beginning at about age two, children begin to name groups of objects. The ability to instantly know how many are in a group, called *subitizing,* begins at about age three. By age eight, with instruction and number experience, most children can identify groups of items and use place values and multiplication skills to count them. Most children follow a natural developmental progression in learning to count with recognizable stages or levels. This developmental path can be described as part of a learning trajectory.

Age Range	Level Name	Level	Description
2	Small Collection Namer	1	The first sign occurs when the child can name groups of 1 to 2, sometimes 3. For example, when shown a pair of shoes, this young child says, "two shoes."
3	Maker of Small Collections	2	At this level, a child can nonverbally make a small collection (no more than 4, usually 1 to 3) with the same number as another collection. For example, when shown a collection of 3, the child makes another collection of 3.
4	Perceptual Subitizer to 4	3	Progress is made when a child instantly recognizes collections up to 4 and verbally names the number of items. For example, when shown 4 objects briefly, the child says "4."
5	Perceptual Subitizer to 5	4	This level is the ability to instantly recognize collections up to 5 and verbally name the number of items. For example, when shown 5 objects briefly, the child says "5."
5	Conceptual Subitizer to 5	5	At this level, the child can verbally label all arrangements to about 5, when shown only briefly. For example, a child at this level might say, "I saw 2 and 2, and so I saw 4."
5	Conceptual Subitizer to 10	6	This step is when the child can verbally label most arrangements to 6 shown briefly, then up to 10, using groups. For example, a child at this level might say, "In my mind, I made 2 groups of 3 and 1 more, so 7."
6	Conceptual Subitizer to 20	7	Next, a child can verbally label structured arrangements up to 20 shown briefly, using groups. For example, the child may say, "I saw 3 fives, so 5, 10, 15."
7	Conceptual Subitizer with Place Value and Skip Counting	8	At this level, a child is able to use groups, skip counting, and place value to verbally label structured arrangements shown briefly. For example, the child may say, "I saw groups of tens and twos, so 10, 20, 30, 40, 42, 44, 46…46!"
8+	Conceptual Subitizer with Place Value and Multiplication	9	As children develop their ability to subitize, they use groups, multiplication, and place value to verbally label structured arrangements shown briefly. At this level, a child may say, "I saw groups of tens and threes, so I thought, 5 tens is 50 and 4 threes is 12, so 62 in all."

Learning Trajectories for Math

Developmental Levels for Composing (Knowing Combinations of Numbers)

Composing and decomposing are combining and separating operations that allow children to build concepts of "parts" and "wholes." Most prekindergartners can "see" that two items and one item make three items. Later, children learn to separate a group into parts in various ways and then to count to produce all of the number "partners" of a given number. Eventually children think of a number and know the different addition facts that make that number. Most children follow a natural developmental progression in learning to compose and decompose numbers with recognizable stages or levels. This developmental path can be described as part of a learning trajectory.

Age Range	Level Name	Level	Description
4	Pre-Part-Whole Recognizer	1	At the earliest levels of composing, a child only nonverbally recognizes parts and wholes. For example, when shown 4 red blocks and 2 blue blocks, a young child may intuitively appreciate that "all the blocks" includes the red and blue blocks, but when asked how many there are in all, the child may name a small number, such as 1.
5	Inexact Part-Whole Recognizer	2	A sign of development is that the child knows a whole is bigger than parts, but does not accurately quantify. For example, when shown 4 red blocks and 2 blue blocks and asked how many there are in all, the child may name a "large number," such as 5 or 10.
5	Composer to 4, then 5	3	At this level, a child knows number combinations. A child at this level quickly names parts of any whole, or the whole given the parts. For example, when shown 4, then 1 is secretly hidden, and then shown the 3 remaining, the child may quickly say "1" is hidden.
6	Composer to 7	4	The next sign of development is when a child knows number combinations to totals of 7. A child at this level quickly names parts of any whole, or the whole when given parts, and can double numbers to 10. For example, when shown 6, then 4 are secretly hidden, and then shown the 2 remaining, the child may quickly say "4" are hidden.
6	Composer to 10	5	This level is when a child knows number combinations to totals of 10. A child at this level may quickly name parts of any whole, or the whole when given parts, and can double numbers to 20. For example, this child would be able to say "9 and 9 is 18."
7	Composer with Tens and Ones	6	At this level, the child understands two-digit numbers as tens and ones, can count with dimes and pennies, and can perform two-digit addition with regrouping. For example, a child at this level may explain, "17 and 36 is like 17 and 3, which is 20, and 33, which is 53."

Developmental Levels for Adding and Subtracting

Single-digit addition and subtraction are generally characterized as "math facts." It is assumed children must memorize these facts, yet research has shown that addition and subtraction have their roots in counting, counting on, number sense, the ability to compose and decompose numbers, and place value. Research has also shown that learning methods for addition and subtraction with understanding is much more effective than rote memorization of seemingly isolated facts. Most children follow an observable developmental progression in learning to add and subtract numbers with recognizable stages or levels. This developmental path can be described as part of a learning trajectory.

Age Range	Level Name	Level	Description
1	Pre +/−	1	At the earliest level, a child shows no sign of being able to add or subtract.
3	Nonverbal +/−	2	The first sign is when a child can add and subtract very small collections nonverbally. For example, when shown 2 objects, then 1 object being hidden under a napkin, the child identifies or makes a set of 3 objects to "match."
4	Small Number +/−	3	This level is when a child can find sums for joining problems up to 3 + 2 by counting with objects. For example, when asked, "You have 2 balls and get 1 more. How many in all?" the child may count out 2, then count out 1 more, then count all 3: "1, 2, 3!"
5	Find Result +/−	4	**Addition** Evidence of this level in addition is when a child can find sums for joining (you had 3 apples and get 3 more; how many do you have in all?) and part-part-whole (there are 6 girls and 5 boys on the playground; how many children are there in all?) problems by direct modeling, counting all, with objects. For example, when asked, "You have 2 red balls and 3 blue balls. How many in all?" the child may count out 2 red, then count out 3 blue, then count all 5. **Subtraction** In subtraction, a child can also solve take-away problems by separating with objects. For example, when asked, "You have 5 balls and give 2 to Tom. How many do you have left?" the child may count out 5 balls, then take away 2, and then count the remaining 3.

Age Range	Level Name	Level	Description
5	Find Change +/–	5	**Addition** At this level, a child can find the missing addend (5 + _ =7) by adding on objects. For example, when asked, "You have 5 balls and then get some more. Now you have 7 in all. How many did you get?" The child may count out 5, then count those 5 again starting at 1, then add more, counting "6, 7," then count the balls added to find the answer, 2. **Subtraction** A child can compare by matching in simple situations. For example, when asked, "Here are 6 dogs and 4 balls. If we give a ball to each dog, how many dogs will not get a ball?" a child at this level may count out 6 dogs, match 4 balls to 4 of them, then count the 2 dogs that have no ball.
5	Make It +/–	6	A significant advancement occurs when a child is able to count on. This child can add on objects to make one number into another without counting from 1. For example, when told, "This puppet has 4 balls, but she should have 6. Make it 6," the child may put up 4 fingers on one hand, immediately count up from 4 while putting up 2 fingers on the other hand, saying, "5, 6," and then count or recognize the 2 fingers.
6	Counting Strategies +/–	7	This level occurs when a child can find sums for joining (you had 8 apples and get 3 more…) and part-part-whole (6 girls and 5 boys…) problems with finger patterns or by adding on objects or counting on. For example, when asked "How much is 4 and 3 more?" the child may answer "4…5, 6, 7. 7!" Children at this level can also solve missing addend (3 + _ = 7) or compare problems by counting on. When asked, for example, "You have 6 balls. How many more would you need to have 8?" the child may say, "6, 7 [puts up first finger], 8 [puts up second finger]. 2!"
6	Part-Whole +/–	8	Further development has occurred when the child has part-whole understanding. This child can solve problems using flexible strategies and some derived facts (for example, "5 + 5 is 10, so 5 + 6 is 11"), can sometimes do start-unknown problems (_ + 6 = 11), but only by trial and error. When asked, "You had some balls. Then you get 6 more. Now you have 11 balls. How many did you start with?" this child may lay out 6, then 3, count, and get 9. The child may put 1 more, say 10, then put 1 more. The child may count up from 6 to 11, then recount the group added, and say, "5!"

Age Range	Level Name	Level	Description
6	Numbers-in-Numbers +/–	9	Evidence of this level is when a child recognizes that a number is part of a whole and can solve problems when the start is unknown (_ + 4 = 9) with counting strategies. For example, when asked, "You have some balls, then you get 4 more balls, now you have 9. How many did you have to start with?" this child may count, putting up fingers, "5, 6, 7, 8, 9." The child may then look at his or her fingers and say, "5!"
7	Deriver +/–	10	At this level, a child can use flexible strategies and derived combinations (for example, "7 + 7 is 14, so 7 + 8 is 15") to solve all types of problems. For example, when asked, "What's 7 plus 8?" this child thinks: 7 + 8 = 7 [7 + 1] = [7 +7] + 1 = 14 + 1 = 15. The child can also solve multidigit problems by incrementing or combining 10s and 1s. For example, when asked "What's 28 + 35?" this child may think: 20 + 30 = 50; + 8 = 58; 2 more is 60, and 3 more is 63. He or she can also combine 10s and 1s: 20 + 30 = 50. 8 + 5 is like 8 plus 2 and 3 more, so it is 13. 50 and 13 is 63.
8+	Problem Solver +/–	11	As children develop their addition and subtraction abilities, they can solve by using flexible strategies and many known combinations. For example, when asked, "If I have 13 and you have 9, how could we have the same number?" this child may say, "9 and 1 is 10, then 3 more makes 13. 1 and 3 is 4. I need 4 more!"
8+	Multidigit +/–	12	Further development is shown when children can use composition of 10s and all previous strategies to solve multidigit +/– problems. For example, when asked, "What's 37 – 18?" this child may say, "Take 1 ten off the 3 tens; that's 2 tens. Take 7 off the 7. That's 2 tens and 0…20. I have one more to take off. That's 19." Or, when asked, "What's 28 + 35?" this child may think, 30 + 35 would be 65. But it's 28, so it's 2 less…63.

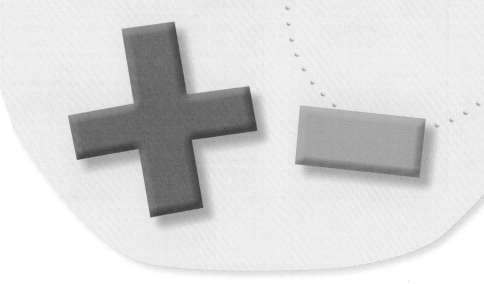

Learning Trajectories for Math

Developmental Levels for Multiplying and Dividing

Multiplication and division build on addition and subtraction understanding and are dependent upon counting and place-value concepts. As children begin to learn to multiply, they make equal groups and count them all. They then learn skip counting and derive related products from products they know. Finding and using patterns aid in learning multiplication and division facts with understanding. Children typically follow an observable developmental progression in learning to multiply and divide numbers with recognizable stages or levels. This developmental path can be described as part of a learning trajectory.

Age Range	Level Name	Level	Description
2	Non-quantitative Sharer "Dumper"	1	Multiplication and division concepts begin very early with the problem of sharing. Early evidence of these concepts can be observed when a child dumps out blocks and gives some (not an equal number) to each person.
3	Beginning Grouper and Distributive Sharer	2	Progression to this level can be observed when a child is able to make small groups (fewer than 5). This child can share by "dealing out," but often only between 2 people, although he or she may not appreciate the numerical result. For example, to share 4 blocks, this child may give each person a block, check that each person has one, and repeat this.
4	Grouper and Distributive Sharer	3	The next level occurs when a child makes small equal groups (fewer than 6). This child can deal out equally between 2 or more recipients, but may not understand that equal quantities are produced. For example, the child may share 6 blocks by dealing out blocks to herself and a friend one at a time.
5	Concrete Modeler ×/÷	4	As children develop, they are able to solve small-number multiplying problems by grouping—making each group and counting all. At this level, a child can solve division/sharing problems with informal strategies, using concrete objects—up to 20 objects and 2 to 5 people—although the child may not understand equivalence of groups. For example, the child may distribute 20 objects by dealing out 2 blocks to each of 5 people, then 1 to each, until the blocks are gone.
6	Parts and Wholes ×/÷	5	A new level is evidenced when the child understands the inverse relation between divisor and quotient. For example, this child may understand "If you share with more people, each person gets fewer."

Age Range	Level Name	Level	Description
7	Skip Counter ×/÷	6	As children develop understanding in multiplication and division, they begin to use skip counting for multiplication and for measurement division (finding out how many groups). For example, given 20 blocks, 4 to each person, and asked how many people, the children may skip count by 4, holding up 1 finger for each count of 4. A child at this level may also use trial and error for partitive division (finding out how many in each group). For example, given 20 blocks, 5 people, and asked how many each should get, this child may give 3 to each, and then 1 more.
8+	Deriver ×/÷	7	At this level, children use strategies and derived combinations to solve multidigit problems by operating on tens and ones separately. For example, a child at this level may explain "7 × 6, five 7s is 35, so 7 more is 42."
8+	Array Quantifier	8	Further development can be observed when a child begins to work with arrays. For example, given 7 × 4 with most of 5 × 4 covered, a child at this level may say, "There are 8 in these 2 rows, and 5 rows of 4 is 20, so 28 in all."
8+	Partitive Divisor	9	This level can be observed when a child is able to figure out how many are in each group. For example, given 20 blocks, 5 people, and asked how many each should get, a child at this level may say, "4, because 5 groups of 4 is 20."
8+	Multidigit ×/÷	10	As children progress, they begin to use multiple strategies for multiplication and division, from compensating to paper-and-pencil procedures. For example, a child becoming fluent in multiplication might explain that "19 times 5 is 95, because 20 fives is 100, and 1 less five is 95."

Developmental Levels for Measuring

Measurement is one of the main real-world applications of mathematics. Counting is a type of measurement which determines how many items are in a collection. Measurement also involves assigning a number to attributes of length, area, and weight. Prekindergarten children know that mass, weight, and length exist, but they do not know how to reason about these or to accurately measure them. As children develop their understanding of measurement, they begin to use tools to measure and understand the need for standard units of measure. Children typically follow an observable developmental progression in learning to measure with recognizable stages or levels. This developmental path can be described as part of a learning trajectory.

Age Range	Level Name	Level	Description
3	Length Quantity Recognizer	1	At the earliest level, children can identify length as an attribute. For example, they might say, "I'm tall, see?"
4	Length Direct Comparer	2	In this level, children can physically align 2 objects to determine which is longer or if they are the same length. For example, they can stand 2 sticks up next to each other on a table and say, "This one's bigger."
5	Indirect Length Comparer	3	A sign of further development is when a child can compare the length of 2 objects by representing them with a third object. For example, a child might compare the length of 2 objects with a piece of string. Additional evidence of this level is that when asked to measure, the child may assign a length by guessing or moving along a length while counting (without equal-length units). For example, the child may move a finger along a line segment, saying 10, 20, 30, 31, 32.
6	Serial Orderer to 6+	4	At this level, a child can order lengths, marked in 1 to 6 units. For example, given towers of cubes, a child at this level may put them in order, 1 to 6.
6	End-to-End Length Measurer	5	At this level, the child can lay units end-to-end, although he or she may not see the need for equal-length units. For example, a child might lay 9-inch cubes in a line beside a book to measure how long it is.
7	Length Unit Iterater	6	A significant change occurs when a child iterates a single unit to measure. He or she sees the need for identical units. The child uses rulers with help.
7	Length Unit Relater	7	At this level, a child can relate size and number of units. For example, the child may explain, "If you measure with centimeters instead of inches, you'll need more of them because each one is smaller."
8+	Length Measurer	8	As a child develops measurement ability, they begin to measure, knowing the need for identical units, the relationships between different units, partitions of unit, and the zero point on rulers. At this level, the child also begins to estimate. The children may explain, "I used a meterstick 3 times, then there was a little left over. So, I lined it up from 0 and found 14 centimeters. So, it's 3 meters, 14 centimeters in all."
8+	Conceptual Ruler Measurer	9	Further development in measurement is evidenced when a child possesses an "internal" measurement tool. At this level, the child mentally moves along an object, segmenting it, and counting the segments. This child also uses arithmetic to measure and estimates with accuracy. For example, a child at this level may explain, "I imagine one meterstick after another along the edge of the room. That's how I estimated the room's length to be 9 meters."

Learning Trajectories for Math

Developmental Levels for Recognizing Geometric Shapes

Geometric shapes can be used to represent and understand objects. Analyzing, comparing, and classifying shapes help create new knowledge of shapes and their relationships. Shapes can be decomposed or composed into other shapes. Through their everyday activities, children build both intuitive and explicit knowledge of geometric figures. Most children can recognize and name basic two-dimensional shapes at four years of age. However, young children can learn richer concepts about shape if they have varied examples and nonexamples of shape, discussions about shapes and their characteristics, a wide variety of shape classes, and interesting tasks. Children typically follow an observable developmental progression in learning about shapes with recognizable stages or levels. This developmental path can be described as part of a learning trajectory.

Age Range	Level Name	Level	Description
2	Shape Matcher—Identical	1	The earliest sign of understanding shape is when a child can match basic shapes (circle, square, typical triangle) with the same size and orientation.
2	Shape Matcher—Sizes	2	A sign of development is when a child can match basic shapes with different sizes.
2	Shape Matcher—Orientations	3	This level of development is when a child can match basic shapes with different orientations.
3	Shape Recognizer—Typical	4	A sign of development is when a child can recognize and name a prototypical circle, square, and, less often, a typical triangle. For example, the child names this a square. Some children may name different sizes, shapes, and orientations of rectangles, but also accept some shapes that look rectangular but are not rectangles. Children name these shapes "rectangles" (including the nonrectangular parallelogram).
3	Shape Matcher—More Shapes	5	As children develop understanding of shape, they can match a wider variety of shapes with the same size and orientation.
3	Shape Matcher—Sizes and Orientations	6	The child matches a wider variety of shapes with different sizes and orientations.
3	Shape Matcher—Combinations	7	The child matches combinations of shapes to each other.
4	Shape Recognizer—Circles, Squares, and Triangles	8	This sign of development is when a child can recognize some nonprototypical squares and triangles and may recognize some rectangles, but usually not rhombi (diamonds). Often, the child does not differentiate sides/corners. The child at this level may name these as triangles.
4	Constructor of Shapes from Parts—Looks Like *Representing*	9	A significant sign of development is when a child represents a shape by making a shape "look like" a goal shape. For example, when asked to make a triangle with sticks, the child may create the following: △.

Age Range	Level Name	Level	Description
5	Shape Recognizer— All Rectangles	10	As children develop understanding of shape, they recognize more rectangle sizes, shapes, and orientations of rectangles. For example, a child at this level may correctly name these shapes "rectangles."
5	Side Recognizer *Parts*	11	A sign of development is when a child recognizes parts of shapes and identifies sides as distinct geometric objects. For example, when asked what this shape is, the child may say it is a quadrilateral (or has 4 sides) after counting and running a finger along the length of each side.
5	Angle Recognizer *Parts*	12	At this level, a child can recognize angles as separate geometric objects. For example, when asked, "Why is this a triangle," the child may say, "It has three angles" and count them, pointing clearly to each vertex (point at the corner).
5	Shape Recognizer— More Shapes	13	As children develop, they are able to recognize most basic shapes and prototypical examples of other shapes, such as hexagon, rhombus (diamond), and trapezoid. For example, a child can correctly identify and name all the following shapes:
6	Shape Identifier	14	At this level, the child can name most common shapes, including rhombi, without making mistakes such as calling ovals circles. A child at this level implicitly recognizes right angles, so distinguishes between a rectangle and a parallelogram without right angles. A child may correctly name all the following shapes:
6	Angle Matcher *Parts*	15	A sign of development is when the child can match angles concretely. For example, given several triangles, the child may find two with the same angles by laying the angles on top of one another.

Age Range	Level Name	Level	Description
7	Parts of Shapes Identifier	16	At this level, the child can identify shapes in terms of their components. For example, the child may say, "No matter how skinny it looks, that's a triangle because it has 3 sides and 3 angles."
7	Constructor of Shapes from Parts—Exact Representing	17	A significant step is when the child can represent a shape with completely correct construction, based on knowledge of components and relationships. For example, when asked to make a triangle with sticks, the child may create the following:
8	Shape Class Identifier	18	As children develop, they begin to use class membership (for example, to sort) not explicitly based on properties. For example, a child at this level may say, "I put the triangles over here, and the quadrilaterals, including squares, rectangles, rhombi, and trapezoids, over there."
8	Shape Property Identifier	19	At this level, a child can use properties explicitly. For example, a child may say, "I put the shapes with opposite sides that are parallel over here, and those with 4 sides but not both pairs of sides parallel over there."
8	Angle Size Comparer	20	The next sign of development is when a child can separate and compare angle sizes. For example, the child may say, "I put all the shapes that have right angles here, and all the ones that have bigger or smaller angles over there."
8	Angle Measurer	21	A significant step in development is when a child can use a protractor to measure angles.
8	Property Class Identifier	22	The next sign of development is when a child can use class membership for shapes (for example, to sort or consider shapes "similar") explicitly based on properties, including angle measure. For example, the child may say, "I put the equilateral triangles over here, and the right triangles over here."
8	Angle Synthesizer	23	As children develop understanding of shape, they can combine various meanings of angle (turn, corner, slant). For example, a child at this level could explain, "This ramp is at a 45° angle to the ground."

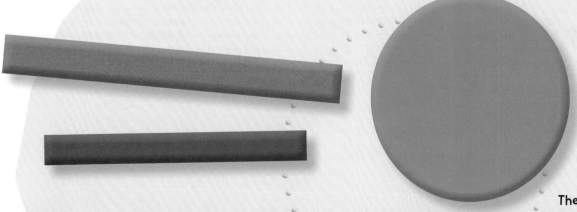

Learning Trajectories for Math

Developmental Levels for Composing Geometric Shapes

Children move through levels in the composition and decomposition of two-dimensional figures. Very young children cannot compose shapes but then gain ability to combine shapes into pictures, synthesize combinations of shapes into new shapes, and eventually substitute and build different kinds of shapes. Children typically follow an observable developmental progression in learning to compose shapes with recognizable stages or levels. This developmental path can be described as part of a learning trajectory.

Age Range	Level Name	Level	Description
2	Pre-Composer	1	The earliest sign of development is when a child can manipulate shapes as individuals, but is unable to combine them to compose a larger shape.
3	Pre-Decomposer	2	At this level, a child can decompose shapes, but only by trial and error.
4	Piece Assembler	3	Around age 4, a child can begin to make pictures in which each shape represents a unique role (for example, one shape for each body part) and shapes touch. A child at this level can fill simple outline puzzles using trial and error.
5	Picture Maker	4	As children develop, they are able to put several shapes together to make one part of a picture (for example, 2 shapes for 1 arm). A child at this level uses trial and error and does not anticipate creation of the new geometric shape. The children can choose shapes using "general shape" or side length, and fill "easy" outline puzzles that suggest the placement of each shape (but note that the child is trying to put a square in the puzzle where its right angles will not fit).
5	Simple Decomposer	5	A significant step occurs when the child is able to decompose ("take apart" into smaller shapes) simple shapes that have obvious clues as to their decomposition.

Age Range	Level Name	Level	Description
5	Shape Composer	6	A sign of development is when a child composes shapes with anticipation ("I know what will fit!"). A child at this level chooses shapes using angles as well as side lengths. Rotation and flipping are used intentionally to select and place shapes.
6	Substitution Composer	7	A sign of development is when a child is able to make new shapes out of smaller shapes and uses trial and error to substitute groups of shapes for other shapes in order to create new shapes in different ways. For example, the child can substitute shapes to fill outline puzzles in different ways.
6	Shape Decomposer (with Help)	8	As children develop, they can decompose shapes by using imagery that is suggested and supported by the task or environment.
7	Shape Composite Repeater	9	This level is demonstrated when the child can construct and duplicate units of units (shapes made from other shapes) intentionally, and understands each as being both multiple, small shapes and one larger shape. For example, the child may continue a pattern of shapes that leads to tiling.
7	Shape Decomposer with Imagery	10	A significant sign of development is when a child is able to decompose shapes flexibly by using independently generated imagery.
8	Shape Composer— Units of Units	11	Children demonstrate further understanding when they are able to build and apply units of units (shapes made from other shapes). For example, in constructing spatial patterns, the child can extend patterning activity to create a tiling with a new unit shape—a unit of unit shapes that he or she recognizes and consciously constructs. For example, the child may build Ts out of 4 squares, use 4 Ts to build squares, and use squares to tile a rectangle.
8	Shape Decomposer — Units of Units	12	As children develop understanding of shape, they can decompose shapes flexibly by using independently generated imagery and planned decompositions of shapes that themselves are decompositions.

Developmental Levels for Comparing Geometric Shapes

As early as four years of age, children can create and use strategies, such as moving shapes to compare their parts or to place one on top of the other, for judging whether two figures are the same shape. From Pre-K to Grade 2, they can develop sophisticated and accurate mathematical procedures for comparing geometric shapes. Children typically follow an observable developmental progression in learning about how shapes are the same and different with recognizable stages or levels. This developmental path can be described as part of a learning trajectory.

Age Range	Level Name	Level	Description
3	"Same Thing" Comparer	1	The first sign of understanding is when the child can compare real-world objects. For example, the children may say two pictures of houses are the same or different.
4	"Similar" Comparer	2	This sign of development occurs when the child judges two shapes to be the same if they are more visually similar than different. For example, the child may say, "These are the same. They are pointy at the top."
4	Part Comparer	3	At this level, a child can say that two shapes are the same after matching one side on each. For example, a child may say, "These are the same" (matching the two sides).
4	Some Attributes Comparer	4	As children develop, they look for differences in attributes, but may examine only part of a shape. For example, a child at this level may say, "These are the same" (indicating the top halves of the shapes are similar by laying them on top of each other).
5	Most Attributes Comparer	5	At this level, the child looks for differences in attributes, examining full shapes, but may ignore some spatial relationships. For example, a child may say, "These are the same."
7	Congruence Determiner	6	A sign of development is when a child determines congruence by comparing all attributes and all spatial relationships. For example, a child at this level may say that two shapes are the same shape and the same size after comparing every one of their sides and angles.
7	Congruence Superposer	7	As children develop understanding, they can move and place objects on top of each other to determine congruence. For example, a child at this level may say that two shapes are the same shape and the same size after laying them on top of each other.
8+	Congruence Representer	8	Continued development is evidenced as children refer to geometric properties and explain with transformations. For example, a child at this level may say, "These must be congruent because they have equal sides, all square corners, and I can move them on top of each other exactly."

Developmental Levels for Spatial Sense and Motions

Infants and toddlers spend a great deal of time learning about the properties and relations of objects in space. Very young children know and use the shape of their environment in navigation activities. With guidance they can learn to "mathematize" this knowledge. They can learn about direction, perspective, distance, symbolization, location, and coordinates. Children typically follow an observable developmental progression in developing spatial sense with recognizable stages or levels. This developmental path can be described as part of a learning trajectory.

Age Range	Level Name	Level	Description
4	Simple Turner	1	An early sign of spatial sense is when a child mentally turns an object to perform easy tasks. For example, given a shape with the top marked with color, the child may correctly identify which of three shapes it would look like if it were turned "like this" (90 degree turn demonstrated), before physically moving the shape.
5	Beginning Slider, Flipper, Turner	2	This sign of development occurs when a child can use the correct motions, but is not always accurate in direction and amount. For example, a child at this level may know a shape has to be flipped to match another shape, but flips it in the wrong direction.
6	Slider, Flipper, Turner	3	As children develop spatial sense, they can perform slides and flips, often only horizontal and vertical, by using manipulatives. For example, a child at this level may perform turns of 45, 90, and 180 degrees. For example, a child knows a shape must be turned 90 degrees to the right to fit into a puzzle.
7	Diagonal Mover	4	A sign of development is when a child can perform diagonal slides and flips. For example, children at this level may know a shape must be turned or flipped over an oblique line (45 degree orientation) to fit into a puzzle.
8	Mental Mover	5	Further signs of development occur when a child can predict results of moving shapes using mental images. A child at this level may say, "If you turned this 120 degrees, it would be just like this one."

Learning Trajectories for Math

Developmental Levels for Patterning and Early Algebra

Algebra begins with a search for patterns. Identifying patterns helps bring order, cohesion, and predictability to seemingly unorganized situations and allows one to make generalizations beyond the information directly available. The recognition and analysis of patterns are important components of young children's intellectual development because they provide a foundation for the development of algebraic thinking. Although prekindergarten children engage in pattern-related activities and recognize patterns in their everyday environment, research has revealed that an abstract understanding of patterns develops gradually during the early childhood years. Children typically follow an observable developmental progression in learning about patterns with recognizable stages or levels. This developmental path can be described as part of a learning trajectory.

Age Range	Level Name	Level	Description
2	Pre-Patterner	1	A child at the earliest level does not recognize patterns. For example, a child may name a striped shirt with no repeating unit a "pattern."
3	Pattern Recognizer	2	At this level, the child can recognize a simple pattern. For example, a child at this level may say, "I'm wearing a pattern" about a shirt with black and white stripes.
4	Pattern Fixer	3	At this level the child fills in missing elements of a pattern, first with ABABAB patterns. When given items in a row with an item missing, such as ABAB_BAB, the child identifies and fills in the missing element (A).
4	Pattern Duplicator AB	4	A sign of development is when the child can duplicate an ABABAB pattern, although the children may have to work alongside the model pattern. For example, given objects in a row, ABABAB, the child may make his or her own ABABAB row in a different location.
4	Pattern Extender AB	5	At this level the child extends AB repeating patterns. For example, given items in a row—ABABAB—the child adds ABAB to the end of the row.
4	Pattern Duplicator	6	At this level, the child is able to duplicate simple patterns (not just alongside the model pattern). For example, given objects in a row, ABBABBABB, the child may make his or her own ABBABBABB row in a different location.
5	Pattern Extender	7	A sign of development is when the child can extend simple patterns. For example, given objects in a row, ABBABBABB, he or she may add ABBABB to the end of the row.
7	Pattern Unit Recognizer	8	At this level, a child can identify the smallest unit of a pattern. For example, given objects in a row with one missing, ABBAB_ABB, he or she may identify and fill in the missing element.

Developmental Levels for Classifying and Analyzing Data

Data analysis contains one big idea: classifying, organizing, representing, and using information to ask and answer questions. The developmental continuum for data analysis includes growth in classifying and counting to sort objects and quantify their groups. Children eventually become capable of simultaneously classifying and counting; for example, counting the number of colors in a group of objects. Children typically follow an observable developmental progression in learning about patterns with recognizable stages or levels. This developmental path can be described as part of a learning trajectory.

Age Range	Level Name	Level	Description
2	Similarity Recognizer	1	The first sign that a child can classify is when he or she recognizes, intuitively, two or more objects as "similar" in some way. For example, "that's another doggie."
2	Informal Sorter	2	A sign of development is when a child places objects that are alike in some attribute together, but switches criteria and may use functional relationships as the basis for sorting. A child at this level might stack blocks of the same shape or put a cup with its saucer.
3	Attribute Identifier	3	The next level is when the child names attributes of objects and places objects together with a given attribute, but cannot then move to sorting by a new rule. For example, the child may say, "These are both red."
4	Attribute Sorter	4	At the next level the child sorts objects according to given attributes, forming categories, but may switch attributes during the sorting. A child at this stage can switch rules for sorting if guided. For example, the child might start putting red beads on a string, but switches to spheres of different colors.
5	Consistent Sorter	5	A sign of development is when the child can sort consistently by a given attribute. For example, the child might put several identical blocks together.
6	Exhaustive Sorter	6	At the next level, the child can sort consistently and exhaustively by an attribute, given or created. This child can use terms "some" and "all" meaningfully. For example, a child at this stage would be able to find all the attribute blocks of a certain size and color.

Age Range	Level Name	Level	Description
6	Multiple Attribute Sorter	7	A sign of development is when the child can sort consistently and exhaustively by more than one attribute, sequentially. For example, a child at this level can put all the attribute blocks together by color, then by shape.
7	Classifier and Counter	8	At the next level, the child is capable of simultaneously classifying and counting. For example, the child counts the number of colors in a group of objects.
7	List Grapher	9	In the early stage of graphing, the child graphs by simply listing all cases. For example, the child may list each child in the class and each child's response to a question.
8+	Multiple Attribute Classifier	10	A sign of development is when the child can intentionally sort according to multiple attributes, naming and relating the attributes. This child understands that objects could belong to more than one group. For example, the child can complete a two-dimensional classification matrix or form subgroups within groups.
8+	Classifying Grapher	11	At the next level the child can graph by classifying data (e.g., responses) and represent it according to categories. For example, the child can take a survey, classify the responses, and graph the result.
8+	Classifier	12	A sign of development is when the child creates complete, conscious classifications logically connected to a specific property. For example, a child at this level gives a definition of a class in terms of a more general class and one or more specific differences and begins to understand the inclusion relation.
8+	Hierarchical Classifier	13	At the next level, the child can perform hierarchical classifications. For example, the child recognizes that all squares are rectangles, but not all rectangles are squares.
8+	Data Representer	14	Signs of development are when the child organizes and displays data through both simple numerical summaries such as counts, tables, and tallies, and graphical displays, including picture graphs, line plots, and bar graphs. At this level the child creates graphs and tables, compares parts of the data, makes statements about the data as a whole, and determines whether the graphs answer the questions posed initially.